250 Delicious Soup Recipes

(250 Delicious Soup Recipes - Volume 1)

Mary Taylor

Copyright: Published in the United States by Mary Taylor/ © MARY TAYLOR

Published on November, 19 2020

All rights reserved. No part of this publication may be reproduced, stored in retrieval system, copied in any form or by any means, electronic, mechanical, photocopying, recording or otherwise transmitted without written permission from the publisher. Please do not participate in or encourage piracy of this material in any way. You must not circulate this book in any format. MARY TAYLOR does not control or direct users' actions and is not responsible for the information or content shared, harm and/or actions of the book readers.

In accordance with the U.S. Copyright Act of 1976, the scanning, uploading and electronic sharing of any part of this book without the permission of the publisher constitute unlawful piracy and theft of the author's intellectual property. If you would like to use material from the book (other than just simply for reviewing the book), prior permission must be obtained by contacting the author at author@shrimpcookbook.com

Thank you for your support of the author's rights.

Content

CHAPTER 1: CHILI SOUP RECIPES 7

1. 1 2 3 Vegetable Chili 7
2. 25 Minute Chili Cheeseburger Skillet Recipe 7
3. 3 Bean Chili 8
4. 30 Minute White Bean Chili 8
5. A.1. Chili 9
6. BBQ Steakhouse Chili 9
7. BBQ Turkey Chili 10
8. BOCA Roasted Vegetable Vegan Chili 10
9. Best Chili Recipe 11
10. Butternut Squash & Black Bean Chili 11
11. Cheesy Beef Burritos 12
12. Cheesy Beef Tostadas 12
13. Cheesy Chicken Chili 13
14. Cheesy Chili For A Crowd 13
15. Cheesy Slow Cooker Chili Recipe 13
16. Chili Cheese Dip 14
17. Chili And Cheese Stuffed Jalapeño Peppers 14
18. Chipotle Quinoa Chili 15
19. Easy Italian Style Chili 15
20. Famous Queso Dip 16
21. Four Star Chili 16
22. Green Enchilada Pork Chili 17
23. Grilled Steak And Chorizo Chili 17
24. Meatless Chili Recipe 18
25. Quick Turkey Chili 18
26. Red Bean Chili 19
27. Slow Cooker Beef Chili 19
28. Slow Cooker Sweet And Spicy Three Bean Chili 20
29. Slow Cooker Tuscan Chili 20
30. Slow Cooker Vegetable Chili Con Queso . 21
31. Sweet Potato And Black Bean Chili 21
32. Three Bean Chili 22
33. Two Bean Vegetarian Chili 23
34. Vegetarian Chili Mac 23
35. Veggie Chili 23
36. Veggie Chili Recipe 24
37. White Chicken Chili 24
38. White Chicken Chili Recipe 25

CHAPTER 2: CHICKEN SOUP RECIPES 26

39. Broccoli Cheddar Soup Recipe 26
40. Butternut Squash Soup With Sour Cream 26
41. Chicken Tortilla Soup 27
42. Chicken And Biscuits 27
43. Crisp & Creamy Baked Chicken Recipe 28
44. Easy Chicken Cordon Bleu 28
45. Easy Chicken Soup 29
46. Easy Chicken And Broccoli 29
47. Gram's Chicken Pot Pie Updated 30
48. Hearty Cabbage Soup Recipe 30
49. Hearty Mexican Chicken Soup 31
50. Homemade Chicken Pot Pie Recipe 31
51. Loaded Potato Soup 32
52. STOVE TOP Stuffed Chicken Rolls 32
53. Santa Fe Chicken Fajita Soup 33
54. Santa Fe Chicken Recipe 33
55. Shortcut Chicken Manicotti Recipe 34
56. Slow Cooker Chicken Taco Soup 34
57. Slow Cooked Chicken & Dumplings 35
58. Smothered Chicken & Green Bean Skillet 35
59. Speedy Asian Soup Recipe 36
60. Speedy Ginger Chicken Soup Bowls 36
61. VELVEETA® Chicken Enchilada Casserole Recipe 37
62. Wonton Soup 37

CHAPTER 3: CHICKEN CHILI SOUP RECIPES 38

63. 15 Minute Chicken Chili 38
64. Beef Enchilada Casserole 38
65. Black & White Bean Chicken Chili 39
66. Cheesy Chicken Quesadilla 39
67. Chicken In Roasted Poblano Sauce 40
68. Chili Chicken Mac & Cheese 40
69. Crispy Simple Baked Chicken 41
70. Fiesta Chicken Enchiladas Recipe 41
71. Fiesta Chicken Soup Recipe 41
72. Green Enchiladas Recipe 42
73. Grilled Chicken Wraps 42
74. How To Cook Chicken 43
75. Kung Pao Chicken Recipe 44
76. Make Ahead Smoky Chipotle Chicken Chili 44
77. Pulled Pork Chili 45
78. Salsa Mac Chicken Supper 45

79. Slow Cooker Buffalo Chicken Chili 46
80. Slow Cooker Chicken Tortilla Soup Recipe 46
81. Slow Cooker Chunky Chicken Chili 47
82. Southwest Four Cheese Chicken 47
83. Southwestern White Chili Recipe 48
84. Spicy Chili Recipe 48
85. Two Bite Fried Chicken 49
86. VELVEETA Cheesy Chicken Chili 49
87. VELVEETA® Spicy Chicken Spaghetti .. 50
88. Weeknight Chicken Fajita Recipe 50

CHAPTER 4: AWESOME SOUP RECIPES 51

89. 15 Minute Jambalaya 51
90. American Chowder 51
91. Andouille Sausage Jambalaya 52
92. BBQ Ham And Bean Soup 52
93. BOCA Jambalaya 53
94. BOCA Vegetarian Minestrone Soup Recipe 53
95. Bacon, Cheese & Potato Chowder 54
96. Baked Potato Soup With Bacon 54
97. Barley And Bean Soup Recipe 55
98. Bean Soup 55
99. Beef Barley Soup 56
100. Beef Brisket 56
101. Big Batch Leek Soup 57
102. Black Bean Minestrone Soup 57
103. Black Bean And Rice Soup 58
104. Broccoli Cheese Soup Recipe 58
105. Broccoli And Cheese Soup With Potato ... 59
106. Cape Anne Chowder 59
107. Caramelized Butternut Squash Soup 60
108. Carrot & Parsnip Soup 60
109. Carrot Soup Recipe 61
110. Cheddar Broccoli Soup 61
111. Cheese & Ale Soup 62
112. Cheeseburger Soup 62
113. Cheesy Broccoli Noodle Soup 63
114. Cheesy Green Chili Soup 63
115. Cheesy Minestrone Pasta 64
116. Cheesy Tortilla Soup 64
117. Cheesy VELVEETA Salmon & Potato Soup 65
118. Chicken Corn Chowder 66
119. Chicken Pozole 66
120. Chicken Tortilla Lime Soup 66
121. Chipotle, Sweet Potato And Black Bean Stew 67
122. Chunky Chicken Vegetable Soup 68
123. Chunky Veggie & Cannellini Bean Soup ... 68
124. Classic Minestrone Soup 69
125. Cold Cucumber Soup 69
126. Corn And Salmon Chowder With Bacon . 70
127. Country Cheese Soup 70
128. Crab Bisque 71
129. Cracker Chicken Casserole 71
130. Cream Of Broccoli Soup Recipe 72
131. Cream Of Broccoli, Bacon & Potato Soup 72
132. Cream Of Mushroom Tortellini Soup 73
133. Cream Of Potato Chowder 73
134. Cream Of Spinach Soup 74
135. Creamed Asparagus Soup 74
136. Creamy Beer Cheese Soup 75
137. Creamy Broccoli & Potato Soup 75
138. Creamy Chicken & Corn Soup 76
139. Creamy Chicken Tortilla Soup 77
140. Creamy Corn & Frank Chowder 77
141. Creamy Italian Sausage And Kale Soup ... 78
142. Creamy Mushroom Soup 78
143. Creamy Potato Soup 79
144. Creamy Roasted Garlic Cauliflower Soup . 79
145. Creamy Roasted Red Pepper Tomato Soup 80
146. Creamy Wild Rice Soup 81
147. Curry Tomato Soup 81
148. Dijon Roasted Veggie Soup 82
149. Easy Clam Chowder 82
150. Easy Clam Chowder Recipe 83
151. Easy Jambalaya Recipe 83
152. Easy Layered Cabbage Casserole 84
153. Easy Seafood Gumbo 85
154. Easy Vegetable Soup 85
155. Fast Black Bean Soup 86
156. Fisherman's Chowder 86
157. French Onion Soup With Bacon 87
158. Hearty French Onion Soup Recipe 87
159. Hearty Golden Chowder 88
160. Hearty Italian Chicken Chowder 88
161. Hearty Mushroom Beef Barley Soup 89
162. Hearty Vegetable Beef Soup 89
163. Homemade Chicken Soup With Rice 90

164. Italian Pasta E Fagioli 90
165. Italian Style Gumbo Recipe 91
166. Kale & Barley Soup 91
167. Kale And Farro Soup 92
168. La Ceiba Conch Soup 92
169. Lasagna Soup 93
170. Lentil Soup 93
171. Lima Bean Soup 94
172. Luscious Potato, Leek & Bacon Soup 94
173. Mac & Grilled Cheese Tomato Soup 95
174. Mac 'N Double Cheese Soup 96
175. Manhattan Clam Chowder 96
176. Marvelous Minestrone 97
177. Mediterranean Sun Dried Tomato Lentil Soup 97
178. Mediterranean Style Seafood Chowder 98
179. Mexican Soup With Tortilla Chips 98
180. Midwest Chowder 99
181. Minestrone Soup 99
182. Minestrone Soup With Poblano Chile 100
183. Mom's Cheesy Potato Chowder With Bacon Bits 100
184. Nana's Cheese Soup 101
185. New England Chowder 101
186. New England Clam Chowder 102
187. No Cream Creamy Broccoli Soup 102
188. ORE IDA Loaded Potato Soup Recipe .. 103
189. Old Fashioned Potato Soup 103
190. PHILADELPHIA® Corn Chowder 104
191. Plantain Garlic Soup 105
192. Potato Cheese Soup 105
193. Princess Fiona's Royal Swamp Soup 106
194. Quick Chicken Jambalaya 106
195. Quick Chicken Minestrone 106
196. Ravioli & Italian Sausage Soup With Parmesan 107
197. Refreshing Gazpacho 107
198. Roasted Corn & Poblano Soup 108
199. Roasted Poblano Tomato Soup 109
200. Roasted Root Vegetable Soup 109
201. Salmon Vegetable Chowder 110
202. Santa Fe Chicken Enchilada Stew 110
203. Santa Fe Soup 111
204. Savory Seafood Chowder 111
205. Shrimp Corn Chowder 112
206. Slow Cooker Beef & Potato Vegetable Soup 112
207. Slow Cooked Winter Vegetable Soup 113
208. Slow Cooker Bean And Barley Soup 113
209. Slow Cooker Cheesy Potato Soup With Bacon 114
210. Slow Cooker Chicken Enchilada Soup ... 115
211. Slow Cooker Chicken And Broccoli Cheese Soup 115
212. Slow Cooker Chicken And Wild Rice Soup 116
213. Slow Cooker Creamy Lentil Soup 116
214. Slow Cooker Cuban Black Bean Soup 117
215. Slow Cooker French Onion Soup 117
216. Slow Cooker Jambalaya Stuffed Peppers 118
217. Slow Cooker Lemon Chicken And Orzo Soup 118
218. Slow Cooker Loaded Baked Potato Soup 119
219. Slow Cooker Pot Roast 119
220. Slow Cooker Southwest Wedding Soup . 120
221. Slow Cooker Split Pea Soup 120
222. Slow Cooker Tomato Soup With Croutons 121
223. Southwest Cheese Soup 121
224. Southwest Chicken And Rice Soup 122
225. Southwest Creamy Tomato Soup 122
226. Southwest Slow Cooker Chicken Ramen Soup 123
227. Spicy Mixed Bean Taco Soup 123
228. Spicy Southwest Corn Cheese Soup 124
229. Spring Pea Soup 124
230. Squash Soup 125
231. Sweet Potato And Black Bean Soup 125
232. Taco Soup 126
233. Tasty Tuna Casserole 126
234. Tex Mex Minestrone Recipe 127
235. Tex Mex Soup 127
236. Three Onion French Onion Soup 128
237. Tomato Bisque 128
238. Tomato Soup With Chipotle Peppers 129
239. Tomato Soup With Grilled Cheese 129
240. Tortilla Soup 130
241. Turkey Jambalaya 130
242. Turkey Pozole Soup 131
243. VELVEETA Jambalaya Skillet 132
244. VELVEETA® Cheesy Broccoli Soup ... 132
245. VELVEETA® Easy Spicy Chicken Spaghetti 133

246. Vegetable And Cheese Chowder 133
247. Vegetables And Corn Dumpling Soup 134
248. Vegetarian Slow Cooker Minestrone 134
249. Velvety Vegetable Cheese Soup 135
250. Western Bean And Burger Soup 135

INDEX 137
CONCLUSION 140

Chapter 1: Chili Soup Recipes

***

1. 1 2 3 Vegetable Chili

Serving: 0 | Prep: 5mins | Cook: 20mins | Ready in: 25mins

Ingredients

- 1 can (28 oz.) whole tomatoes, undrained, cut up
- 1 jar (16 oz.) TACO BELL® Thick & Chunky Salsa
- 1 can (15 oz.) black beans, rinsed
- 1 pkg. (10 oz.) frozen corn
- 1 cup halved zucchini slices
- 1 tsp. chili powder
- 1 pkg. (7 oz.) KRAFT 2% Milk Shredded Mild Cheddar Cheese, divided

Direction

- Combine all ingredients except cheese in saucepan.
- Bring to boil on medium-high heat; simmer on low heat 10 min., stirring occasionally.
- Spoon 2 Tbsp. cheese into each of 8 soup bowls; top with chili and remaining cheese.

Nutrition Information

- Calories: 220
- Saturated Fat: 3 g
- Total Carbohydrate: 0 g
- Total Fat: 6 g
- Protein: 13 g
- Sodium: 730 mg
- Fiber: 7 g
- Sugar: 0 g
- Cholesterol: 15 mg

2. 25 Minute Chili Cheeseburger Skillet Recipe

Serving: 4 | Prep: 25mins | Cook: | Ready in: 25mins

Ingredients

- 1 lb. lean ground beef
- 2 cups water
- 1 pkg. (7-1/4 oz.) KRAFT Macaroni & Cheese Dinner
- 1 tsp. chili powder
- 3 cups chopped broccoli
- 1/4 cup HEINZ Tomato Ketchup

Direction

- Brown meat in large skillet; drain. Return meat to skillet.
- Stir in water, Macaroni and chili powder. Bring to boil; cover. Simmer on medium-low heat 5 min., stirring occasionally.
- Add broccoli; simmer 5 min. or until macaroni is tender. Remove from heat.
- Stir in Cheese Sauce Mix and ketchup until blended.

Nutrition Information

- Calories: 360
- Total Carbohydrate: 0 g
- Protein: 24 g
- Sodium: 650 mg
- Saturated Fat: 4 g
- Cholesterol: 55 mg
- Fiber: 3 g
- Sugar: 0 g
- Total Fat: 10 g

3. 3 Bean Chili

Serving: 0 | Prep: 25mins | Cook: 20mins | Ready in: 45mins

Ingredients

- 2 lb. lean ground beef
- 1 small yellow onion, chopped
- 1 small green pepper, chopped
- 2 cans (15.5 oz. each) dark red kidney beans, undrained
- 2 cans (15.5 oz. each) pinto beans, undrained
- 2 cans (15.5 oz. each) black beans, undrained
- 1 can (14.5 oz.) diced tomatoes, undrained
- 1 can (6 oz.) tomato paste
- 2 env. (1 oz. each) chili seasoning mix
- 1/2 tsp. ground cinnamon
- 1-1/4 cups BREAKSTONE'S or KNUDSEN Sour Cream

Direction

- Brown meat in Dutch oven or small stockpot on medium heat; drain. Add onions and peppers; cook 5 min. or until crisp-tender, stirring frequently.
- Add all remaining ingredients except sour cream; mix well. Bring to boil; cover. Simmer on medium-low heat 20 min., stirring occasionally.
- Serve topped with sour cream.

Nutrition Information

- Calories: 300
- Protein: 21 g
- Total Carbohydrate: 33 g
- Saturated Fat: 4 g
- Sugar: 5 g
- Cholesterol: 50 mg
- Sodium: 990 mg
- Fiber: 10 g
- Total Fat: 9 g

4. 30 Minute White Bean Chili

Serving: 0 | Prep: 10mins | Cook: 20mins | Ready in: 30mins

Ingredients

- 1 cup chopped onions
- 1 clove garlic, minced
- 1 Tbsp. oil
- 1 pkg. (16 oz.) frozen ground turkey, thawed
- 1 cup chicken broth
- 1 can (14-1/2 oz.) stewed tomatoes, undrained
- 1/4 cup GREY POUPON Dijon Mustard
- 1 Tbsp. chili powder
- 1/8 to 1/4 tsp. ground red pepper (cayenne)
- 1 can (15 oz.) cannellini beans, drained, rinsed
- 1 can (8 oz.) whole kernel corn, drained
- 1 cup KRAFT Shredded Cheddar Cheese

Direction

- Cook and stir onions and garlic in hot oil in 3-quart saucepan on medium-high heat until tender. Stir in turkey. Cook until turkey is cooked through, stirring occasionally to break up the turkey. Drain.
- Add broth, tomatoes with their liquid, mustard, chili powder and pepper; mix well. Bring to boil; reduce heat to medium-low. Simmer 10 minutes, stirring occasionally.
- Stir in beans and corn; cook 5 minutes, stirring occasionally. Serve topped with the cheese.

Nutrition Information

- Calories: 350
- Total Fat: 17 g
- Fiber: 6 g
- Sodium: 780 mg
- Saturated Fat: 6 g
- Cholesterol: 75 mg
- Total Carbohydrate: 0 g
- Sugar: 0 g
- Protein: 25 g

5. A.1. Chili

Serving: 0 | Prep: 10mins | Cook: 35mins | Ready in: 45mins

Ingredients

- 1-1/2 lb. lean ground beef
- 1 large green pepper, chopped
- 1 large onion, chopped
- 1 clove garlic, minced
- 3 Tbsp. chili powder
- 1 can (14-1/2 oz.) diced tomatoes, undrained
- 1/2 cup water
- 1 can (15.5 oz.) kidney beans, rinsed
- 1/3 cup A.1. Original Sauce

Direction

- Brown meat with peppers, onions and garlic in large saucepan. Stir in chili powder; cook and stir 1 min.
- Stir in tomatoes and water. Bring to boil; cover. Simmer on low heat 15 min., stirring occasionally.
- Add beans and steak sauce; mix well. Simmer, covered, 5 min.

Nutrition Information

- Calories: 220
- Fiber: 4 g
- Protein: 19 g
- Total Fat: 8 g
- Saturated Fat: 3 g
- Total Carbohydrate: 0 g
- Cholesterol: 50 mg
- Sugar: 0 g
- Sodium: 520 mg

6. BBQ Steakhouse Chili

Serving: 0 | Prep: 30mins | Cook: 7hours | Ready in: 7hours30mins

Ingredients

- 2 Tbsp. oil
- 1 lb. beef top round steak, cut into 1/2-inch pieces
- 1 lb. extra-lean ground beef
- 1 onion, finely chopped
- 1/4 cup A.1. Dry Rub Bold Original
- 3 cloves garlic, minced
- 2 cans (16 oz. each) kidney beans, rinsed
- 2-1/2 cups undrained canned no-salt-added diced tomatoes
- 1 bottle (18 oz.) KRAFT Hickory Smoke Barbecue Sauce
- 3/4 cup KRAFT Shredded Cheddar Cheese

Direction

- Heat oil in large skillet on medium heat. Add next 5 ingredients; stir. Cook 10 min. or until meat is evenly browned, stirring frequently. Spoon into slow cooker sprayed with cooking spray.
- Add all remaining ingredients except cheese; stir. Cover with lid. Cook on LOW 7 to 8 hours (or on HIGH 4 to 5 hours).
- Serve topped with cheese.

Nutrition Information

- Calories: 250
- Fiber: 4 g
- Sodium: 600 mg
- Sugar: 14 g
- Saturated Fat: 2.5 g
- Cholesterol: 40 mg
- Total Fat: 7 g
- Total Carbohydrate: 28 g
- Protein: 18 g

7. BBQ Turkey Chili

Serving: 0 | Prep: | Cook: | Ready in:

Ingredients

- 2 Tbsp. oil
- 2 onions, finely chopped
- 1 each red and yellow pepper, chopped
- 4 cloves garlic, finely chopped
- 1/4 cup chili powder
- 2 Tbsp. ground cumin
- 1 Tbsp. smoked paprika
- 2 tsp. dried oregano leaves
- 1 lb. each ground turkey and hot Italian turkey sausage, casings removed
- 1/2 cup lager-style beer
- 1 can (28 oz.) diced tomatoes, drained
- 1 can (15 oz.) each kidney and pinto beans, rinsed
- 3/4 cup KRAFT Hickory Smoke Barbecue Sauce
- 1-3/4 cups KRAFT Shredded Cheddar Cheese

Direction

- Heat oil in large skillet on medium heat. Add onions, peppers, garlic and seasonings; stir. Cook 10 min., stirring frequently.
- Add meat; mix well, using back of spoon to break sausage into smaller pieces. Cook 5 min. or until meat is done, stirring frequently. Add beer; stir to scrape any browned bits from bottom of skillet. Spoon into slow cooker sprayed with cooking spray.
- Stir in tomatoes, beans and barbecue sauce; cover with lid. Cook on LOW 8 hours (or on HIGH 5 hours.)
- Serve topped with cheese.

Nutrition Information

- Calories: 0 g
- Protein: 0 g
- Fiber: 0 g
- Cholesterol: 0 g
- Sodium: 0 g
- Saturated Fat: 0 g
- Total Carbohydrate: 0 g
- Sugar: 0 g
- Total Fat: 0 g

8. BOCA Roasted Vegetable Vegan Chili

Serving: 0 | Prep: 30mins | Cook: 15mins | Ready in: 45mins

Ingredients

- 1 g yellow pepper, chopped
- 1 g yellow squash, chopped
- 2-1/2 g cubed peeled eggplant
- 1/4 g chopped red onions
- 2 g garlic, minced
- 2 g oil
- 1 g (15 oz.) tomato sauce
- 1 can (15 oz.) chili beans
- 1 g (12 oz.) frozen BOCA Veggie Ground Crumbles

Direction

- Heat oven to 450°F.
- Combine vegetables, garlic and oil in 13x9-inch pan.
- Bake 15 min. or until vegetables are golden brown, stirring occasionally. Transfer to large saucepan. Stir in remaining ingredients; cover.
- Cook on medium-high heat 10 min. or until crumbles are cooked through (160°F), stirring occasionally.

Nutrition Information

- Calories: 200
- Fiber: 10 g
- Saturated Fat: 0.5 g
- Total Fat: 6 g
- Protein: 18 g
- Cholesterol: 0 mg

- Sugar: 0 g
- Sodium: 890 mg
- Total Carbohydrate: 0 g

9. Best Chili Recipe

Serving: 0 | Prep: 30mins | Cook: | Ready in: 30mins

Ingredients

- 1/2 lb. extra-lean ground beef
- 1 can (15 oz.) no-salt-added red kidney beans, rinsed
- 1 can (14.5 oz.) fire-roasted diced tomatoes, undrained
- 1 cup TACO BELL® Thick & Chunky Salsa
- 1 tsp. chili powder
- 1/2 cup KRAFT 2% Milk Shredded Sharp Cheddar Cheese
- 1/4 cup BREAKSTONE'S or KNUDSEN Sour Cream

Direction

- Brown meat in large skillet.
- Add beans, tomatoes, salsa and chili powder; mix well. Bring to boil. Cover; simmer on medium-low heat 10 min., stirring occasionally.
- Serve topped with cheese and sour cream.

Nutrition Information

- Calories: 290
- Cholesterol: 55 mg
- Fiber: 7 g
- Saturated Fat: 4.5 g
- Sodium: 870 mg
- Total Carbohydrate: 0 g
- Protein: 24 g
- Total Fat: 9 g
- Sugar: 0 g

10. Butternut Squash & Black Bean Chili

Serving: 0 | Prep: 25mins | Cook: 35mins | Ready in: 1hours

Ingredients

- 1/4 cup KRAFT Sun Dried Tomato Vinaigrette Dressing made with Extra Virgin Olive Oil
- 2 cups cubed butternut squash (1-inch pieces)
- 1 yellow onion, chopped
- 4 large cloves garlic, minced
- 2 tsp. chili powder
- 1 tsp. ground cumin
- 1 can (28 oz.) diced tomatoes, undrained
- 1 can (15.5 oz.) black beans, rinsed
- 4 green onions, chopped
- 1/4 cup chopped fresh cilantro
- 1/2 cup KRAFT Mexican Style Shredded Four Cheese with a TOUCH OF PHILADELPHIA

Direction

- Heat dressing in Dutch oven or large deep skillet on medium heat. Add squash, yellow onions and garlic; cook and stir 7 min. or until squash is slightly softened.
- Add seasonings; cook and stir 30 sec. Stir in tomatoes and beans; bring to boil. Cover; simmer on medium-low heat 35 min. or until squash is tender, stirring occasionally.
- Stir in green onions and cilantro. Top with cheese.

Nutrition Information

- Calories: 190
- Sodium: 460 mg
- Protein: 9 g
- Saturated Fat: 2 g
- Total Fat: 5 g
- Total Carbohydrate: 29 g
- Fiber: 9 g
- Cholesterol: 10 mg

- Sugar: 9 g

11. Cheesy Beef Burritos

Serving: 4 | Prep: 20mins | Cook: |Ready in: 20mins

Ingredients

- 1/2 lb. extra-lean ground beef
- 2 tsp. chili powder
- 1 can (15 oz.) black beans, rinsed
- 1/2 cup TACO BELL® Thick & Chunky Salsa
- 2/3 cup KRAFT 2% Milk Shredded Sharp Cheddar Cheese
- 4 flour tortillas (10 inch)
- 1/4 cup BREAKSTONE'S Reduced Fat or KNUDSEN Light Sour Cream
- 1 tomato, chopped
- 1 cup loosely packed shredded romaine lettuce

Direction

- Cook meat and chili powder in large skillet on medium-high heat 5 min. or until meat is done, stirring frequently. Add beans and salsa; cook 5 min. or until heated through, stirring occasionally. Remove from heat. Stir in cheese.
- Spoon meat mixture down centers of tortillas; top with remaining ingredients.
- Fold in opposite sides of each tortilla, then roll up burrito-style.

Nutrition Information

- Calories: 490
- Total Carbohydrate: 0 g
- Saturated Fat: 6 g
- Total Fat: 14 g
- Sodium: 990 mg
- Cholesterol: 55 mg
- Sugar: 0 g
- Protein: 30 g
- Fiber: 10 g

12. Cheesy Beef Tostadas

Serving: 0 | Prep: 10mins | Cook: 15mins |Ready in: 25mins

Ingredients

- 4 flour tortillas (6 inch)
- 2 tsp. chili powder, divided
- 1/2 lb. extra-lean ground beef
- 1 can (15 oz.) no-salt-added black beans, rinsed
- 1/2 cup TACO BELL® Thick & Chunky Salsa
- 3/4 cup KRAFT Mexican Style 2% Milk Finely Shredded Four Cheese, divided
- 1/2 cup shredded romaine lettuce
- 1 large tomato, chopped
- 1/4 cup BREAKSTONE'S Reduced Fat or KNUDSEN Light Sour Cream

Direction

- Heat oven to 400ºF.
- Place tortillas in single layer on baking sheet; spray with cooking spray. Sprinkle evenly with 1 tsp. chili powder. Bake 7 to 8 min. or until crisp.
- Meanwhile, brown meat in large skillet. Add beans, salsa and remaining chili powder; cook 4 min. or until heated through, stirring occasionally. Remove from heat. Stir in half the cheese.
- Spread meat mixture onto tortillas; top with remaining cheese, lettuce, tomatoes and sour cream.

Nutrition Information

- Calories: 100
- Cholesterol: 40 mg
- Fiber: 0 g
- Sugar: 0 g
- Saturated Fat: 2 g
- Protein: 13 g
- Sodium: 50 mg
- Total Fat: 4.5 g

- Total Carbohydrate: 0 g

13. Cheesy Chicken Chili

Serving: 6 | Prep: 25mins | Cook: | Ready in: 25mins

Ingredients

- 1-1/4 lb. boneless skinless chicken breasts, cut into bite-size pieces
- 2 cans (15 oz. each) tomato sauce
- 1 can (15 oz.) kidney beans, rinsed
- 1/2 lb. (8 oz.) VELVEETA, cut into 1/2-inch cubes

Direction

- Spray 5-qt. Dutch oven or large saucepan with cooking spray.
- Add chicken; cook and stir on medium heat 8 to 10 min. or until done.
- Stir in remaining ingredients; cook on medium heat 5 min. or until heated through and VELVEETA is melted, stirring frequently.

Nutrition Information

- Calories: 300
- Cholesterol: 85 mg
- Protein: 31 g
- Total Carbohydrate: 21 g
- Sugar: 4 g
- Total Fat: 11 g
- Sodium: 820 mg
- Fiber: 4 g
- Saturated Fat: 6 g

14. Cheesy Chili For A Crowd

Serving: 12 | Prep: 30mins | Cook: | Ready in: 30mins

Ingredients

- 2 lb. lean ground beef
- 1 onion, chopped
- 1 can (15 oz.) kidney beans, rinsed
- 1 can (14-1/2 oz.) diced tomatoes, undrained
- 1 can (6 oz.) tomato paste
- 1/2 cup water
- 3 Tbsp. chili powder
- 2 tsp. ground cumin
- 1/2 lb. (8 oz.) VELVEETA, cut into 1/2-inch cubes
- 4 cups hot cooked wagon wheel pasta

Direction

- Brown meat with onions in Dutch oven or stockpot on medium-high heat; drain.
- Add beans, tomatoes, tomato paste, water and seasonings; mix well. Cover; simmer on medium-low heat 10 min. or until heated through, stirring occasionally.
- Add VELVEETA; cook 3 to 5 min. or until completely melted, stirring frequently. Stir in pasta.

Nutrition Information

- Calories: 300
- Total Fat: 11 g
- Fiber: 4 g
- Sugar: 5 g
- Saturated Fat: 5 g
- Sodium: 560 mg
- Cholesterol: 60 mg
- Total Carbohydrate: 28 g
- Protein: 24 g

15. Cheesy Slow Cooker Chili Recipe

Serving: 6 | Prep: 10mins | Cook: | Ready in: 10mins

Ingredients

- 1 lb. ground beef

- 1 can (15 oz.) red kidney beans (drained and rinsed)
- 1 medium red onion, chopped
- 1 cup chicken broth
- 1/2 cup tomato sauce with Italian spices
- 1 cup KRAFT Shredded Three Cheese with a TOUCH OF PHILADELPHIA

Direction

- Brown beef in skillet until cooked through.
- Add browned beef and all ingredients except tomatoes and shredded cheese to slow cooker and cook on high for 3 hours, or low for 6 hours.
- Add tomatoes and cover; cook additional 30 minutes in slow cooker on low.
- Ladle chili into individual bowls and top with cheese.

Nutrition Information

- Calories: 270
- Total Fat: 16 g
- Saturated Fat: 7 g
- Sodium: 440 mg
- Total Carbohydrate: 15 g
- Fiber: 4 g
- Protein: 18 g
- Sugar: 2 g
- Cholesterol: 55 mg

16. Chili Cheese Dip

Serving: 0 | Prep: 10mins | Cook: | Ready in: 10mins

Ingredients

- 1 pkg. (8 oz.) PHILADELPHIA Cream Cheese, softened
- 1 can (15 oz.) chili with beans
- 1 cup KRAFT Shredded Cheddar Cheese
- 2 green onions, sliced
- 1 tomato, seeded, chopped

Direction

- Heat oven to 325°F.
- Spread cream cheese onto bottom of pie plate; top with chili and cheddar.
- Bake 15 to 18 min. or until dip is heated through and cheddar is melted.
- Top with onions and tomatoes.

Nutrition Information

- Calories: 70
- Protein: 3 g
- Sodium: 135 mg
- Fiber: 0.7623 g
- Sugar: 0 g
- Saturated Fat: 3 g
- Total Fat: 5 g
- Total Carbohydrate: 0 g
- Cholesterol: 15 mg

17. Chili And Cheese Stuffed Jalapeño Peppers

Serving: 12 | Prep: 30mins | Cook: 10mins | Ready in: 40mins

Ingredients

- 2 Tbsp. KRAFT Zesty Italian Dressing
- 1/2 lb. lean ground beef, cooked, drained
- 1/2 cup chopped tomatoes
- 2 Tbsp. PLANTERS Slivered Almonds
- 2 Tbsp. raisins
- 1 cup KRAFT Shredded Cheddar Cheese, divided
- 12 jalapeño peppers, cut lengthwise in half, seeded

Direction

- Heat oven to 350°F.
- Heat dressing in medium saucepan on medium-high heat. Add meat, tomatoes, nuts

and raisins; stir. Cook 3 to 5 min. or until heated through, stirring occasionally; drain. Return meat mixture to pan; stir in 1/4 cup cheese.
- Place peppers on foil-covered baking sheet; fill with meat mixture.
- Bake 10 min. Sprinkle with remaining cheese; bake 3 to 5 min. or until melted.

Nutrition Information

- Calories: 80
- Cholesterol: 15 mg
- Total Fat: 5 g
- Protein: 5 g
- Saturated Fat: 2.5 g
- Total Carbohydrate: 0 g
- Sugar: 0 g
- Sodium: 90 mg
- Fiber: 0.9797 g

18. Chipotle Quinoa Chili

Serving: 0 | Prep: 20mins | Cook: 25mins | Ready in: 45mins

Ingredients

- 1 Tbsp. oil
- 1 yellow onion, chopped
- 4 cloves garlic, minced
- 2 Tbsp. chili powder
- 1 Tbsp. ground cumin
- 1 tsp. chipotle chile pepper powder
- 2 cans (28 oz. each) diced tomatoes, undrained
- 1 can (15.5 oz.) no-salt-added black beans, rinsed
- 1 can (15.5 oz.) no-salt-added red kidney beans, rinsed
- 2 red peppers, coarsely chopped
- 1 cup frozen corn
- 1 cup quinoa, rinsed
- 4 green onions, chopped
- 1/2 cup chopped fresh cilantro
- 1 cup KRAFT Shredded Three Cheese with a TOUCH OF PHILADELPHIA

Direction

- Heat oil in Dutch oven or large deep skillet on medium-high heat. Add yellow onions and garlic; cook and stir 5 min. or until onions are crisp-tender.
- Stir in seasonings; cook 1 min. Add tomatoes, beans, peppers, corn and quinoa; stir. Bring to boil; cover. Simmer on medium-low heat 25 min. or until quinoa is tender, stirring occasionally.
- Remove from heat. Stir in green onions and cilantro. Serve topped with cheese.

Nutrition Information

- Calories: 220
- Cholesterol: 10 mg
- Sodium: 300 mg
- Total Fat: 6 g
- Protein: 11 g
- Fiber: 9 g
- Sugar: 0 g
- Total Carbohydrate: 0 g
- Saturated Fat: 2 g

19. Easy Italian Style Chili

Serving: 0 | Prep: 30mins | Cook: | Ready in: 30mins

Ingredients

- 1 lb. lean ground beef
- 1 jar (24 oz.) CLASSICO Tomato and Basil Pasta Sauce
- 2 cups water
- 2 cups medium-size pasta shapes, any variety, uncooked
- 1 can (15 oz.) kidney beans, rinsed
- 1 onion, chopped

- 1/3 cup KRAFT Grated Parmesan Cheese, divided
- 1 Tbsp. chili powder

Direction

- Brown meat in Dutch oven or large deep skillet; drain.
- Add pasta sauce, water, pasta, beans, onions, 1/4 cup cheese and chili powder; stir. Cover; cook on medium heat 10 to 12 min. or until pasta is tender, stirring occasionally.
- Top with remaining cheese.

Nutrition Information

- Calories: 400
- Fiber: 5 g
- Saturated Fat: 4.5 g
- Cholesterol: 60 mg
- Total Fat: 12 g
- Sodium: 700 mg
- Total Carbohydrate: 0 g
- Sugar: 0 g
- Protein: 28 g

20. Famous Queso Dip

Serving: 0 | Prep: 10mins | Cook: | Ready in: 10mins

Ingredients

- 1 lb. (16 oz.) VELVEETA, cut into 1/2-inch cubes
- 1 can (10 oz.) RO*TEL Diced Tomatoes & Green Chilies, undrained

Direction

- Combine ingredients in microwaveable bowl.
- Microwave on HIGH 5 min. or until VELVEETA is completely melted and mixture is well blended, stirring after 3 min.

Nutrition Information

- Calories: 50
- Cholesterol: 10 mg
- Protein: 3 g
- Sugar: 0 g
- Total Fat: 3 g
- Saturated Fat: 1.5 g
- Fiber: 0 g
- Total Carbohydrate: 0 g
- Sodium: 320 mg

21. Four Star Chili

Serving: 0 | Prep: 15mins | Cook: 1hours45mins | Ready in: 2hours

Ingredients

- 1 lb. each boneless beef stew meat and pork for stew, cut into 1/2-inch pieces
- 1 large onion, chopped
- 1/2 cup KRAFT Zesty Italian Dressing
- 1 large each green and red bell pepper, chopped
- 1 jar (16 oz.) TACO BELL® Thick & Chunky Salsa
- 1 can (14-1/2 oz.) fat-free reduced-sodium beef broth
- 1 Tbsp. chili powder
- 2 cans (15 oz. each) black beans, rinsed
- 4 cups hot cooked long-grain brown rice

Direction

- Brown meat with onions in dressing in Dutch oven or large deep skillet on medium-high heat 5 min., stirring occasionally. Add peppers; cook 2 to 3 min. or until crisp-tender.
- Add salsa, broth and chili powder; stir. Bring to boil. Cover; simmer on medium-low heat 1 hour or until meat is tender.
- Stir in beans; cook, uncovered, 30 min. Serve over rice.

Nutrition Information

- Calories: 380
- Saturated Fat: 2.5 g
- Cholesterol: 65 mg
- Sugar: 0 g
- Fiber: 7 g
- Sodium: 960 mg
- Total Carbohydrate: 0 g
- Protein: 31 g
- Total Fat: 9 g

22. Green Enchilada Pork Chili

Serving: 0 | Prep: 45mins | Cook: | Ready in: 45mins

Ingredients

- 1/4 cup KRAFT Zesty Italian Dressing
- 1-1/2 lb. pork tenderloin, cut into bite-size pieces
- 1 onion, chopped
- 2 cloves garlic, minced
- 1/4 cup chopped fresh cilantro, divided
- 2 cans (15 oz. each) pinto beans, rinsed, divided
- 1 jar (16 oz.) green salsa
- 1 can (14.5 oz.) fat-free reduced-sodium chicken broth
- 1 cup frozen corn
- 2 cups coarsely crushed tortilla chips
- 1/2 cup BREAKSTONE'S or KNUDSEN Sour Cream
- 1/2 cup KRAFT Mexican Style Finely Shredded Four Cheese

Direction

- Heat dressing in Dutch oven or small stockpot on medium-high heat. Add meat, onions, garlic and 2 Tbsp. cilantro; cook 6 to 8 min. or until meat is done, stirring frequently. Meanwhile, mash half the beans in small bowl.
- Add mashed beans, remaining whole beans, salsa, broth and corn to meat mixture in pan; mix well. Bring to boil; cover. Simmer on low heat 15 min., stirring occasionally.
- Place 1/4 cup chips in each of 8 serving bowls; top with chili, sour cream, cheese and remaining cilantro.

Nutrition Information

- Calories: 280
- Sodium: 990 mg
- Total Carbohydrate: 27 g
- Saturated Fat: 4 g
- Protein: 19 g
- Fiber: 7 g
- Sugar: 5 g
- Total Fat: 10 g
- Cholesterol: 50 mg

23. Grilled Steak And Chorizo Chili

Serving: 0 | Prep: 30mins | Cook: 20mins | Ready in: 50mins

Ingredients

- 1/2 lb. Mexican chorizo
- 1 beef skirt steak (1-1/2 lb.)
- 1 each green and red pepper, quartered
- 1 red onion, cut into 1/2-inch-thick slices
- 1/4 cup KRAFT Zesty Italian Dressing
- 1 Tbsp. chili powder
- 3 cloves garlic, minced
- 1 can (28 oz.) diced tomatoes, undrained
- 1/2 cup KRAFT Original Barbecue Sauce

Direction

- Heat grill for indirect grilling: Light one side of grill, leaving other side unlit. Close lid; heat grill to 350ºF.
- Crumble chorizo into 13x9-inch disposable foil pan. Brush steak, peppers and onions with dressing; place over unlit area of grill. Place

chorizo (in foil pan) next to steak and vegetables. Cover grill with lid.
- Grill 20 min. or until steak is medium doneness and chorizo is done, stirring chorizo and turning steak and vegetables after 10 min.
- Remove steak and vegetables from grill; cut into 1-inch pieces. Add chili powder and garlic to chorizo; cook and stir 30 sec. to 1 min. or until garlic is fragrant. Add steak, grilled vegetables, tomatoes and barbecue sauce to pan; mix well. Grill 10 min. or until heated through, stirring occasionally.

Nutrition Information

- Calories: 280
- Total Fat: 14 g
- Sugar: 0 g
- Protein: 23 g
- Total Carbohydrate: 0 g
- Fiber: 2 g
- Sodium: 540 mg
- Cholesterol: 70 mg
- Saturated Fat: 5 g

24. Meatless Chili Recipe

Serving: 0 | Prep: 15mins | Cook: 30mins | Ready in: 45mins

Ingredients

- 2 red peppers, chopped
- 1 onion, chopped
- 2 cloves garlic, minced
- 2 tsp. oil
- 1 pkg. (12 oz.) frozen BOCA Veggie Ground Crumbles
- 1 can (15 oz.) black beans, rinsed
- 1 can (15 oz.) chili beans
- 1 can (15 oz.) tomato sauce
- 1 can (14-1/2 oz.) diced tomatoes, undrained
- 1 can (4 oz.) chopped green chiles, undrained
- 1 Tbsp. chili powder

- 1/2 tsp. ground cumin

Direction

- Cook and stir peppers, onions and garlic in hot oil in large saucepan on medium-high heat 2 min. or until crisp-tender.
- Stir in crumbles; cook 2 min.
- Add remaining ingredients; mix well. Bring to boil. Simmer on medium-low 30 min. or until crumbles are cooked through (160°F), stirring occasionally.

Nutrition Information

- Calories: 180
- Total Carbohydrate: 26 g
- Total Fat: 2 g
- Sodium: 1050 mg
- Sugar: 5 g
- Protein: 16 g
- Cholesterol: 0 mg
- Fiber: 9 g
- Saturated Fat: 0 g

25. Quick Turkey Chili

Serving: 0 | Prep: 15mins | Cook: 3hours | Ready in: 3hours15mins

Ingredients

- 1/2 lb. ground turkey breast
- 1 can (28 oz.) diced tomatoes, undrained
- 1 jar (16 oz.) TACO BELL® Thick & Chunky Salsa
- 1 can (15.5 oz.) black beans, rinsed
- 1 can (15.5 oz.) kidney beans, rinsed
- 1 can (15.5 oz.) great Northern beans, rinsed
- 1 tsp. chili powder
- 1 tsp. ground cumin
- 1 pkg. (7 oz.) KRAFT 2% Milk Shredded Cheddar Cheese

Direction

- Cook turkey in large saucepan on medium heat 10 min. or until no longer pink, stirring occasionally.
- Add to slow cooker with all remaining ingredients except cheese; stir. Cover with lid.
- Cook on HIGH 3 to 4 hours (or on LOW 5 to 6 hours).
- Spoon into soup bowls; top with cheese.

Nutrition Information

- Calories: 280
- Fiber: 10 g
- Sodium: 890 mg
- Total Carbohydrate: 0 g
- Sugar: 0 g
- Total Fat: 6 g
- Saturated Fat: 3 g
- Cholesterol: 25 mg
- Protein: 22 g

26. Red Bean Chili

Serving: 0 | Prep: 20mins | Cook: 30mins | Ready in: 50mins

Ingredients

- 1/2 lb. lean ground beef
- 1 tsp. adobo seasoning with pepper
- 1 Tbsp. extra virgin olive oil
- 1 onion, chopped
- 1/2 cup chopped green peppers
- 1 tsp. minced garlic
- 1 Tbsp. chili powder
- 1 tsp. ground cumin
- 2 Tbsp. tomato paste
- 1 Tbsp. chopped fresh cilantro
- 1 can (15.5 oz.) small red beans, undrained
- 1 can (14.5 oz.) diced tomatoes, undrained
- 1 cup KRAFT Shredded Mild Cheddar Cheese

Direction

- Season meat with adobo. Brown in hot oil in large saucepan on medium heat; drain. Add onions, peppers and garlic; cook 5 min. or until tender, stirring occasionally.
- Stir in chili powder and cumin; cook 2 min. Stir in all remaining ingredients except cheese. Bring to boil; simmer on low heat 30 min., stirring occasionally.
- Serve topped with cheese.

Nutrition Information

- Calories: 360
- Saturated Fat: 9 g
- Total Fat: 18 g
- Total Carbohydrate: 27 g
- Sugar: 5 g
- Protein: 22 g
- Sodium: 780 mg
- Cholesterol: 55 mg
- Fiber: 9 g

27. Slow Cooker Beef Chili

Serving: 0 | Prep: 15mins | Cook: 5hours | Ready in: 5hours15mins

Ingredients

- 1-1/2 lb. lean ground beef
- 2 cans (15.5 oz. each) kidney beans, rinsed
- 1 can (16 oz.) no-salt-added tomato sauce
- 1-1/2 cups TACO BELL® Thick & Chunky Mild Salsa
- 1 cup frozen corn
- 1 onion, chopped
- 2 Tbsp. chili powder
- 1 cup KRAFT Mexican Style Finely Shredded Four Cheese

Direction

- Brown meat; drain. Spoon into slow cooker sprayed with cooking spray. Add all remaining ingredients except cheese; mix well. Cover with lid.
- Cook on LOW 5 to 6 hours (or on HIGH 3 to 4 hours).
- Stir chili. Serve topped with cheese.

Nutrition Information

- Calories: 280
- Fiber: 8 g
- Saturated Fat: 5 g
- Total Fat: 11 g
- Cholesterol: 55 mg
- Protein: 21 g
- Total Carbohydrate: 23 g
- Sodium: 560 mg
- Sugar: 6 g

28. Slow Cooker Sweet And Spicy Three Bean Chili

Serving: 0 | Prep: 15mins | Cook: 6hours | Ready in: 6hours15mins

Ingredients

- 2 Tbsp. olive oil
- 1 lb. ground beef
- 1 can (15.5 oz.) dark red kidney beans, drained and rinsed
- 1 can (15.5 oz.) red kidney beans, drained and rinsed
- 1 can (15.5 oz.) black beans, drained and rinsed
- 2 cans (15.25 oz) corn, drained and rinsed
- 1 can (14.5 oz.) diced tomatoes
- 1 can (15 oz.) tomato sauce
- 1/2 large sweet onion, chopped (about 1 cup)
- 1/2 green pepper, seeds removed, chopped (about 1 cup)
- 1 jalapeño pepper, seeds removed, chopped (optional)
- 1/2 cup KRAFT Spicy Honey Barbecue Sauce
- 2 Tbsp. chili powder
- 1 tsp. cumin seed
- 1/4 tsp. cayenne pepper
- season to taste
- Garnish:
- KRAFT Mexican Style Finely Shredded Four Cheese
- fresh cilantro
- red onion
- BREAKSTONE'S or KNUDSEN Sour Cream

Direction

- In a large skillet heat olive oil over medium high heat. Add the ground beef and cook until browned and cooked through.
- Add the ground beef and all other ingredients to slow cooker except the garnishes.
- Stir to combine and cook on high for 5-6 hours or low for 3-4 hours. Serve warm with your favorite garnishes like cheese, freshly chopped cilantro, chopped red onion and sour cream.

Nutrition Information

- Calories: 0 g
- Sodium: 0 g
- Cholesterol: 0 g
- Sugar: 0 g
- Total Fat: 0 g
- Fiber: 0 g
- Total Carbohydrate: 0 g
- Protein: 0 g
- Saturated Fat: 0 g

29. Slow Cooker Tuscan Chili

Serving: 0 | Prep: 30mins | Cook: 3hours40mins | Ready in: 4hours10mins

Ingredients

- 1 lb. Italian sausage

- 1 onion, chopped
- 1 can (14.5 oz.) diced tomatoes, undrained
- 1 each green and yellow pepper, chopped
- 1 can (6 oz.) tomato paste
- 1 can (15 oz.) cannellini beans, rinsed
- 1/2 tsp. dried basil leaves
- 1/2 tsp. dried oregano leaves
- 1-1/2 cups KRAFT Shredded Italian* Five Cheese with a TOUCH OF PHILADELPHIA

Direction

- Crumble sausage into large skillet. Add onions; cook until sausage is browned, stirring frequently. Drain. Transfer to slow cooker.
- Add tomatoes, peppers and tomato paste; mix well. Stir in beans; cover with lid. Cook on LOW 3-1/2 to 4 hours (or on HIGH 2-1/2 to 3 hours).
- Stir in herbs; cover. Cook on HIGH 10 min.; stir. Serve topped with cheese.

Nutrition Information

- Calories: 320
- Sodium: 660 mg
- Saturated Fat: 8 g
- Cholesterol: 50 mg
- Fiber: 8 g
- Protein: 18 g
- Total Fat: 18 g
- Total Carbohydrate: 21 g
- Sugar: 6 g

30. Slow Cooker Vegetable Chili Con Queso

Serving: 0 | Prep: 15mins | Cook: 3hours40mins | Ready in: 3hours55mins

Ingredients

- 1 qt. (4 cups) fat-free reduced-sodium vegetable broth
- 1 can (28 oz.) diced tomatoes, undrained
- 1 can (15 oz.) black beans, rinsed
- 1 can (15 oz.) chickpeas (garbanzo beans), rinsed
- 1 can (15 oz.) kidney beans, rinsed
- 1 onion, chopped
- 1 zucchini, chopped
- 1 green pepper, chopped
- 1 cup frozen corn
- 1 pkg. (1-1/4 oz.) TACO BELL® Taco Seasoning Mix
- 6 oz. VELVEETA, cut into 1/2-inch cubes

Direction

- Combine all ingredients except VELVEETA in slower cooker; cover with lid.
- Cook on HIGH 3-1/2 to 4 hours (or on LOW 5 to 6 hours).
- Stir in VELVEETA; cook, covered, 10 min. or until VELVEETA is completely melted. Stir before serving.

Nutrition Information

- Calories: 160
- Total Carbohydrate: 25 g
- Fiber: 6 g
- Total Fat: 3.5 g
- Sugar: 7 g
- Saturated Fat: 1.5 g
- Cholesterol: 10 mg
- Sodium: 500 mg
- Protein: 9 g

31. Sweet Potato And Black Bean Chili

Serving: 0 | Prep: 20mins | Cook: 30mins | Ready in: 50mins

Ingredients

- 2 Tbsp. olive oil

- 1 onion, chopped
- 2 Tbsp. chili powder
- 1 tsp. ground cumin
- 2 lb. sweet potatoes (about 4 large), peeled, cut into 1/2-inch chunks
- 3 cans (15 oz. each) crushed tomatoes
- 1 can (15.5 oz.) black beans, rinsed
- 1 can (14.5 oz) fat-free reduced-sodium chicken broth
- 1 pkg. (12 oz.) BOCA Veggie Ground Crumbles
- 2 canned chipotle peppers in adobo sauce, finely chopped
- 1/2 cup chopped fresh cilantro, divided
- 1 cup BREAKSTONE'S or KNUDSEN Sour Cream

Direction

- Heat oil in Dutch oven on medium-high heat. Add onions; cook 5 to 7 min. or until lightly browned, stirring occasionally. Add chili powder and cumin; mix well.
- Add all remaining ingredients except cilantro and sour cream; stir. Bring to boil; simmer on medium-low heat 25 to 30 min. or until potatoes are tender, stirring occasionally. Remove from heat. Stir in half the cilantro.
- Serve topped with sour cream and remaining cilantro.

Nutrition Information

- Calories: 270
- Protein: 15 g
- Cholesterol: 20 mg
- Total Carbohydrate: 0 g
- Saturated Fat: 3.5 g
- Sodium: 610 mg
- Sugar: 0 g
- Fiber: 10 g
- Total Fat: 9 g

32. Three Bean Chili

Serving: 0 | Prep: 20mins | Cook: |Ready in: 20mins

Ingredients

- 1 can (28 oz.) fire-roasted crushed tomatoes
- 1 jar (16 oz.) TACO BELL® Thick & Chunky Salsa
- 1 can (15 oz.) no-salt-added black beans, drained
- 1 can (15 oz.) no-salt-added red kidney beans, drained
- 1 can (15 oz.) no-salt-added pinto beans, drained
- 1 tsp. chili powder
- 1 tsp. ground cumin
- 1 cup KRAFT Mexican Style 2% Milk Finely Shredded Four Cheese
- 1/2 cup BREAKSTONE'S Reduced Fat or KNUDSEN Light Sour Cream
- 1/4 cup chopped fresh cilantro

Direction

- Bring all ingredients except cheese, sour cream and cilantro to boil in saucepan, stirring occasionally. Simmer on medium-low heat 10 min., stirring occasionally.
- Serve topped with remaining ingredients.

Nutrition Information

- Calories: 270
- Fiber: 11 g
- Total Carbohydrate: 40 g
- Sugar: 9 g
- Cholesterol: 20 mg
- Sodium: 750 mg
- Total Fat: 6 g
- Saturated Fat: 3.5 g
- Protein: 16 g

33. Two Bean Vegetarian Chili

Serving: 8 | Prep: 30mins | Cook: 30mins | Ready in: 1hours

Ingredients

- 2 cups long-grain brown rice, uncooked
- 2 Tbsp. KRAFT Lite Balsamic Vinaigrette Dressing
- 2 carrots, cut into 1/4-inch-thick slices
- 1 onion, chopped
- 1 red pepper, chopped
- 3 cloves garlic, minced
- 2 cans (14.5 oz. each) diced tomatoes, undrained
- 1 can (15.5 oz.) red kidney beans, rinsed
- 1 can (15.5 oz.) cannellini beans, rinsed
- 1/2 cup KRAFT Original Barbecue Sauce
- 3 Tbsp. chili powder
- 1 cup frozen corn
- 1-1/2 cups KRAFT Mexican Style Finely Shredded Four Cheese

Direction

- Cook rice as directed on package.
- Meanwhile, heat dressing in large saucepan on medium-high heat. Add carrots, onions, peppers and garlic; cook and stir 6 to 8 min. or until vegetables are crisp-tender. Add all remaining ingredients except corn and cheese; stir. Bring to boil; simmer on medium-low heat 30 min., stirring occasionally. Stir in corn; cook 5 min. or until heated through.
- Serve chili over rice; top with cheese.

Nutrition Information

- Calories: 450
- Fiber: 12 g
- Sodium: 710 mg
- Protein: 17 g
- Total Carbohydrate: 0 g
- Total Fat: 9 g
- Saturated Fat: 4.5 g
- Cholesterol: 20 mg
- Sugar: 0 g

34. Vegetarian Chili Mac

Serving: 4 | Prep: 25mins | Cook: | Ready in: 25mins

Ingredients

- 1 pkg. (7-1/4 oz.) KRAFT Macaroni & Cheese Dinner
- 1 cup canned kidney beans, rinsed
- 1 cup drained canned diced tomatoes
- 1 tsp. chili powder

Direction

- Prepare Dinner as directed on package, using the Light Prep directions.
- Add remaining ingredients; cook 5 min. or until heated through, stirring occasionally.

Nutrition Information

- Calories: 280
- Sugar: 0 g
- Fiber: 5 g
- Total Carbohydrate: 0 g
- Protein: 12 g
- Sodium: 570 mg
- Total Fat: 2 g
- Saturated Fat: 1.5 g
- Cholesterol: 15 mg

35. Veggie Chili

Serving: 4 | Prep: 25mins | Cook: | Ready in: 25mins

Ingredients

- 1 Tbsp. oil
- 1 onion, chopped
- dash crushed red pepper

- 1 can (15.5 oz.) black beans, rinsed
- 1 can (14.5 oz.) stewed tomatoes, undrained
- 1 can (12 oz.) corn, drained
- 1 cup vegetable broth
- 1 Tbsp. chili powder
- 1/2 cup KRAFT Cheddar & Asadero Cheese Deliciously Paired for Tacos
- 1/4 cup BREAKSTONE'S Reduced Fat or KNUDSEN Light Sour Cream

Direction

- Heat oil in large saucepan on medium-high heat. Add onions and crushed pepper; cook and stir 5 min. or until onions are crisp-tender.
- Add beans, tomatoes, corn, vegetable broth and chili powder; stir. Bring to boil, stirring frequently; simmer on medium-low heat 10 min. or until heated through, stirring occasionally.
- Serve topped with cheese and sour cream.

Nutrition Information

- Calories: 280
- Fiber: 8 g
- Cholesterol: 20 mg
- Sodium: 830 mg
- Protein: 11 g
- Total Carbohydrate: 0 g
- Sugar: 0 g
- Saturated Fat: 4 g
- Total Fat: 10 g

36. Veggie Chili Recipe

Serving: 0 | Prep: 15mins | Cook: 45mins | Ready in: 1hours

Ingredients

- 1/4 cup KRAFT Zesty Italian Dressing
- 2 medium onions, chopped
- 10 arbol chiles, stemmed, torn into pieces
- 1 medium butternut squash, peeled, cubed (about 3 cups)
- 4 large carrots (1 lb.), chopped
- 2 red peppers, seeded and chopped
- 2 cans (15.5 oz. each) red kidney beans, drained
- 2 cans (14.5 oz. each) diced tomatoes, undrained
- 2 cans (8 oz. each) tomato sauce
- 1 cinnamon stick
- 5 cups hot cooked rice
- 1 pkg. (8 oz.) KRAFT 2% Milk Shredded Colby & Monterey Jack Cheeses
- 1/2 cup chopped cilantro, divided

Direction

- Heat dressing in large stockpot on medium-high heat. Add onions; cook 5 to 7 min. or until crisp-tender, stirring frequently. Stir in chiles; cook 1 min.
- Add squash, carrots, red peppers, beans, tomatoes, tomato sauce and cinnamon stick; bring to boil. Simmer on medium-low 30 min. or until squash is tender.
- Discard cinnamon stick. Serve chili over rice; top with cheese and cilantro.

Nutrition Information

- Calories: 350
- Total Fat: 7 g
- Cholesterol: 15 mg
- Protein: 16 g
- Fiber: 9 g
- Total Carbohydrate: 0 g
- Sugar: 0 g
- Sodium: 630 mg
- Saturated Fat: 3 g

37. White Chicken Chili

Serving: 0 | Prep: 25mins | Cook: | Ready in: 25mins

Ingredients

- 1-1/2 lb. boneless skinless chicken breasts, cut into bite-size pieces
- 1 large onion, chopped
- 1 tub (8 oz.) PHILADELPHIA Cream Cheese Spread
- 2 Tbsp. milk
- 1/2 tsp. each dried oregano leaves, garlic powder and ground cumin
- 1 can (15 oz.) white beans, rinsed
- 1 cup fat-free reduced-sodium chicken broth
- 1 can (4 oz.) green chiles, undrained
- 1/2 cup KRAFT Mexican Style Finely Shredded Four Cheese
- 1/2 cup chopped tomatoes
- 2 Tbsp. chopped fresh cilantro

Direction

- Cook chicken and onions in large saucepan sprayed with cooking spray on medium heat 8 to 10 min. or until chicken is done, stirring frequently.
- Mix cream cheese spread, milk and seasonings until blended. Add to chicken mixture along with the beans, broth and chiles; mix well. Simmer on medium-low heat 5 min. or until heated through, stirring occasionally.
- Serve topped with remaining ingredients.

Nutrition Information

- Calories: 350
- Fiber: 6 g
- Total Fat: 15 g
- Saturated Fat: 8 g
- Protein: 33 g
- Sodium: 500 mg
- Cholesterol: 100 mg
- Total Carbohydrate: 0 g
- Sugar: 0 g

38. White Chicken Chili Recipe

Serving: 0 | Prep: 30mins | Cook: 20mins | Ready in: 50mins

Ingredients

- 1/3 cup KRAFT Italian Vinaigrette Dressing made with Extra Virgin Olive Oil
- 1 onion, chopped
- 1 carrot, peeled, chopped
- 4 cloves garlic, minced
- 1-1/2 lb. boneless skinless chicken thighs, cut into bite-size pieces
- 1 jalapeño pepper, seeded, finely chopped
- 1 Tbsp. ground cumin
- 1/2 tsp. each ground coriander and oregano
- 1 can (15 oz.) cannellini beans, rinsed
- 1 can (15 oz.) fat-free reduced-sodium chicken broth
- 1 bottle (7.5 oz.) TACO BELL® Verde Salsa
- 1/2 cup BREAKSTONE'S or KNUDSEN Sour Cream

Direction

- Heat dressing in Dutch oven on medium heat. Add onions, carrots and garlic; cook 5 min. or until crisp-tender, stirring frequently.
- Add chicken and peppers; cook 7 to 8 min. or until lightly browned, stirring frequently. Add cumin, coriander and oregano; mix well.
- Add beans, broth and salsa; mix well. Bring to boil, stirring occasionally. Simmer, partially covered, on medium-low heat 20 min., stirring occasionally.
- Serve topped with sour cream.

Nutrition Information

- Calories: 270
- Protein: 23 g
- Sugar: 0 g
- Cholesterol: 120 mg
- Total Fat: 13 g
- Total Carbohydrate: 0 g
- Saturated Fat: 4 g

- Fiber: 3 g
- Sodium: 750 mg

Chapter 2: Chicken Soup Recipes

***

39. Broccoli Cheddar Soup Recipe

Serving: 0 | Prep: 10mins | Cook: 30mins | Ready in: 40mins

Ingredients

- 1 onion, chopped
- 2 Tbsp. KRAFT Lite House Italian Dressing
- 1 can (10-1/2 oz.) condensed chicken broth
- 2 broth cans water
- 4 cups chopped broccoli
- 1 cup fat-free milk
- 1/2 cup instant white rice, uncooked
- 1 cup KRAFT 2% Milk Cheddar Cheese

Direction

- Cook onions in dressing in large saucepan until crisp-tender.
- Add broth, water and broccoli; stir. Bring to boil; cook 8 to 10 min. or until broccoli is tender. Stir in milk and rice; simmer on medium heat 5 min.
- Pour into blender in batches; blend until smooth. Return to saucepan; cook on low heat until heated through, stirring frequently. Serve topped with cheese.

Nutrition Information

- Calories: 140
- Saturated Fat: 2.5 g
- Cholesterol: 15 mg
- Sodium: 580 mg
- Total Carbohydrate: 0 g
- Sugar: 0 g
- Protein: 11 g
- Total Fat: 5 g
- Fiber: 2 g

40. Butternut Squash Soup With Sour Cream

Serving: 0 | Prep: 20mins | Cook: 25mins | Ready in: 45mins

Ingredients

- 1 Tbsp. olive oil
- 2 butternut squash (4 lb.), peeled, seeded and cut into chunks
- 1 onion, chopped
- 1 clove garlic, minced
- 1/2 tsp. ground allspice
- 2 WYLER'S Instant Bouillon Chicken Flavored Cubes
- 3-3/4 cups water
- 1/2 cup BREAKSTONE'S Reduced Fat or KNUDSEN Light Sour Cream

Direction

- Heat oil in large saucepan on medium heat. Add squash, onions and garlic; cook 5 min. or until crisp-tender, stirring occasionally. Stir in allspice; cook and stir 1 min.
- Add bouillon and water. Bring to boil; cover. Simmer on low heat 15 min. or until squash is tender. Process, in batches, in food processor until smooth. Return to saucepan; cook until heated through, stirring occasionally.
- Ladle into 8 bowls. Top with sour cream.

Nutrition Information

- Calories: 200
- Sugar: 0 g
- Protein: 6 g
- Saturated Fat: 1.5 g
- Total Carbohydrate: 0 g
- Sodium: 480 mg
- Fiber: 7 g
- Cholesterol: 5 mg
- Total Fat: 5 g

41. Chicken Tortilla Soup

Serving: 0 | Prep: 20mins | Cook: 25mins | Ready in: 45mins

Ingredients

- 6 corn tortillas (6 inch), divided
- 1-1/2 tsp. oil, divided
- 1/2 lb. boneless skinless chicken breasts, cut into bite-size pieces
- 2 cans (14-1/2 oz. each) chicken broth
- 1 cup TACO BELL® Thick & Chunky Medium Salsa
- 1 cup frozen corn
- 1 cup KRAFT Shredded Cheddar Cheese

Direction

- Heat oven to 400°F.
- Cut 2 tortillas into strips; toss with 1/2 tsp. oil. Spread onto rimmed baking sheet. Bake 10 to 12 min. or until crisp, stirring occasionally.
- Meanwhile, finely chop remaining tortillas. Heat remaining oil in large saucepan on medium-high heat. Add chicken; cook and stir 5 min. Add chopped tortillas, broth, salsa and corn. Bring to boil; simmer on medium-low heat 15 min.
- Serve topped with cheese and tortilla strips.

Nutrition Information

- Calories: 220

- Sugar: 3 g
- Total Fat: 9 g
- Sodium: 920 mg
- Saturated Fat: 4.5 g
- Cholesterol: 40 mg
- Total Carbohydrate: 19 g
- Fiber: 4 g
- Protein: 15 g

42. Chicken And Biscuits

Serving: 6 | Prep: 15mins | Cook: 35mins | Ready in: 50mins

Ingredients

- 1 can (10-3/4 oz.) condensed cream of chicken soup
- 3/4 cup BREAKSTONE'S or KNUDSEN Sour Cream, divided
- 2 cups chopped cooked chicken
- 1 pkg. (16 oz.) frozen mixed vegetables (carrots, corn, green beans, peas), thawed
- 1 cup KRAFT Shredded Mild Cheddar Cheese
- 1 cup all-purpose baking mix
- 3 Tbsp. milk

Direction

- Heat oven to 375°F.
- Mix soup and 1/2 cup sour cream until blended. Combine chicken, vegetables and cheese in large bowl. Add soup mixture; mix lightly.
- Spoon into 8-inch square baking dish sprayed with cooking spray.
- Stir baking mix, milk and remaining sour cream just until mixture forms soft dough. Spoon into 6 mounds over chicken mixture.
- Bake 35 min. or until chicken mixture is hot and bubbly, and biscuit topping is golden brown.

Nutrition Information

- Calories: 400
- Total Fat: 21 g
- Fiber: 3 g
- Protein: 23 g
- Sugar: 7 g
- Saturated Fat: 10 g
- Sodium: 750 mg
- Cholesterol: 85 mg
- Total Carbohydrate: 30 g

43. Crisp & Creamy Baked Chicken Recipe

Serving: 4 | Prep: 15mins | Cook: 20mins | Ready in: 35mins

Ingredients

- 4 small boneless skinless chicken breasts (1 lb.)
- 6 Tbsp. (about 1/2 of pkt.) SHAKE 'N BAKE Extra Crispy Seasoned Coating Mix
- 1 cup long-grain white rice, uncooked
- 2/3 cup (about 1/2 of 10-3/4-oz. can) condensed cream of celery soup
- 1/4 cup milk
- 1 cup KRAFT Shredded Three Cheese with a TOUCH OF PHILADELPHIA

Direction

- Heat oven to 400°F.
- Coat chicken with coating mix as directed on package; place in 13x9-inch baking dish sprayed with cooking spray. Discard any remaining coating mix.
- Bake 20 min. or until chicken is done (165°F). Meanwhile, cook rice as directed on package, omitting salt.
- Mix soup and milk until blended; pour over chicken. Top with cheese. Bake 5 min. or until cheese is melted and sauce is hot and bubbly. Serve with rice.

Nutrition Information

- Calories: 490
- Cholesterol: 100 mg
- Saturated Fat: 7 g
- Total Carbohydrate: 52 g
- Total Fat: 15 g
- Protein: 36 g
- Fiber: 1 g
- Sodium: 840 mg
- Sugar: 2 g

44. Easy Chicken Cordon Bleu

Serving: 6 | Prep: 20mins | Cook: 25mins | Ready in: 45mins

Ingredients

- 1 pkg. (6 oz.) STOVE TOP Lower Sodium Stuffing Mix for Chicken
- 6 small boneless skinless chicken breasts (1-1/2 lb.)
- 6 slices OSCAR MAYER Deli Fresh Smoked Ham
- 1 can (10-3/4 oz.) reduced-sodium condensed cream of chicken soup
- 1 Tbsp. GREY POUPON Savory Honey Mustard
- 6 KRAFT Big Slice Swiss Cheese Slices

Direction

- Heat oven to 400°F.
- Prepare stuffing mix as directed on package.
- Place chicken in 13x9-inch baking dish sprayed with cooking spray; cover with ham. Mix soup and mustard; spoon over chicken. Top with stuffing.
- Bake 25 min. or until chicken is done (165°F). Top with cheese; bake 5 min. or until cheese is melted.

Nutrition Information

- Calories: 430

- Sodium: 730 mg
- Cholesterol: 95 mg
- Total Fat: 18 g
- Total Carbohydrate: 0 g
- Sugar: 0 g
- Fiber: 1 g
- Saturated Fat: 7 g
- Protein: 36 g

45. Easy Chicken Soup

Serving: 0 | Prep: 10mins | Cook: 20mins | Ready in: 30mins

Ingredients

- 1 lb. boneless skinless chicken breasts, cut into 1-inch chunks
- 1/4 cup chopped onion
- 2 tsp. oil
- 2 cans (14-1/2 oz. each) chicken broth
- 3 cups water
- 2 cups carrot slices
- 1 env. GOOD SEASONS Italian Dressing Mix
- 2 Tbsp. chopped fresh parsley
- Quick & Easy Matzo Balls

Direction

- Cook and stir chicken and onion in hot oil in large saucepan on medium-high heat until chicken is cooked through.
- Add broth, water, carrots and dressing mix. Bring to boil. Reduce heat to low; cover. Simmer 5 min. or until carrots are tender.
- Stir in parsley. Serve with Quick & Easy Matzo Balls.

Nutrition Information

- Calories: 250
- Saturated Fat: 2 g
- Sodium: 920 mg
- Sugar: 0 g
- Total Fat: 11 g
- Total Carbohydrate: 0 g
- Fiber: 1 g
- Cholesterol: 125 mg
- Protein: 17 g

46. Easy Chicken And Broccoli

Serving: 4 | Prep: 20mins | Cook: | Ready in: 20mins

Ingredients

- 1 lb. boneless skinless chicken breasts, cut into bite-size pieces
- 3 cups frozen broccoli florets
- 1 can (10-3/4 oz.) condensed cream of mushroom soup
- 1 cup plus 2 Tbsp. water
- 1-1/2 cups instant white rice, uncooked
- 1 cup KRAFT Shredded Three Cheese with a TOUCH OF PHILADELPHIA

Direction

- Cook and stir chicken in large skillet sprayed with cooking spray on medium-high heat 2 to 3 min. or until evenly browned.
- Add broccoli, soup and water; stir. Bring to boil.
- Stir in rice; sprinkle with cheese. Cover; simmer on low heat 5 min.

Nutrition Information

- Calories: 450
- Cholesterol: 95 mg
- Sugar: 3 g
- Fiber: 5 g
- Total Carbohydrate: 39 g
- Total Fat: 16 g
- Sodium: 810 mg
- Saturated Fat: 7 g
- Protein: 37 g

47. Gram's Chicken Pot Pie Updated

Serving: 6 | Prep: 15mins | Cook: 30mins | Ready in: 45mins

Ingredients

- 1 lb. boneless skinless chicken breasts, cut into bite-size pieces
- 2 Tbsp. KRAFT Zesty Italian Dressing
- 2 cups frozen mixed vegetables (carrots, corn, green beans, peas)
- 1 can (10-3/4 oz.) condensed cream of chicken soup
- 1/4 lb. (4 oz.) VELVEETA, cut into 1/2-inch cubes
- 1 sheet frozen puff pastry (1/2 of 17.3-oz. pkg.), thawed
- 1 egg, beaten

Direction

- Heat oven to 400°F.
- Cook and stir chicken in dressing in large skillet on medium heat 5 min. or until done. Stir in vegetables and soup. Spoon into 9-inch square baking dish sprayed with cooking spray; top with VELVEETA.
- Unfold pastry sheet; place over chicken mixture. Fold under edges of pastry; press onto top of baking dish to seal. Brush with egg. Cut several slits in pastry to permit steam to escape. Place dish on baking sheet.
- Bake 30 min. or until crust is deep golden brown. Let stand 5 min. before serving.

Nutrition Information

- Calories: 460
- Sugar: 4 g
- Total Carbohydrate: 30 g
- Fiber: 2 g
- Sodium: 820 mg
- Total Fat: 26 g
- Cholesterol: 90 mg
- Protein: 25 g
- Saturated Fat: 8 g

48. Hearty Cabbage Soup Recipe

Serving: 0 | Prep: 10mins | Cook: 40mins | Ready in: 50mins

Ingredients

- 4 cups chopped green cabbage
- 2 carrots, sliced
- 2 stalks celery, sliced
- 1 onion, chopped
- 1 pkg. (10 oz.) frozen green beans, slightly thawed
- 1 can (15-1/2 oz.) cannellini beans, rinsed
- 1-1/2 qt. (6 cups) water
- 2 cans (14-1/2 oz. each) fat-free reduced-sodium chicken broth
- 2 cups canned crushed tomatoes, undrained
- 1 env. (0.7 oz.) GOOD SEASONS Italian Dressing Mix

Direction

- Combine ingredients in Dutch oven.
- Bring to boil on high heat; simmer on medium-low 30 min. or until vegetables are tender, stirring occasionally.

Nutrition Information

- Calories: 60
- Total Carbohydrate: 0 g
- Fiber: 4 g
- Saturated Fat: 0 g
- Total Fat: 0 g
- Sodium: 400 mg
- Protein: 3 g
- Cholesterol: 0 mg
- Sugar: 0 g

49. Hearty Mexican Chicken Soup

Serving: 0 | Prep: 30mins | Cook: | Ready in: 30mins

Ingredients

- 1 large yellow onion, chopped
- 1 Tbsp. oil
- 1 clove garlic, minced
- 1/2 tsp. ground cumin
- 1 qt. (4 cups) fat-free reduced-sodium chicken broth
- 1 can (15.5 oz.) cannellini beans, rinsed
- 1 cup TACO BELL® Thick & Chunky Salsa
- 2 cups shredded rotisserie chicken
- 1 cup frozen corn
- 2 green onions, chopped
- 1/4 cup chopped fresh cilantro
- 1 cup KRAFT Mexican Style Finely Shredded Four Cheese

Direction

- Cook yellow onions in hot oil in large saucepan on medium heat 6 to 7 min. or until tender, stirring frequently. Add garlic and cumin; cook and stir 1 min.
- Add broth, beans and salsa; stir. Bring to boil. Stir in chicken and corn. Return to boil; simmer 5 min., stirring occasionally. Remove from heat.
- Stir in green onions and cilantro. Serve topped with cheese.

Nutrition Information

- Calories: 230
- Cholesterol: 50 mg
- Fiber: 5 g
- Sodium: 690 mg
- Total Carbohydrate: 0 g
- Sugar: 0 g
- Saturated Fat: 4.5 g
- Protein: 15 g
- Total Fat: 11 g

50. Homemade Chicken Pot Pie Recipe

Serving: 5 | Prep: 15mins | Cook: 30mins | Ready in: 45mins

Ingredients

- 2 cups frozen mixed vegetables (peas, carrots, green beans, corn)
- 2 pkg. (6 oz. each) OSCAR MAYER CARVING BOARD Flame Grilled Chicken Breast Strips
- 1 can (10-3/4 oz.) condensed cream of chicken soup
- 1/2 cup KRAFT Shredded Cheddar Cheese
- 1 cup flour
- 2 tsp. CALUMET Baking Powder
- 1/2 cup (1/2 of 8-oz. tub) PHILADELPHIA Cream Cheese Spread
- 1/4 cup milk

Direction

- Heat oven to 400°F.
- Combine vegetables, chicken and soup; spoon into 5 (2-cup) ovenproof bowls. Top with cheddar.
- Mix flour and baking powder in medium bowl. Cut in cream cheese spread until mixture resembles coarse crumbs. Stir in milk with fork until mixture forms dough.
- Divide into 5 balls. Pat each into 5-inch circle on lightly floured surface. Prick several times with fork to allow steam to escape.
- Place biscuits on top of chicken mixture. Bake 25 to 30 min. or until crusts are golden brown.

Nutrition Information

- Calories: 380
- Protein: 27 g
- Total Fat: 15 g
- Fiber: 2 g

- Sugar: 4 g
- Sodium: 1180 mg
- Cholesterol: 80 mg
- Total Carbohydrate: 34 g
- Saturated Fat: 7 g

51. Loaded Potato Soup

Serving: 0 | Prep: 30mins | Cook: | Ready in: 30mins

Ingredients

- 1 lb. baking potato es (about 3), cubed
- 1 can (14-1/2 oz.) fat-free reduced-sodium chicken broth
- 1 cup milk
- 3 slices OSCAR MAYER Bacon, cooked, crumbled and divided
- 1 cup KRAFT Shredded Cheddar Cheese, divided
- 1 green onion sliced, divided
- 1/4 cup BREAKSTONE'S or KNUDSEN Sour Cream

Direction

- Microwave potatoes in large microwaveable bowl on HIGH 5 min., stirring after 2-1/2 min. Stir in broth and milk. Microwave 10 min., stirring after 5 min. Carefully smash potatoes with potato masher.
- Reserve 2 Tbsp. each bacon and cheese, and 1 Tbsp. onions for topping. Stir remaining bacon, cheese and onions into soup.
- Serve topped with sour cream and reserved ingredients.

Nutrition Information

- Calories: 290
- Sugar: 4 g
- Total Carbohydrate: 25 g
- Protein: 13 g
- Total Fat: 16 g

- Cholesterol: 50 mg
- Sodium: 530 mg
- Fiber: 3 g
- Saturated Fat: 9 g

52. STOVE TOP Stuffed Chicken Rolls

Serving: 6 | Prep: 15mins | Cook: 30mins | Ready in: 45mins

Ingredients

- 1 pkg. (6 oz.) STOVE TOP Stuffing Mix for Chicken
- 1 cup water
- 2 eggs, beaten
- 6 small boneless skinless chicken breasts (1-1/2 lb.), pounded to 1/4-inch thickness
- 1 can (10-3/4 oz.) condensed cream of chicken soup
- 1/2 cup milk
- 1 tsp. paprika

Direction

- Heat oven to 400°F.
- Combine stuffing mix and water in medium bowl. Let stand 5 min. Stir in eggs.
- Place chicken, top sides down, on cutting board; spread with stuffing mixture. Starting at one short end, tightly roll up each chicken breast; place, seam side down, in 13x9-inch baking dish sprayed with cooking spray.
- Mix soup and milk; pour over chicken. Sprinkle with paprika.
- Bake 25 to 30 min. or until chicken is done (165°F).

Nutrition Information

- Calories: 320
- Saturated Fat: 2.5 g
- Sugar: 4 g

- Protein: 32 g
- Cholesterol: 145 mg
- Total Fat: 9 g
- Total Carbohydrate: 26 g
- Fiber: 1 g
- Sodium: 920 mg

53. Santa Fe Chicken Fajita Soup

Serving: 8 | Prep: 30mins | Cook: 30mins | Ready in: 1hours

Ingredients

- 1 pkg. (1.4 oz.) TACO BELL® Fajita Seasoning Mix
- 1/3 cup water
- 1 lb. boneless skinless chicken breasts, cut into thin strips
- 4 large cloves garlic, minced
- 2 Tbsp. chopped fresh cilantro
- 1 large red onion, chopped
- 1 small green pepper, chopped
- 1 pkg. (8 oz.) PHILADELPHIA Neufchatel Cheese, cubed
- 8 oz. 2% Milk VELVEETA, cut into 1/2-inch cubes
- 2 cans (14.5 oz. each) fat-free reduced-sodium chicken broth

Direction

- Combine seasoning mix and water in medium bowl. Add chicken; toss to evenly coat. Refrigerate 30 min.
- Cook garlic and cilantro in large nonstick saucepan on medium-high heat 1 min. Stir in chicken mixture, onions and peppers; cook 10 min. or until chicken is done, stirring frequently.
- Add Neufchatel, VELVEETA and broth; mix well. Cook on medium heat until Neufchatel and VELVEETA are completely melted and soup is heated through, stirring occasionally.

Nutrition Information

- Calories: 210
- Total Carbohydrate: 11 g
- Total Fat: 10 g
- Saturated Fat: 6 g
- Fiber: 0 g
- Sodium: 990 mg
- Cholesterol: 65 mg
- Sugar: 6 g
- Protein: 16 g

54. Santa Fe Chicken Recipe

Serving: 0 | Prep: 10mins | Cook: 45mins | Ready in: 55mins

Ingredients

- 2 cups instant white rice, uncooked
- 1 can (15 oz.) black beans, rinsed
- 1 yellow pepper, chopped
- 1 can (10-1/2 oz.) condensed cream of chicken soup
- 2 cups water
- 1/4 cup chopped fresh cilantro
- 4 small boneless skinless chicken breasts (1 lb.)
- 1/2 cup TACO BELL® Thick & Chunky Salsa
- 1 cup KRAFT Mexican Style Finely Shredded Four Cheese

Direction

- Heat oven to 400°F.
- Combine rice, beans and peppers in 13x9-inch baking dish. Mix soup, water and cilantro; pour over rice mixture.
- Top with chicken and salsa.
- Bake 45 min. or until chicken is done (165°F), topping with cheese for the last 10 min.

Nutrition Information

- Calories: 500
- Fiber: 8 g

- Cholesterol: 85 mg
- Sugar: 3 g
- Total Fat: 12 g
- Saturated Fat: 6 g
- Total Carbohydrate: 65 g
- Sodium: 860 mg
- Protein: 33 g

55. Shortcut Chicken Manicotti Recipe

Serving: 4 | Prep: 20mins | Cook: 50mins | Ready in: 1hours10mins

Ingredients

- 1 can (10-3/4 oz.) condensed cream of chicken soup
- 1-1/2 cups water
- 1/4 lb. (4 oz.) VELVEETA, cut into 1/2-inch cubes
- 12 manicotti shells, uncooked
- 1 lb. boneless skinless chicken breasts, cut into thin strips
- 2 cups frozen broccoli florets
- 1/4 cup KRAFT Grated Parmesan Cheese

Direction

- Heat oven to 400ºF.
- Microwave soup, water and VELVEETA in microwaveable bowl on HIGH 3 min. or until VELVEETA is completely melted and mixture is well blended, stirring after 2 min.
- Spread 1/3 of the VELVEETA mixture onto bottom of 13x9-inch baking dish sprayed with cooking spray. Stuff pasta shells with chicken; place in baking dish.
- Stir broccoli into remaining soup mixture; spoon over pasta shells. Sprinkle with Parmesan; cover.
- Bake 45 to 50 min. or until pasta is tender and chicken is done.

Nutrition Information

- Calories: 390
- Sugar: 4 g
- Total Fat: 14 g
- Sodium: 1070 mg
- Total Carbohydrate: 32 g
- Cholesterol: 90 mg
- Protein: 32 g
- Saturated Fat: 6 g
- Fiber: 2 g

56. Slow Cooker Chicken Taco Soup

Serving: 8 | Prep: 1hours | Cook: 6hours | Ready in: 7hours

Ingredients

- 2 lb. boneless skinless chicken breast tenderloins
- 1 cup chopped onion
- 2 cloves finely chopped garlic
- 2 Tbsp. ground cumin
- 1 Tbsp. dried Mexican oregano
- 1 Tbsp. smoked paprika
- 1 tsp. chili powder
- 1 can (15 oz.) whole kernel corn, drained
- 1 can (15 oz.) green beans, drained
- 1 can (15 oz.) black beans, rinsed and drained
- 1 can (15 oz) red kidney beans, rinsed and drained
- 2 cans (15 oz.) diced tomatoes and green chiles, undrained
- 1 can (6 oz.) tomato paste
- 1 qt. chicken stock
- 1 cup KRAFT Mexican Style Shredded Four Cheese with a TOUCH OF PHILADELPHIA
- 1/4 cup fresh cilantro, for garnish

Direction

- Add chicken, onion and garlic to slow cooker. Turn slow cooker to high and cook for up to an hour.
- Add all spices, corn, green beans, black beans, kidney beans, diced tomatoes, tomato paste and chicken stock. Mix well to combine. Turn the cooker's heat to low to cook for an additional 6 – 7 hours, or until chicken is very tender and falling apart.
- Before serving, remove chicken tenderloins and shred. Add chicken back to soup.
- Serve your soup topped with cheese and a pinch fresh cilantro.

Nutrition Information

- Calories: 0 g
- Cholesterol: 0 g
- Total Fat: 0 g
- Total Carbohydrate: 0 g
- Protein: 0 g
- Sugar: 0 g
- Sodium: 0 g
- Fiber: 0 g
- Saturated Fat: 0 g

57. Slow Cooked Chicken & Dumplings

Serving: 0 | Prep: 15mins | Cook: 8hours45mins | Ready in: 9hours

Ingredients

- 1-1/2 lb. boneless skinless chicken thighs
- 2-1/2 cups fat-free reduced-sodium chicken broth
- 1-1/2 cups each chopped carrots, celery and onions
- 2 cups frozen peas
- 1/2 cup (1/2 of 8-oz. tub) PHILADELPHIA Chive & Onion Cream Cheese Spread
- 2 eggs, beaten
- 1 pkg. (6 oz.) STOVE TOP Stuffing Mix for Chicken
- 3/4 cup hot water

Direction

- Place chicken in slow cooker sprayed with cooking spray. Add broth, carrots, celery and onions; stir. Cover with lid.
- Cook on LOW 8 to 10 hours (or on HIGH 3-1/2 hours).
- Add peas and cream cheese spread; stir until cream cheese is completely melted and sauce is well blended.
- Mix eggs, stuffing mix and hot water until blended; drop in heaping 2-Tbsp. portions over chicken mixture.
- Cook, covered, on HIGH 30 min. Gently turn dumplings; cook, covered, 15 min.

Nutrition Information

- Calories: 410
- Total Fat: 14 g
- Cholesterol: 190 mg
- Sodium: 940 mg
- Sugar: 0 g
- Saturated Fat: 5 g
- Fiber: 5 g
- Protein: 32 g
- Total Carbohydrate: 0 g

58. Smothered Chicken & Green Bean Skillet

Serving: 0 | Prep: 5mins | Cook: 22mins | Ready in: 27mins

Ingredients

- 4 small boneless skinless chicken breasts (1 lb.)
- 2 cups frozen green beans
- 1 can (10-1/2 oz.) condensed low-fat condensed cream of mushroom soup

- 1/2 cup water
- 1/4 tsp. dried thyme leaves
- 1 cup KRAFT 2% Milk Shredded Sharp Cheddar Cheese

Direction

- Heat large nonstick skillet on medium-high heat. Add chicken; cover. Cook 5 to 7 min. on each side or until done (165°F). Remove chicken from skillet.
- Add beans, soup, water and thyme to skillet; cover. Cook 6 min., stirring frequently.
- Return chicken to skillet. Cook 1 min. or until hot. Top with cheese.

Nutrition Information

- Calories: 270
- Total Fat: 10 g
- Sodium: 780 mg
- Protein: 33 g
- Cholesterol: 90 mg
- Fiber: 2 g
- Total Carbohydrate: 0 g
- Saturated Fat: 5 g
- Sugar: 0 g

59. Speedy Asian Soup Recipe

Serving: 0 | Prep: 5mins | Cook: 12mins | Ready in: 17mins

Ingredients

- 1 cup instant brown rice, uncooked
- 1/4 cup KRAFT Asian Toasted Sesame Dressing
- 2 tsp. lite soy sauce
- 2 cups chopped cooked chicken
- 2 cups each fat-free reduced-sodium chicken broth and water

Direction

- Combine 1/4 cup rice, 1 Tbsp. dressing and 1/2 tsp. soy sauce in each of 4 microwaveable soup bowls.
- Add 1/2 cup of each of the remaining ingredients to each bowl; stir. Cover with waxed paper.
- Microwave on HIGH 5 to 7 min. or until heated through. Let stand 5 min. before serving.

Nutrition Information

- Calories: 280
- Fiber: 2 g
- Total Fat: 9 g
- Total Carbohydrate: 0 g
- Cholesterol: 60 mg
- Sugar: 0 g
- Saturated Fat: 2 g
- Sodium: 570 mg
- Protein: 24 g

60. Speedy Ginger Chicken Soup Bowls

Serving: 4 | Prep: 15mins | Cook: | Ready in: 15mins

Ingredients

- 3/4 cup instant white rice, uncooked
- 4 mL minced fresh ginger
- 1 mL OSCAR MAYER CARVING BOARD Flame Grilled Chicken Breast Strips
- 2 mL cut-up fresh vegetables (thin red pepper strips, sliced carrots and sliced green onions)
- 2 mL fat-free reduced-sodium chicken broth
- 2 cups water

Direction

- Combine 3 Tbsp. rice and 1 tsp. ginger in each of 4 microwaveable soup bowls.
- Top each with 1/4 cup chicken and 1/2 cup vegetables; stir.

- Add 1/2 cup each broth and water to each bowl; cover with waxed paper. Microwave on HIGH 2 min. Let stand 5 min. before serving.

Nutrition Information

- Calories: 130
- Total Carbohydrate: 0 g
- Sugar: 0 g
- Protein: 11 g
- Sodium: 420 mg
- Total Fat: 1 g
- Cholesterol: 25 mg
- Fiber: 2 g
- Saturated Fat: 0 g

61. VELVEETA® Chicken Enchilada Casserole Recipe

Serving: 6 | Prep: 15mins | Cook: 35mins | Ready in: 50mins

Ingredients

- 3/4 cup TACO BELL® Thick & Chunky Salsa, divided
- 2 cups chopped cooked chicken
- 1 can (10-3/4 oz.) condensed cream of chicken soup
- 1/2 lb. (8 oz.) Mexican VELVEETA, cut into 1/2-inch cubes
- 6 corn tortillas (6 inch), cut in half

Direction

- Heat oven to 350°F. Reserve 1/4 cup salsa for later use. Mix chicken, soup and VELVEETA until well blended; spread 1 cup onto bottom of 8-inch square baking dish.
- Top with layers of 6 tortilla halves and 1/2 each of the remaining remaining salsa and chicken mixture; repeat layers.
- Bake 30 to 35 min. or until heated through. Serve topped with reserved salsa.

Nutrition Information

- Calories: 290
- Total Fat: 15 g
- Saturated Fat: 6 g
- Protein: 18 g
- Sodium: 1270 mg
- Total Carbohydrate: 21 g
- Sugar: 5 g
- Cholesterol: 55 mg
- Fiber: 3 g

62. Wonton Soup

Serving: 0 | Prep: 55mins | Cook: | Ready in: 55mins

Ingredients

- 4 green onions, divided
- 1-1/2 cups sliced shiitake mushrooms, divided
- 1 can (8 oz.) sliced water chestnuts, drained, divided
- 1/2 lb. ground pork
- 2 Tbsp. KRAFT Asian Toasted Sesame Dressing
- 1 egg, separated
- 32 wonton wrappers
- 2 qt. (8 cups) fat-free reduced-sodium chicken broth

Direction

- Chop 2 onions. Finely chop enough mushrooms to measure 1/4 cup and enough water chestnuts to measure 2 Tbsp. Mix chopped vegetables and chopped water chestnuts with meat, dressing and egg yolk until blended. Spoon onto centers of wonton wrappers, adding about 1 tsp. to each.
- Beat egg white lightly. Brush onto edges of wrappers; fold diagonally in half. Press edges together to seal. Bring opposite corners of long edge of each triangle together, overlapping

corners; brush with remaining egg white to seal.
- Slice remaining onions; place in large saucepan. Add chicken broth, remaining mushrooms and remaining water chestnuts; bring to boil on medium heat. Carefully add wontons; simmer 4 min. or until wontons are done, stirring occasionally.

Nutrition Information

- Calories: 200
- Protein: 10 g
- Sugar: 0 g
- Saturated Fat: 2 g
- Total Carbohydrate: 0 g
- Total Fat: 6 g
- Fiber: 2 g
- Sodium: 660 mg
- Cholesterol: 45 mg

Chapter 3: Chicken Chili Soup Recipes

***

63. 15 Minute Chicken Chili

Serving: 0 | Prep: 15mins | Cook: | Ready in: 15mins

Ingredients

- 2-1/2 cups shredded cooked chicken
- 1 can (15.5 oz.) chili beans
- 1 can (10 oz.) diced tomatoes and green chiles, undrained
- 2 Tbsp. A.1. Sweet Hickory Sauce
- 1/2 cup KRAFT 2% Milk Shredded Cheddar Cheese
- 1 Tbsp. chopped fresh cilantro

Direction

- Cook all ingredients except cheese and cilantro in saucepan on medium heat 5 min. or until heated through, stirring occasionally.
- Serve topped with the cheese and cilantro.

Nutrition Information

- Calories: 340
- Protein: 34 g
- Sodium: 910 mg
- Total Fat: 10 g
- Sugar: 0 g
- Cholesterol: 85 mg
- Saturated Fat: 3.5 g
- Total Carbohydrate: 0 g
- Fiber: 8 g

64. Beef Enchilada Casserole

Serving: 0 | Prep: 20mins | Cook: 25mins | Ready in: 45mins

Ingredients

- 1 lb. lean ground beef
- 1 can (10-3/4 oz.) reduced-sodium condensed cream of chicken soup
- 1-1/4 cups cubed VELVEETA (1/2-inch cubes), divided
- 6 corn tortillas (6 inch), cut in half
- 1 can (10 oz.) RO*TEL Diced Tomatoes & Green Chilies, undrained

Direction

- Heat oven to 350°F.
- Brown meat in large skillet; drain. Stir in soup and 1 cup VELVEETA.
- Spoon 1/3 of the meat mixture into 8-inch square baking dish; cover with 6 tortilla halves and 1/4 cup tomatoes. Repeat layers. Top with remaining meat mixture, tomatoes and VELVEETA; cover.

- Bake 25 min. or until heated through.

Nutrition Information

- Calories: 290
- Fiber: 2 g
- Sugar: 4 g
- Cholesterol: 70 mg
- Sodium: 840 mg
- Total Fat: 13 g
- Protein: 22 g
- Saturated Fat: 6 g
- Total Carbohydrate: 21 g

65. Black & White Bean Chicken Chili

Serving: 0 | Prep: 30mins | Cook: | Ready in: 30mins

Ingredients

- 1 can (28 oz.) diced tomatoes, undrained
- 1 lb. boneless skinless chicken breasts, cooked, cut into bite-size pieces
- 1 can (15 oz.) black beans, rinsed
- 1 can (15 oz.) cannellini beans, rinsed
- 1 cup KRAFT Original Barbecue Sauce
- 1 onion, chopped
- 1 tsp. chili powder
- 1 tsp. ground cumin

Direction

- Combine ingredients in large saucepan.
- Bring to boil on medium-high heat; simmer on medium-low heat 10 min. or until heated through, stirring occasionally.

Nutrition Information

- Calories: 200
- Total Carbohydrate: 0 g
- Sodium: 620 mg
- Sugar: 0 g
- Protein: 17 g
- Total Fat: 2 g
- Cholesterol: 35 mg
- Fiber: 4 g
- Saturated Fat: 0 g

66. Cheesy Chicken Quesadilla

Serving: 4 | Prep: 30mins | Cook: | Ready in: 30mins

Ingredients

- 1/2 cup TACO BELL® Thick & Chunky Salsa
- 2 Tbsp. MIRACLE WHIP Dressing
- 1/2 tsp. chili powder
- 1/2 lb. cooked boneless skinless chicken breasts, sliced
- 8 flour tortillas (6 inch)
- 1 cup KRAFT Mexican Style Finely Shredded Four Cheese

Direction

- Mix salsa, dressing and chili powder until blended; spread onto tortillas.
- Place chicken on half of each tortilla; top with cheese. Fold tortillas in half to enclose filling.
- Heat large heavy skillet sprayed with cooking spray on medium heat. Add quesadillas, 2 at a time; cook 4 to 5 min. on each side or until cheese is melted and quesadillas are lightly browned on both sides. Repeat with remaining quesadillas.
- Cut quesadillas into wedges to serve.

Nutrition Information

- Calories: 450
- Fiber: 4 g
- Sodium: 1110 mg
- Total Fat: 18 g
- Total Carbohydrate: 0 g
- Cholesterol: 75 mg
- Protein: 30 g

- Sugar: 0 g
- Saturated Fat: 8 g

67. Chicken In Roasted Poblano Sauce

Serving: 8 | Prep: 15mins | Cook: 10mins | Ready in: 25mins

Ingredients

- 1/4 cup KRAFT Zesty Italian Dressing, divided
- 8 small boneless skinless chicken breasts (2 lb.)
- 4 large poblano chiles, roasted, peeled and deveined
- 1 cup BREAKSTONE'S or KNUDSEN Sour Cream
- 1 chicken bouillon cube

Direction

- Heat 2 Tbsp. dressing in large skillet on medium-high heat. Add chicken; cook 5 min. on each side or until breasts are evenly browned on both sides.
- Meanwhile, blend chiles, sour cream and bouillon cube in blender until smooth.
- Add remaining dressing to skillet. Pour chile mixture over chicken; bring to boil. Cover; simmer on medium-low heat 10 min. or until chicken is done (165°F).

Nutrition Information

- Calories: 210
- Fiber: 1 g
- Total Fat: 10 g
- Cholesterol: 90 mg
- Total Carbohydrate: 0 g
- Sodium: 310 mg
- Sugar: 0 g
- Protein: 25 g
- Saturated Fat: 4.5 g

68. Chili Chicken Mac & Cheese

Serving: 0 | Prep: 10mins | Cook: 15mins | Ready in: 25mins

Ingredients

- 1 pkg. (7-1/4 oz.) KRAFT Macaroni & Cheese Dinner
- 3/4 lb. boneless skinless chicken breasts, cut into bite-size pieces
- 1 tsp. chili powder
- 1/4 cup KRAFT 2% Milk Shredded Sharp Cheddar Cheese
- 1/4 cup TACO BELL® Thick & Chunky Salsa

Direction

- Prepare Dinner as directed on package, using the Light Prep directions. Meanwhile, toss chicken with chili powder in large skillet sprayed with cooking spray; cook and stir on medium heat 5 min. or until chicken is done.
- Add prepared Dinner to chicken; mix lightly.
- Serve topped with remaining ingredients.

Nutrition Information

- Calories: 340
- Sodium: 650 mg
- Total Carbohydrate: 0 g
- Sugar: 0 g
- Total Fat: 8 g
- Saturated Fat: 4 g
- Cholesterol: 70 mg
- Fiber: 1 g
- Protein: 28 g

69. Crispy Simple Baked Chicken

Serving: 0 | Prep: 10mins | Cook: 20mins | Ready in: 30mins

Ingredients

- 2 Tbsp. (about 1/4 pkt.) SHAKE 'N BAKE Chicken Coating Mix
- 1 tsp. chili powder
- 1/4 tsp. garlic powder
- 2 small boneless skinless chicken breasts (1/2 lb.)

Direction

- Heat oven to 425°F.
- Mix coating mix, chili and garlic powder. Use to coat chicken as directed on package.
- Place on baking sheet.
- Bake 20 min. or until chicken is done (165°F).

Nutrition Information

- Calories: 150
- Saturated Fat: 1 g
- Sugar: 0 g
- Cholesterol: 55 mg
- Fiber: 0.5488 g
- Total Fat: 3.5 g
- Total Carbohydrate: 0 g
- Sodium: 360 mg
- Protein: 19 g

70. Fiesta Chicken Enchiladas Recipe

Serving: 4 | Prep: 25mins | Cook: 20mins | Ready in: 45mins

Ingredients

- 1 lb. boneless skinless chicken breasts, cut into bite-size pieces
- 1 each large green and red pepper, chopped
- 1 Tbsp. chili powder
- 3/4 cup TACO BELL® Thick & Chunky Salsa, divided
- 2 oz. (1/4 of 8-oz. pkg) PHILADELPHIA 1/3 Less Fat than Cream Cheese, cubed
- 3/4 cup KRAFT Mexican Style 2% Milk Finely Shredded Four Cheese, divided
- 8 whole wheat tortillas (6 inch)

Direction

- Heat oven to 375°F.
- Cook chicken, peppers and chili powder in large skillet sprayed with cooking spray on medium heat 8 min. or until chicken is done, stirring frequently. Stir in 1/4 cup salsa and Neufchatel; cook and stir 3 to 5 min. or until Neufchatel is completely melted and mixture is well blended. Stir in 1/4 cup shredded cheese.
- Spoon heaping 1/3 cup chicken mixture down center of each tortilla; roll up. Place, seam sides down, in 13x9-inch baking dish sprayed with cooking spray; top with remaining salsa and shredded cheese. Cover.
- Bake 20 min. or until heated through.

Nutrition Information

- Calories: 170
- Protein: 27 g
- Saturated Fat: 2.5 g
- Cholesterol: 95 mg
- Fiber: 0 g
- Sugar: 0 g
- Total Fat: 6 g
- Sodium: 110 mg
- Total Carbohydrate: 0 g

71. Fiesta Chicken Soup Recipe

Serving: 0 | Prep: 30mins | Cook: | Ready in: 30mins

Ingredients

- 1/4 cup KRAFT Zesty Italian Dressing
- 3/4 lb. boneless skinless chicken breasts, cut into bite-size pieces
- 1 onion, chopped
- 1 cup (about 1/2 of 14-1/2-oz. can) stewed tomatoes, undrained
- 1 can (14-1/2 oz.) fat-free reduced-sodium chicken broth
- 1-1/4 cups water
- 1 can (8-1/2 oz.) peas and diced carrots, drained
- 1 tsp. chili powder
- 3/4 cup KRAFT Mexican Style Shredded Four Cheese with a TOUCH OF PHILADELPHIA

Direction

- Heat dressing in large saucepan on medium-high heat. Add chicken and onions; cook 5 min., stirring occasionally.
- Add all remaining ingredients except cheese; stir. Bring to boil; simmer on medium heat 8 min. or until chicken is done and onions are tender. Meanwhile, heat broiler.
- Ladle soup into 8 ovenproof bowls; top with cheese. Broil, 6 inches from heat, 2 to 3 min. or until cheese is melted.

Nutrition Information

- Calories: 130
- Sodium: 400 mg
- Total Fat: 5 g
- Saturated Fat: 2.5 g
- Total Carbohydrate: 0 g
- Fiber: 2 g
- Sugar: 0 g
- Protein: 12 g
- Cholesterol: 35 mg

72. Green Enchiladas Recipe

Serving: 0 | Prep: 20mins | Cook: 20mins | Ready in: 40mins

Ingredients

- 1 lb. boneless skinless chicken breasts, cooked, shredded
- 2 cans (12 oz. each) green enchilada sauce, divided
- 6 oz. Queso Blanco VELVEETA, cut into 1/2-inch cubes, divided
- 12 corn tortillas (6 inch)

Direction

- Heat oven to 375°F.
- Combine chicken, 1/2 cup enchilada sauce and half the VELVEETA. Pour 1/2 cup of the remaining sauce onto bottom of 13x9-inch baking dish sprayed with cooking spray.
- Spoon 1/4 cup chicken mixture down center of each tortilla, roll up. Place, seam-sides down, in dish; top with remaining sauce and VELVEETA. Cover.
- Bake 20 min. or until enchiladas are heated through and VELVEETA is melted.

Nutrition Information

- Calories: 310
- Sodium: 1070 mg
- Fiber: 3 g
- Saturated Fat: 3 g
- Total Carbohydrate: 31 g
- Sugar: 6 g
- Protein: 22 g
- Total Fat: 10 g
- Cholesterol: 60 mg

73. Grilled Chicken Wraps

Serving: 4 | Prep: 35mins | Cook: 10mins | Ready in: 45mins

Ingredients

- 1 lb. boneless skinless chicken breast s
- 2 tsp. oil

- 1 cup KRAFT Mexican Style Shredded Four Cheese with a TOUCH OF PHILADELPHIA
- 1 tomato, chopped
- 3 Tbsp. KRAFT Zesty Italian Dressing
- 2 tsp. chili powder
- 4 flour tortilla s (8 inch)

Direction

- Heat grill to medium heat.
- Brush chicken with oil. Grill 6 to 8 min. on each side or until done (165°F); cool slightly.
- Cut chicken into strips; place in medium bowl. Add cheese, tomatoes, dressing and chili powder; mix lightly. Spoon down centers of tortillas. Fold in opposite sides of tortillas, then roll up burrito-style.
- Place, seam sides down, on grill grate. Grill 4 to 5 min. on each side or until evenly browned.

Nutrition Information

- Calories: 430
- Total Fat: 19 g
- Sugar: 2 g
- Cholesterol: 95 mg
- Sodium: 720 mg
- Total Carbohydrate: 29 g
- Fiber: 3 g
- Saturated Fat: 7 g
- Protein: 35 g

74. How To Cook Chicken

Serving: 0 | Prep: | Cook: | Ready in:

Ingredients

- Chicken

Direction

- *Food Safety and Chicken
- Chicken is a versatile ingredient that can be used in a variety of cooking methods, ethnic cuisines and flavor combinations.
- For proper food safety, always wash your hands before and after handling raw chicken. Also, be sure to use clean knives, cutting boards and counters when working with chicken. Wash all with hot soapy water after using to prepare other ingredients.
- A meat thermometer or instant-read thermometer is the best way to check for the doneness of cooked chicken. The internal temperature should be at least 165°F when tested at the thickest part of the chicken.
- *How to Cut Up Chicken
- Bone-in chicken pieces or whole chickens take longer to cook but provide the best flavor in recipe use. Check out these delicious and easy ideas using whole or cut-up chickens.
- Cutting boneless skinless chicken breasts into pieces can be a slippery task. To make it safer to cut the chicken breasts, partially freeze the chicken before cutting. The firmer chicken is much easier to cut and handle.
- If you want to stretch your dollar, purchase boneless chicken breasts and butterfly them. This simple technique can take a larger, thicker breast and turn it into 2 servings. To butterfly a chicken breast, place chicken breast, smooth-side down, on a cutting board with the tip end facing you. Place hand on top of breast. Carefully cut into the thickest part of the breast, being careful to not cut all the way through to opposite side of breast. Open breast like a book, then lightly pound it to the desired thickness. If desired, you can cut the breast in half before cooking.
- *How to Grill Chicken
- Let's grill! Boneless chicken breasts are popular for the grill but can easily dry out from their lack of internal fat. To lessen this problem, consider marinating chicken breasts in your favorite KRAFT Dressing for at least 30 minutes before grilling. (Be sure to discard the marinade after removing the marinated chicken.) Brush the chicken with additional

dressing or KRAFT Barbecue Sauce for the last few minutes of the grilling time.

75. Kung Pao Chicken Recipe

Serving: 0 | Prep: 30mins | Cook: | Ready in: 30mins

Ingredients

- 1/4 cup water
- 5 cups small fresh broccoli florets
- 1/4 cup creamy peanut butter
- 1 Tbsp. lite soy sauce
- 2 tsp. Thai chili sauce
- 1/4 cup KRAFT Classic CATALINA Dressing, divided
- 2 cloves garlic, minced
- 1 Tbsp. minced fresh ginger
- 1 lb. boneless skinless chicken thighs, cut into bite-size pieces
- 2 green onions, sliced

Direction

- Bring water to boil in large nonstick skillet. Add broccoli; cover. Simmer on medium-low heat 5 min. or until crisp-tender. Meanwhile, mix peanut butter, soy sauce, chili sauce and 2 Tbsp. dressing until blended.
- Transfer broccoli to serving plate; cover to keep warm. Heat remaining dressing in same skillet on medium-high heat. Add garlic and ginger; cook and stir 1 min. Add chicken; cook 2 min., stirring frequently. Stir in peanut butter mixture; cook 5 to 7 min. or until chicken is done and sauce is thickened, stirring frequently to scrape browned bits from bottom of skillet.
- Spoon chicken mixture next to broccoli; sprinkle with onions.

Nutrition Information

- Calories: 290
- Total Fat: 15 g
- Saturated Fat: 3.5 g
- Total Carbohydrate: 0 g
- Protein: 25 g
- Sugar: 0 g
- Cholesterol: 100 mg
- Sodium: 340 mg
- Fiber: 4 g

76. Make Ahead Smoky Chipotle Chicken Chili

Serving: 0 | Prep: 1hours | Cook: | Ready in: 1hours

Ingredients

- 1 lb. lean ground chicken
- 1 yellow onion, chopped
- 2 cloves garlic, minced
- 1 can (28 oz.) diced tomatoes, undrained
- 1 can (15.5 oz.) black beans, rinsed
- 1 green pepper, chopped
- 1/3 cup KRAFT Sweet & Spicy Barbecue Sauce
- 1 Tbsp. chili powder
- 1 tsp. chipotle chile pepper powder
- 1/4 cup chopped fresh cilantro
- 3/4 cup KRAFT Mexican Style Shredded Four Cheese with a TOUCH OF PHILADELPHIA
- 2 green onions, chopped

Direction

- Cook and stir first 3 ingredients in large nonstick skillet on high heat 8 to 10 min. or until chicken is done. Add tomatoes, beans, green peppers, barbecue sauce, chili powder and chipotle chile pepper powder; mix well. Bring to boil; simmer on medium-low heat 25 min., stirring occasionally. Cool completely.
- Spoon chili into freezer container; freeze up to 1 month.
- Thaw chili in refrigerator overnight. When ready to serve, bring to boil in saucepan, then simmer on medium-low heat 10 to 15 min. or until heated through, stirring occasionally. Stir

in cilantro just before serving. Top with cheese and green onions.

Nutrition Information

- Calories: 280
- Sodium: 610 mg
- Cholesterol: 60 mg
- Total Carbohydrate: 0 g
- Total Fat: 6 g
- Fiber: 8 g
- Protein: 27 g
- Sugar: 0 g
- Saturated Fat: 3 g

77. Pulled Pork Chili

Serving: 0 | Prep: 20mins | Cook: 10hours | Ready in: 10hours20mins

Ingredients

- 2 cans (14-1/2 oz. each) fat-free reduced-sodium chicken broth
- 2 cans (14-1/2 oz. each) chili-ready diced tomatoes, undrained
- 1 can (15-1/2 oz.) kidney beans, rinsed
- 1 can (15 oz.) black beans, rinsed
- 1 large onion, chopped
- 2 Tbsp. chili powder
- 2 tsp. ground cumin
- 1 boneless pork shoulder (2-1/2 lb.)
- 1 pkg. (8 oz.) KRAFT Shredded Cheddar Cheese
- 1-1/4 cups BREAKSTONE'S or KNUDSEN Sour Cream

Direction

- Combine all ingredients except meat, cheese and sour cream in slow cooker. Add meat; cover with lid. Cook on LOW 10 to 12 hours (or on HIGH 7 hours).
- Remove meat from slow cooker. Shred meat; return to slow cooker. Stir.
- Spoon into bowls; top with cheese and sour cream.

Nutrition Information

- Calories: 440
- Saturated Fat: 14 g
- Cholesterol: 115 mg
- Sugar: 4 g
- Total Carbohydrate: 14 g
- Sodium: 620 mg
- Total Fat: 29 g
- Fiber: 5 g
- Protein: 29 g

78. Salsa Mac Chicken Supper

Serving: 4 | Prep: 5mins | Cook: 15mins | Ready in: 20mins

Ingredients

- 1 pkg. (14 oz.) KRAFT Deluxe Macaroni & Cheese Dinner Made With 2% Milk Cheese
- 1 tsp. chili powder
- 4 small boneless skinless chicken breasts (1 lb.)
- 3 cups baby carrots (12 oz.)
- 1/2 cup TACO BELL® Thick & Chunky Salsa

Direction

- Prepare Dinner as directed on package.
- Meanwhile, sprinkle chili powder over chicken; place, seasoned-sides down, in large nonstick skillet sprayed with cooking spray. Cook on medium-high heat 3 min.; turn.
- Top with carrots and salsa; cover. Simmer on medium-low heat 10 to 12 min. or until chicken is done (165°F) and carrots are tender. Serve with prepared Dinner.

Nutrition Information

- Calories: 460
- Saturated Fat: 2.5 g
- Sugar: 11 g
- Protein: 39 g
- Total Carbohydrate: 59 g
- Fiber: 5 g
- Total Fat: 7 g
- Cholesterol: 80 mg
- Sodium: 1270 mg

79. Slow Cooker Buffalo Chicken Chili

Serving: 0 | Prep: 15mins | Cook: 5hours | Ready in: 5hours15mins

Ingredients

- 2 Tbsp. flour
- 1/4 cup KRAFT Zesty Italian Dressing
- 2 lb. boneless skinless chicken thighs, cut into bite-size pieces
- 1 can (14.5 oz.) fire-roasted diced tomatoes, drained
- 1 onion, chopped
- 1 cup fat-free reduced-sodium vegetable broth
- 1 can (15 oz.) white beans, rinsed
- 1 stalk celery, finely chopped
- 1/2 cup Buffalo wing sauce
- 1 pkg. (4.5 oz.) ATHENOS Crumbled Blue Cheese

Direction

- Whisk flour and dressing in large bowl until blended. Add chicken; toss to evenly coat. Place in slow cooker. Add tomatoes, onions and broth; cover with lid.
- Cook on LOW 5 to 6 hours (or on HIGH 3 to 4 hours), adding beans, celery and wing sauce for the last 30 min.
- Serve topped with cheese.

Nutrition Information

- Calories: 290
- Saturated Fat: 5 g
- Fiber: 5 g
- Total Fat: 13 g
- Sugar: 0 g
- Cholesterol: 115 mg
- Protein: 26 g
- Total Carbohydrate: 0 g
- Sodium: 680 mg

80. Slow Cooker Chicken Tortilla Soup Recipe

Serving: 0 | Prep: 15mins | Cook: 4hours15mins | Ready in: 4hours30mins

Ingredients

- 4 boneless skinless chicken thighs (1 lb.)
- 1 can (10 oz.) diced tomatoes and green chiles, undrained
- 2 carrots, cut diagonally into thin slices
- 1 onion, chopped
- 1 tsp. chili powder
- 1 tsp. ground cumin
- 2 cans (14.5 oz. each) fat-free reduced-sodium chicken broth
- 4 cups tortilla chips
- 3/4 cup KRAFT Mexican Style Shredded Four Cheese with a TOUCH OF PHILADELPHIA

Direction

- Place chicken in Slow Cooker. Add tomatoes, carrots, onions, chili powder, cumin and broth; cover with lid. Cook on LOW 4 to 5 hours (or on HIGH 2 to 3 hours).
- Use slotted spoon to remove chicken from Slow Cooker; cool slightly. Coarsely chop chicken; return to Slow Cooker. Stir.
- Crush chips coarsely; place in 8 soup bowls. Ladle soup into bowls; top with cheese.

Nutrition Information

- Calories: 180
- Fiber: 2 g
- Sugar: 0 g
- Protein: 13 g
- Saturated Fat: 3 g
- Sodium: 510 mg
- Total Carbohydrate: 0 g
- Cholesterol: 60 mg
- Total Fat: 9 g

81. Slow Cooker Chunky Chicken Chili

Serving: 0 | Prep: 10mins | Cook: 6hours | Ready in: 6hours10mins

Ingredients

- 1 can (15.5 oz.) dark red kidney beans, rinsed
- 1 can (15.5 oz.) light red kidney beans, rinsed
- 1-1/2 cups TACO BELL® Thick & Chunky Mild Salsa
- 1 can (15 oz.) no-salt-added tomato sauce
- 2 Tbsp. chili powder
- 1-1/2 lb. boneless skinless chicken thighs, cut into bite-size pieces
- 1 onion, chopped
- 1 cup frozen corn
- 1 cup KRAFT Mexican Style Finely Shredded Four Cheese

Direction

- Combine beans, salsa, tomato sauce and chili powder in Slow Cooker. Top with chicken, onions and corn. (Do not stir.) Cover with lid.
- Cook on LOW 6 to 8 hours (or on HIGH 4 to 5 hours); stir.
- Serve topped with cheese.

Nutrition Information

- Calories: 310
- Total Carbohydrate: 0 g

- Fiber: 7 g
- Total Fat: 10 g
- Cholesterol: 90 mg
- Protein: 26 g
- Sugar: 0 g
- Saturated Fat: 4 g
- Sodium: 650 mg

82. Southwest Four Cheese Chicken

Serving: 6 | Prep: 10mins | Cook: 30mins | Ready in: 40mins

Ingredients

- 1 pkt. SHAKE 'N BAKE Seasoned Panko Seasoned Coating Mix
- 1/2 tsp. chili powder
- 1/4 tsp. garlic powder
- 1/4 tsp. onion powder
- 1/4 tsp. ground cumin
- 1 cup KRAFT Mexican Style Finely Shredded Four Cheese
- 6 small boneless skinless chicken breasts (1-1/2 lb.)

Direction

- Heat oven to 375°F.
- Combine bread crumbs and seasonings in medium bowl; stir in cheese.
- Moisten chicken with water. Coat with cheese mixture, 1 piece at a time. Lightly press cheese mixture onto both sides of chicken. (Chicken will not be completely coated.) Place on baking sheet sprayed with cooking spray; top with any remaining cheese mixture.
- Bake 28 to 30 min. or until chicken is done (165°F).

Nutrition Information

- Calories: 230
- Cholesterol: 85 mg

- Sugar: 0 g
- Fiber: 0 g
- Sodium: 400 mg
- Total Fat: 9 g
- Total Carbohydrate: 8 g
- Protein: 29 g
- Saturated Fat: 4 g

83. Southwestern White Chili Recipe

Serving: 0 | Prep: 30mins | Cook: | Ready in: 30mins

Ingredients

- 2 Tbsp. KRAFT Zesty Italian Dressing
- 1 lb. boneless skinless chicken breasts, cut into bite-size pieces
- 1 small onion, chopped
- 2 cans (15 oz. each) white beans, rinsed
- 1 can (14-1/2 oz.) fat-free reduced-sodium chicken broth
- 1 can (4 oz.) green chiles, undrained
- 1 tsp. ground cumin
- 1-1/2 cups KRAFT Mexican Style Finely Shredded Four Cheese
- 2 Tbsp. chopped fresh cilantro

Direction

- Heat dressing in large saucepan on medium-high heat. Add chicken and onions; cook 7 min. or until chicken is done, stirring occasionally.
- Stir in beans, broth, chiles and cumin. Bring to boil. Simmer on medium-low heat 10 min., stirring occasionally.
- Serve topped with cheese and cilantro.

Nutrition Information

- Calories: 320
- Cholesterol: 70 mg
- Total Carbohydrate: 24 g

- Fiber: 6 g
- Sugar: 2 g
- Saturated Fat: 6 g
- Total Fat: 11 g
- Sodium: 940 mg
- Protein: 30 g

84. Spicy Chili Recipe

Serving: 6 | Prep: 30mins | Cook: 40mins | Ready in: 1hours10mins

Ingredients

- 1 Tbsp. oil
- 1 lb. boneless beef chuck steak, cut into bite-size pieces
- 2 cups chopped onions
- 1 can (14-1/2 oz.) diced tomatoes, undrained
- 1/3 cup A.1. Bold & Spicy Sauce
- 1 can (15-1/4 oz.) red kidney beans, rinsed
- 3 cups hot cooked long-grain white rice

Direction

- Heat oil in Dutch oven or large saucepan on medium heat. Add meat and onions; cook 4 to 5 min. or until meat is evenly browned, stirring frequently.
- Add tomatoes and A.1.; mix well. Bring to boil; simmer on medium-low heat 30 to 40 min. or until meat is tender, stirring frequently.
- Stir in beans; cook 5 min. or until heated through, stirring frequently.
- Serve over rice.

Nutrition Information

- Calories: 370
- Saturated Fat: 1.5 g
- Protein: 25 g
- Fiber: 6 g
- Total Fat: 8 g

- Cholesterol: 50 mg
- Sodium: 390 mg
- Total Carbohydrate: 49 g
- Sugar: 6 g

- Saturated Fat: 1 g
- Total Fat: 6 g
- Cholesterol: 40 mg
- Protein: 11 g

85. Two Bite Fried Chicken

Serving: 8 | Prep: 30mins | Cook: 1hours | Ready in: 1hours30mins

Ingredients

- 8 boneless skinless chicken thighs (2 lb.), cut in half
- 1/4 cup KRAFT Zesty Italian Dressing
- 2 Tbsp. A.1. Original Sauce
- 2 Tbsp. lime juice
- 1/2 cup flour
- 1/2 tsp. black pepper
- 1/2 tsp. chili powder
- 1 cup PLANTERS Peanut Oil

Direction

- Place chicken in shallow dish. Mix dressing, A.1. and lime juice until blended; pour over chicken. Turn to evenly coat each piece. Refrigerate 1 hour to marinate.
- Drain chicken; discard marinade. Mix flour and seasonings in pie plate. Add chicken, a few pieces at a time; turn to evenly coat each piece. Place on large plate.
- Heat oil in large skillet to 350°F. Add chicken in batches; cook 11 to 13 min. or until golden brown and done (165°F), turning after 6 min. Drain on paper towels.

Nutrition Information

- Calories: 110
- Sugar: 0 g
- Total Carbohydrate: 5 g
- Fiber: 0 g
- Sodium: 100 mg

86. VELVEETA Cheesy Chicken Chili

Serving: 0 | Prep: 10mins | Cook: 30mins | Ready in: 40mins

Ingredients

- 1 lb. boneless skinless chicken breasts, cut into bite-size pieces
- 1 small onion, chopped
- 1 tsp. ground cumin
- 1 tsp. chili powder
- 2 cans (15 oz. each) white beans, drained
- 1 can (14-1/2 oz.) fat-free reduced-sodium chicken broth
- 1 can (4 oz.) green chiles, undrained
- 1/2 lb. (8 oz.) VELVEETA, cut into 1/2-inch cubes

Direction

- Cook chicken and onions in large saucepan sprayed with cooking spray 7 min. or until chicken is done, stirring occasionally. Stir in seasonings; cook and stir 1 min.
- Add beans, broth and chiles; stir. Bring to boil; simmer on medium-low heat 10 min., stirring occasionally.
- Stir in VELVEETA; cook until melted, stirring frequently.

Nutrition Information

- Calories: 310
- Saturated Fat: 4.5 g
- Sugar: 7 g
- Cholesterol: 65 mg
- Fiber: 5 g

- Total Carbohydrate: 28 g
- Protein: 29 g
- Total Fat: 9 g
- Sodium: 1300 mg

87. VELVEETA® Spicy Chicken Spaghetti

Serving: 0 | Prep: 25mins | Cook: 35mins | Ready in: 1hours

Ingredients

- 3/4 lb. spaghetti, uncooked
- 1 lb. boneless skinless chicken breasts, cut into bite-size pieces
- 3/4 lb. (12 oz.) VELVEETA, cut into 1/2-inch cubes
- 1 can (10-3/4 oz.) 98%-fat-free condensed cream of chicken soup
- 1 can (10 oz.) RO*TEL Diced Tomatoes & Green Chilies, undrained
- 1 can (4 oz.) mushroom pieces and stems, drained
- 1/3 cup milk

Direction

- Heat oven to 350ºF.
- Cook spaghetti as directed on package, omitting salt.
- Meanwhile, cook and stir chicken in large skillet sprayed with cooking spray on medium-high heat 8 to 10 min. or until done. Add remaining ingredients; cook and stir 5 min. or until VELVEETA is completely melted and mixture is well blended.
- Drain spaghetti. Add to chicken mixture; mix lightly. Spoon into 13x9-inch pan sprayed with cooking spray.
- Bake 30 to 35 min. or until heated through.

Nutrition Information

- Calories: 300
- Saturated Fat: 4 g
- Protein: 20 g
- Cholesterol: 45 mg
- Fiber: 2 g
- Sodium: 840 mg
- Total Fat: 8 g
- Total Carbohydrate: 0 g
- Sugar: 0 g

88. Weeknight Chicken Fajita Recipe

Serving: 4 | Prep: 20mins | Cook: | Ready in: 20mins

Ingredients

- 1 tsp. oil
- 1 lb. boneless skinless chicken breasts, cut into thin strips
- 1/4 cup KRAFT Zesty Italian Dressing
- 3 cups refrigerated pre-cut mixed stir-fry vegetables (broccoli, carrots, green and red peppers, onions, snow peas)
- 2 tsp. chili powder
- 8 flour tortillas (6 inch)
- 1 cup KRAFT Shredded Cheddar Cheese

Direction

- Heat oil in large nonstick skillet on medium-high heat. Add chicken; cook 5 min. or until done, stirring occasionally.
- Stir in dressing, vegetables and chili powder; cook 5 min. or until vegetables are crisp-tender, stirring occasionally.
- Spoon chicken mixture down centers of tortillas; top with cheese. Roll up.

Nutrition Information

- Calories: 490
- Saturated Fat: 8 g
- Cholesterol: 95 mg

- Total Carbohydrate: 0 g
- Fiber: 4 g
- Sugar: 0 g
- Total Fat: 20 g
- Sodium: 850 mg
- Protein: 36 g

Chapter 4: Awesome Soup Recipes

***

89. 15 Minute Jambalaya

Serving: 4 | Prep: 5mins | Cook: 10mins | Ready in: 15mins

Ingredients

- 2 cans (14-1/2 oz. each) stewed tomatoes, undrained
- 1 cup water
- 6-1/2 oz. (1/2 of 13-oz. pkg.) OSCAR MAYER Natural Uncured Turkey Sausage, sliced
- 3 chicken bouillon cubes
- 1 tsp. hot pepper sauce
- 2 cups instant white rice, uncooked

Direction

- Bring all ingredients except rice to boil in large skillet on medium heat, stirring occasionally. Simmer on medium-low heat 1 to 2 min. or until bouillon is completely dissolved, stirring occasionally.
- Stir in rice; cover. Cook 5 min.
- Fluff with fork.

Nutrition Information

- Calories: 310
- Fiber: 3 g
- Total Carbohydrate: 0 g
- Sugar: 0 g
- Cholesterol: 35 mg
- Saturated Fat: 2 g
- Protein: 14 g
- Total Fat: 7 g
- Sodium: 1900 mg

90. American Chowder

Serving: 0 | Prep: 15mins | Cook: 30mins | Ready in: 45mins

Ingredients

- 1 large onion, sliced
- 2 Tbsp. butter or margarine
- 4 cups cubed potatoes
- 2 cups water
- 1 cup sliced celery
- 1/4 tsp. pepper
- 2 cups milk
- 2 Tbsp. flour
- 1 pkg. (12 oz.) OSCAR MAYER Smokies, sliced
- 1/2 lb. (8 oz.) VELVEETA, cut up

Direction

- Cook and stir onion in butter in large saucepan on medium-high heat until tender. Add potatoes, water, celery and pepper. Bring to boil. Reduce heat to medium-low; cover. Simmer 15 minutes or until vegetables are tender.
- Stir small amount of the milk into flour until well blended. Gradually add flour mixture to hot vegetable mixture, stirring constantly. Stir in remaining milk and the Smokies; cook until mixture boils and thickens, stirring constantly.
- Add VELVEETA; cook until completely melted, stirring frequently.

Nutrition Information

- Calories: 340
- Fiber: 2 g
- Total Fat: 21 g
- Protein: 14 g
- Sugar: 7 g
- Sodium: 940 mg
- Cholesterol: 60 mg
- Saturated Fat: 10 g
- Total Carbohydrate: 23 g

91. Andouille Sausage Jambalaya

Serving: 8 | Prep: 15mins | Cook: 55mins | Ready in: 1hours10mins

Ingredients

- 3 Tbsp. flour
- 2 tsp. dried thyme leaves
- 1/4 tsp. each ground red pepper (cayenne) and black pepper
- 8 bone-in chicken thighs (2-1/2 lb.), skinned
- 1 Tbsp. oil
- 1 large onion, chopped
- 1 large green pepper, chopped
- 4 cloves garlic, minced
- 1 can (28 oz.) fire-roasted diced tomatoes, undrained
- 1/2 cup BULL'S-EYE Texas Style Barbecue Sauce
- 1 pkg. (9 oz.) fully cooked andouille sausage, sliced
- 3 cups fat-free reduced-sodium chicken broth
- 1-1/2 cups long-grain white rice, uncooked
- 1/2 lb. uncooked deveined peeled large shrimp
- 1/4 cup minced fresh parsley

Direction

- Mix flour and seasonings in shallow dish. Add chicken; turn to coat both sides of each thigh. Heat oil in Dutch oven or large deep skillet on medium heat. Add 4 chicken thighs; cook 4 min. on each side or until each is golden brown on both sides. Transfer to plate, reserving drippings in pan. Repeat with remaining chicken.
- Add onions, green peppers and garlic to drippings in pan; cook and stir 5 min. Stir in tomatoes, barbecue sauce and sausage. Return chicken and any juices from plate to tomato mixture; simmer 25 min. or until chicken is done (165ºF), stirring occasionally. Meanwhile, bring broth to boil in medium saucepan. Stir in rice; cover. Simmer on medium-low heat 20 min. or until broth is absorbed and rice is tender.
- Add shrimp to tomato mixture; simmer 8 min. or until shrimp turn pink.
- Spoon rice into shallow bowls; top with chicken mixture and parsley.

Nutrition Information

- Calories: 410
- Saturated Fat: 4 g
- Total Carbohydrate: 45 g
- Sodium: 910 mg
- Total Fat: 14 g
- Fiber: 3 g
- Protein: 26 g
- Sugar: 9 g
- Cholesterol: 120 mg

92. BBQ Ham And Bean Soup

Serving: 0 | Prep: 2hours30mins | Cook: 8hours | Ready in: 10hours30mins

Ingredients

- 20 oz. bag dry mixed beans
- 1-1/2 cups vegetable broth
- 2 cups chicken broth
- 1 can (10 oz.) diced tomatoes and green chiles

- 1 bottle (12.5 oz.) KRAFT Hickory Smoke Barbecue Sauce
- 2 Tbsp. GREY POUPON Dijon Mustard
- 2 cups spicy (or mild) vegetable juice cocktail
- 1 pkg. (7.5 oz.) OSCAR MAYER CARVING BOARD Slow Cooked Ham, chopped
- 3 celery stalks, chopped
- 1 cup sliced carrots
- 1 cup assorted sweet peppers, chopped
- 1/2 cup chopped onion
- 2 Tbsp. apple HEINZ Apple Cider Vinegar
- 2 Tbsp. LEA & PERRINS Worcestershire Sauce
- 1 tsp. chili powder
- 1/2 tsp. black pepper
- 1/2 tsp. garlic powder
- 1/2 tsp. ground cumin

Direction

- Place beans in a large pot; cover with 2 quarts of water. Allow to soak overnight, or at least 8 hours.
- Drain. Add 2 quarts of water. Bring to a boil, reduce heat and simmer uncovered for 1-2 hours or until beans are tender.
- Combine and mix ingredients in slow cooker. Cook on low for 6-8 hours or until vegetables are tender.

Nutrition Information

- Calories: 0 g
- Sugar: 0 g
- Protein: 0 g
- Cholesterol: 0 g
- Total Fat: 0 g
- Fiber: 0 g
- Sodium: 0 g
- Saturated Fat: 0 g
- Total Carbohydrate: 0 g

93. BOCA Jambalaya

Serving: 0 | Prep: 45mins | Cook: | Ready in: 45mins

Ingredients

- 2-1/2 cups water
- 1 pkg. (8 oz.) jambalaya mix
- 1 pkg. (10 oz.) frozen BOCA Veggie Breakfast Links, cut into 1/2-inch-thick slices
- 1 stalk celery, sliced

Direction

- Bring water to boil in large saucepan.
- Stir in remaining ingredients. Return to boil; cover.
- Simmer on low heat 25 to 30 min. or until liquid is absorbed, stirring occasionally.

Nutrition Information

- Calories: 260
- Fiber: 3 g
- Cholesterol: 0 mg
- Protein: 14 g
- Total Fat: 5 g
- Sodium: 1240 mg
- Saturated Fat: 0.5 g
- Total Carbohydrate: 41 g
- Sugar: 1 g

94. BOCA Vegetarian Minestrone Soup Recipe

Serving: 0 | Prep: 40mins | Cook: | Ready in: 40mins

Ingredients

- 2 qt. (8 cups) water
- 2 cans (14-1/2 oz. each) Italian-style diced tomatoes, undrained
- 1 pkg. (10 oz.) frozen chopped spinach
- 2 cups frozen BOCA Veggie Ground Crumbles
- 2 carrots, chopped
- 1 onion, chopped
- 1 cup farfalle (bow-tie pasta), uncooked

Direction

- Bring all ingredients except pasta to boil in Dutch oven or large deep skillet on medium-high heat, stirring occasionally.
- Simmer on medium-low heat 15 to 20 min. or until crumbles are heated through (160°F) and carrots are crisp-tender, stirring occasionally. Meanwhile, cook pasta as directed on package, omitting salt.
- Drain pasta. Stir into soup.

Nutrition Information

- Calories: 80
- Protein: 6 g
- Sodium: 270 mg
- Total Fat: 0 g
- Cholesterol: 0 mg
- Saturated Fat: 0 g
- Total Carbohydrate: 0 g
- Sugar: 0 g
- Fiber: 2 g

95. Bacon, Cheese & Potato Chowder

Serving: 0 | Prep: 20mins | Cook: | Ready in: 20mins

Ingredients

- 1 can (10-3/4 oz.) condensed cream of potato soup
- 3 cups fat-free milk
- 2 cups ORE-IDA Diced Hash Brown Potatoes
- 1 cup KRAFT 2% Milk Shredded Sharp Cheddar Cheese
- 2 slices OSCAR MAYER Bacon, cooked, crumbled
- 2 green onions, thinly sliced

Direction

- Mix soup and milk in large saucepan. Stir in potatoes.
- Bring to boil on high heat, stirring occasionally. Simmer on medium-low heat 10 min. or until heated through, stirring frequently.
- Serve topped with cheese, bacon and onions.

Nutrition Information

- Calories: 180
- Cholesterol: 20 mg
- Protein: 11 g
- Total Fat: 6 g
- Saturated Fat: 3 g
- Total Carbohydrate: 0 g
- Sugar: 0 g
- Fiber: 2 g
- Sodium: 580 mg

96. Baked Potato Soup With Bacon

Serving: 0 | Prep: 30mins | Cook: | Ready in: 30mins

Ingredients

- 1 Tbsp. butter or margarine
- 1/4 cup chopped yellow onions
- 1/4 cup chopped celery
- 1 can (14-1/2 oz.) fat-free reduced-sodium chicken broth
- 1-1/4 cups milk
- 3/4 lb. baking potatoes (about 2), baked, cut into 1/2-inch pieces
- 1/8 tsp. pepper
- 1 green onion, sliced, divided
- 8 slices cooked OSCAR MAYER Center Cut Bacon, crumbled, divided
- 3/4 cup KRAFT Finely Shredded Mild Cheddar Cheese, divided
- 1/4 cup BREAKSTONE'S or KNUDSEN Sour Cream

Direction

- Melt butter in large saucepan or Dutch oven on medium heat. Add yellow onions and celery; cook and stir 5 min. or until crisp-tender. Add next 4 ingredients; bring just to boil, stirring constantly. Lightly crush potatoes with back of spoon. Simmer on medium-low heat 5 min., stirring frequently.
- Reserve 1 Tbsp. green onions and 2 Tbsp. each bacon and cheese. Add remaining green onions, bacon and cheese to soup; cook 5 min. or until cheese is melted, stirring constantly.
- Serve topped with reserved green onions, bacon, cheese and sour cream.

Nutrition Information

- Calories: 210
- Protein: 10 g
- Total Fat: 12 g
- Fiber: 2 g
- Sugar: 0 g
- Saturated Fat: 7 g
- Cholesterol: 40 mg
- Sodium: 410 mg
- Total Carbohydrate: 0 g

97. Barley And Bean Soup Recipe

Serving: 0 | Prep: 10mins | Cook: 30mins | Ready in: 40mins

Ingredients

- 4 OSCAR MAYER Selects Uncured Angus Bun-Length Beef Franks, cut into 1/4-inch-thick slices
- 1 qt. (4 cups) water
- 1 can (15-1/2 oz.) great Northern beans, rinsed
- 1 can (14-1/2 oz.) Italian-style stewed tomatoes, undrained
- 2 carrots, peeled, thinly sliced
- 1/2 cup quick-cooking barley, uncooked
- 2 tsp. LEA & PERRINS Worcestershire Sauce

Direction

- Combine ingredients in Dutch oven or large deep skillet.
- Bring to boil on medium heat 10 min., stirring occasionally. Cover.
- Simmer on medium-low heat 15 min. or until vegetables are crisp-tender, stirring occasionally.

Nutrition Information

- Calories: 180
- Cholesterol: 20 mg
- Protein: 8 g
- Sugar: 4 g
- Saturated Fat: 3.5 g
- Sodium: 460 mg
- Total Carbohydrate: 20 g
- Fiber: 5 g
- Total Fat: 8 g

98. Bean Soup

Serving: 0 | Prep: 30mins | Cook: 4hours | Ready in: 4hours30mins

Ingredients

- 2 cups dry lima beans
- 2 slices OSCAR MAYER Lower Sodium Bacon
- 1 pkg. (10 oz.) frozen corn
- 1/4 lb. OSCAR MAYER Natural Uncured Turkey Sausage, thinly sliced
- 1 onion, chopped
- 4-1/2 tsp. flour
- 1-1/2 cups water
- dash pepper

Direction

- Place beans in large saucepan. Add enough water to cover beans. Bring to boil; simmer on medium-low heat 2-1/2 hours or until tender.

- Cook bacon in large skillet on medium heat until crisp. Drain on paper towels, reserving drippings in skillet for later use.
- Crumble bacon. Add to beans along with the corn, sausage and onions; mix well. Simmer on medium-low heat 1 hour.
- Stir flour into reserved bacon drippings in skillet; cook on medium-low heat until hot and bubbly, stirring frequently. Gradually stir in water until well blended; cook on medium heat until mixture comes to boil and thickens, stirring constantly. Add to soup; simmer 30 min., stirring occasionally. Stir in pepper.

Nutrition Information

- Calories: 180
- Fiber: 4 g
- Protein: 9 g
- Sodium: 240 mg
- Saturated Fat: 2 g
- Sugar: 0 g
- Cholesterol: 20 mg
- Total Fat: 7 g
- Total Carbohydrate: 0 g

99. Beef Barley Soup

Serving: 0 | Prep: 15mins | Cook: 20mins | Ready in: 35mins

Ingredients

- 1/2 lb. ground beef
- 2-1/2 cups cold water
- 1 can (14-1/2 oz.) stewed tomatoes, cut up
- 3/4 cup sliced carrots
- 3/4 cup sliced mushrooms
- 1/2 cup quick-cooking barley, uncooked
- 2 cloves garlic, minced
- 1 tsp. dried oregano leaves
- 1/2 lb. (8 oz.) VELVEETA, cut up

Direction

- Brown meat in large saucepan; drain. Stir in water, tomatoes, carrots, mushrooms, barley, garlic and oregano.
- Bring to boil. Reduce heat to low; cover. Simmer 10 minutes or until barley is tender.
- Add VELVEETA; stir until melted.

Nutrition Information

- Calories: 250
- Cholesterol: 50 mg
- Total Carbohydrate: 19 g
- Fiber: 3 g
- Sugar: 6 g
- Sodium: 770 mg
- Total Fat: 13 g
- Saturated Fat: 7 g
- Protein: 15 g

100. Beef Brisket

Serving: 16 | Prep: 15mins | Cook: 4hours | Ready in: 4hours15mins

Ingredients

- 2 large onions, sliced
- 1 beef brisket (4 lb.)
- 1 can (10-1/2 oz.) condensed French onion soup
- 1-1/4 cups dry red wine
- 1/2 cup HEINZ Tomato Ketchup
- 1/2 cup packed brown sugar
- 1 env. (1 oz.) onion soup mix

Direction

- Heat oven to 350°F.
- Spread onions onto bottom of large shallow pan sprayed with cooking spray; top with meat.
- Mix remaining ingredients until blended; pour over meat. Cover with foil; pierce in several places with sharp knife.

- Bake 3-1/2 to 4 hours or until meat is tender. Let stand, covered, 10 min.
- Transfer meat to cutting board. Cut across the grain into thin slices. Serve topped with wine mixture from bottom of pan.

Nutrition Information

- Calories: 390
- Protein: 20 g
- Sodium: 380 mg
- Fiber: 0 g
- Total Fat: 26 g
- Total Carbohydrate: 0 g
- Sugar: 0 g
- Cholesterol: 80 mg
- Saturated Fat: 10 g

101. Big Batch Leek Soup

Serving: 0 | Prep: 35mins | Cook: 10mins | Ready in: 45mins

Ingredients

- 6 large leeks (about 2 lb.), cut into 1/4-inch-thick slices
- 2 Tbsp. olive oil
- 2 lb. baking potatoes (about 6), peeled, chopped
- 2 qt. (8 cups) water
- 1 tsp. pepper
- 1 pkg. (8 oz.) PHILADELPHIA Cream Cheese, cut up
- 3/4 cup milk
- 1/3 cup chopped fresh chives

Direction

- Cook leeks in hot oil in large stockpot or Dutch oven on medium-high heat 5 min. or until tender, stirring occasionally. Add next 3 ingredients; cover. Bring to boil. Reduce heat to medium-low; simmer 15 to 20 min. or until potatoes are tender. Cool 10 min.
- Puree leek mixture, in batches, in blender; return to stockpot.
- Whisk in cream cheese, a tablespoonful at a time, beating until blended. Cook and stir on medium heat until cream cheese is completely melted. Add milk; cook until heated through, stirring constantly. Sprinkle with chives just before serving.

Nutrition Information

- Calories: 200
- Total Carbohydrate: 26 g
- Cholesterol: 25 mg
- Sodium: 100 mg
- Fiber: 3 g
- Sugar: 5 g
- Protein: 4 g
- Total Fat: 9 g
- Saturated Fat: 4.5 g

102. Black Bean Minestrone Soup

Serving: 0 | Prep: 5mins | Cook: 25mins | Ready in: 30mins

Ingredients

- 3 cans (15 oz. each) black beans, drained, rinsed
- 2 cans (14-1/2 oz. each) fat-free reduced-sodium chicken broth
- 1 can (28 oz.) diced tomatoes, undrained
- 1 each: onion, zucchini and celery stalk, chopped
- 1 carrot, peeled, chopped
- 1 pkg. (6 oz.) OSCAR MAYER Baked Cooked Ham, chopped
- 1 cup water
- 1 pkg. (7-1/4 oz.) KRAFT Macaroni & Cheese Dinner

- 2 cups fresh spinach leaves

Direction

- Combine beans, broth, tomatoes, onions, zucchini, celery, carrots, ham and red pepper in Dutch oven or stockpot. Bring to boil on medium-high heat. Reduce heat to low; cover. Simmer 10 min. or until vegetables are crisp-tender.
- Add water and Macaroni; stir. Cook 7 to 8 min. or until Macaroni is tender.
- Stir in Cheese Sauce Mix and spinach; cook 2 min. or until spinach is wilted, stirring occasionally. Serve immediately.

Nutrition Information

- Calories: 200
- Sodium: 570 mg
- Fiber: 8 g
- Total Carbohydrate: 0 g
- Protein: 13 g
- Cholesterol: 10 mg
- Sugar: 0 g
- Total Fat: 2 g
- Saturated Fat: 1 g

103. Black Bean And Rice Soup

Serving: 0 | Prep: 10mins | Cook: 10mins | Ready in: 20mins

Ingredients

- 2 cans (15 oz. each) black beans, undrained, divided
- 3 cups water
- 1/2 cup chopped onions
- 1 env. (0.7 oz.) GOOD SEASONS Italian Dressing Mix
- 1-1/2 cups instant brown rice, uncooked

Direction

- Blend 1-1/2 cans beans in blender until smooth. Pour into large saucepan.
- Add remaining beans, water, onions and dressing mix; stir until well blended. Bring to boil on medium-high heat.
- Stir in rice; cover. Simmer on low heat 5 min. or until heated through; stir.

Nutrition Information

- Calories: 250
- Sodium: 850 mg
- Protein: 8 g
- Fiber: 8 g
- Cholesterol: 0 mg
- Total Carbohydrate: 0 g
- Total Fat: 1.5 g
- Saturated Fat: 0 g
- Sugar: 0 g

104. Broccoli Cheese Soup Recipe

Serving: 10 | Prep: 20mins | Cook: | Ready in: 20mins

Ingredients

- 3 cups milk
- 1 pkg. (10 oz.) frozen chopped broccoli, thawed
- 1 can (10-3/4 oz.) condensed cream of chicken soup
- 1 can (10-3/4 oz.) condensed cream of celery soup
- 1 can (10-3/4 oz.) condensed cream of potato soup
- 1/2 lb. (8 oz.) VELVEETA, cut into 1/2-inch cubes

Direction

- Bring all ingredients except VELVEETA to boil in large saucepan, stirring constantly; simmer on medium-low heat 5 min., stirring occasionally.
- Add VELVEETA; cook 5 min. or until VELVEETA is melted and soup is well blended, stirring constantly.

Nutrition Information

- Calories: 160
- Total Fat: 7 g
- Saturated Fat: 3.5 g
- Protein: 8 g
- Sodium: 770 mg
- Fiber: 2 g
- Cholesterol: 20 mg
- Sugar: 7 g
- Total Carbohydrate: 15 g

105. Broccoli And Cheese Soup With Potato

Serving: 0 | Prep: 15mins | Cook: 4hours | Ready in: 4hours15mins

Ingredients

- 2 lb. baking potatoes (about 4), peeled, cut into 3/4-inch pieces
- 1 can (14.5 oz.) fat-free reduced-sodium chicken broth
- 1 cup water
- 4 cups small broccoli florets, coarsely chopped
- 1 lb. (16 oz.) VELVEETA, cut into 1/2-inch cubes

Direction

- Line slow cooker with disposable plastic liner as directed on package. Place potatoes in prepared slow cooker. Add broth and water; cover with lid.
- Cook on LOW 4 to 5 hours (or on HIGH 2 to 2-1/2 hours).
- Mash potatoes lightly with potato masher. Stir in VELVEETA and broccoli; cook, covered, 30 min. Stir before serving.

Nutrition Information

- Calories: 250
- Protein: 11 g
- Fiber: 2 g
- Total Fat: 8 g
- Sodium: 920 mg
- Total Carbohydrate: 29 g
- Sugar: 6 g
- Saturated Fat: 5 g
- Cholesterol: 30 mg

106. Cape Anne Chowder

Serving: 0 | Prep: 50mins | Cook: 20mins | Ready in: 1hours10mins

Ingredients

- 6 slices OSCAR MAYER Bacon, chopped
- 1 large onion, coarsely chopped
- 2 Tbsp. flour
- 2 cups water
- 1/2 lb. baking potatoes (about 2), peeled, cubed
- 2 stalks celery, sliced
- 1/4 tsp. pepper
- 1 pkg. (8 oz.) CRACKER BARREL Sharp Cheddar Cheese, shredded
- 2 cups milk
- 1 lb. cod fillets, cut into chunks
- 1 can (6 oz.) crabmeat, drained, flaked

Direction

- Cook and stir bacon in large saucepan on medium heat until crisp. Remove bacon from pan with slotted spoon, reserving 2 Tbsp.

drippings in pan. Drain bacon on paper towels.
- Add onions to drippings in pan; cook 5 to 6 min. or until crisp-tender, stirring occasionally. Add flour; mix well. Gradually stir in water until blended. Add vegetables and pepper; stir. Bring to boil; cover. Simmer on medium-low heat 20 min. or until potatoes are tender.
- Stir in cheese; cook 2 min. or until melted, stirring frequently. Add milk, cod and crabmeat; cook 8 to 10 min. or until fish is done, stirring occasionally. Serve topped with bacon.

Nutrition Information

- Calories: 260
- Total Carbohydrate: 11 g
- Cholesterol: 70 mg
- Protein: 21 g
- Sugar: 4 g
- Total Fat: 15 g
- Sodium: 390 mg
- Saturated Fat: 7 g
- Fiber: 1 g

107. Caramelized Butternut Squash Soup

Serving: 6 | Prep: 30mins | Cook: 1hours30mins | Ready in: 2hours

Ingredients

- 1 butternut squash (3 lb.), peeled, seeded and cut into 2-inch chunks
- 1 large Vidalia onion, quartered
- 1 head garlic, cloves separated and peeled
- 1-1/2 Tbsp. extra virgin olive oil
- 3-1/2 cups fat-free reduced-sodium chicken broth, divided
- 1/2 tsp. pepper
- 2 Tbsp. whipping cream
- 1/2 cup BREAKSTONE'S or KNUDSEN Sour Cream
- 3 slices OSCAR MAYER Butcher Thick Cut Hickory Smoked Bacon, chopped, cooked

Direction

- Heat oven to 350°F.
- Toss squash, onions, garlic and oil; spread onto bottom of 13x9-inch baking dish. Pour 1 cup broth over vegetables.
- Bake 1-1/2 hours or until vegetables are soft and caramelized, checking every 20 min. and if necessary, adding additional broth to keep from scorching, and stirring after 45 min.
- Add vegetables and any liquid from dish to large stockpot. Add remaining broth and pepper; cook on medium-low heat 20 min., stirring occasionally.
- Puree vegetable mixture in blender. Return to pot, stir in cream. Serve soup topped with sour cream and bacon.

Nutrition Information

- Calories: 210
- Total Carbohydrate: 0 g
- Sugar: 0 g
- Cholesterol: 25 mg
- Fiber: 4 g
- Total Fat: 11 g
- Saturated Fat: 4 g
- Protein: 6 g
- Sodium: 390 mg

108. Carrot & Parsnip Soup

Serving: 0 | Prep: 45mins | Cook: 1hours | Ready in: 1hours45mins

Ingredients

- 6 Tbsp. KRAFT Sun Dried Tomato Vinaigrette Dressing made with Extra Virgin Olive Oil, divided

- 1 onion, chopped
- 3 carrots, peeled, chopped
- 3 parsnips, peeled, chopped
- 3-1/2 cups water
- 3 cups fat-free reduced-sodium chicken broth
- 1/2 cup (1/2 of 8-oz. tub) PHILADELPHIA Cream Cheese Spread

Direction

- Heat 1/4 cup dressing in large saucepan on medium heat. Add onions; cook 4 to 6 min. or until crisp-tender, stirring frequently. Add carrots and parsnips; cook and stir 8 to 10 min. or until parsnips are lightly browned.
- Stir in water and broth; cover. Simmer on medium-low heat 40 to 45 min. or until vegetables are softened, stirring occasionally. Remove from heat. Uncover. Cool 15 min.
- Process soup, in batches, in food processor or blender until smooth. Return to saucepan; cook on low heat 5 min. or until heated through, stirring frequently. Add cream cheese spread and remaining dressing; cook and stir 5 min. or until cream cheese is melted and soup is well blended.

Nutrition Information

- Calories: 110
- Total Fat: 6 g
- Protein: 2 g
- Saturated Fat: 3 g
- Sodium: 380 mg
- Sugar: 0 g
- Cholesterol: 20 mg
- Fiber: 3 g
- Total Carbohydrate: 0 g

109. Carrot Soup Recipe

Serving: 0 | Prep: 10mins | Cook: 15mins | Ready in: 25mins

Ingredients

- 1 small onion, chopped
- 1/4 cup KRAFT Lite House Italian Dressing
- 1 lb. carrots, peeled, chopped
- 2 cans (14-1/2 oz. each) fat-free reduced-sodium chicken broth
- 1/4 tsp. ground cumin
- 1/2 cup BREAKSTONE'S Reduced Fat or KNUDSEN Light Sour Cream, divided

Direction

- Cook and stir onions in dressing in large saucepan on medium-high heat 5 min. or until onions are tender. Add carrots, broth and cumin; mix well. Cook 10 min. or until carrots are tender, stirring frequently. Cool slightly.
- Blend broth mixture in blender container until pureed. Add 1/4 cup sour cream; blend until smooth.
- Ladle soup evenly into 4 soup bowls; top each with 1 Tbsp. of remaining sour cream. Serve with crackers.

Nutrition Information

- Calories: 90
- Sugar: 0 g
- Cholesterol: 15 mg
- Fiber: 4 g
- Saturated Fat: 2 g
- Sodium: 450 mg
- Total Carbohydrate: 0 g
- Total Fat: 3 g
- Protein: 2 g

110. Cheddar Broccoli Soup

Serving: 0 | Prep: 30mins | Cook: | Ready in: 30mins

Ingredients

- 1/4 cup chopped onions
- 1 Tbsp. butter or margarine

- 1 Tbsp. flour
- 3-1/2 cups fat-free milk
- 4 oz. (1/2 of 8-oz. pkg.) PHILADELPHIA Neufchatel Cheese, cubed
- 1 pkg. (8 oz.) KRAFT Shredded Triple Cheddar Cheese with a TOUCH OF PHILADELPHIA
- 1 pkg. (10 oz.) frozen chopped broccoli, cooked, drained
- 1/4 tsp. ground nutmeg
- 1/8 tsp. pepper

Direction

- Cook and stir onions in butter in medium saucepan on medium-high heat 3 to 5 min. or until onions are crisp-tender. Whisk in flour until well blended.
- Add milk; cook and stir on medium heat 2 min., stirring occasionally. Add Neufchatel; cook and stir 2 to 3 min. or until melted.
- Stir in remaining ingredients; cook 5 min. or until heated through, stirring occasionally.

Nutrition Information

- Calories: 290
- Saturated Fat: 12 g
- Cholesterol: 60 mg
- Fiber: 2 g
- Total Carbohydrate: 0 g
- Protein: 16 g
- Sugar: 0 g
- Total Fat: 20 g
- Sodium: 420 mg

111. Cheese & Ale Soup

Serving: 0 | Prep: 10mins | Cook: 25mins | Ready in: 35mins

Ingredients

- 5 slices OSCAR MAYER Bacon, chopped
- 1/2 cup finely chopped leeks (white and green parts)
- 3 cloves garlic, minced
- 2 Tbsp. flour
- 1-1/2 qt. (6 cups) milk
- 1 lb. (16 oz.) VELVEETA, cut into 1/2-inch cubes
- 3/4 cup beer or ale
- 3 Tbsp. chopped fresh parsley

Direction

- Cook bacon, leeks and garlic in large saucepan on medium-high heat 7 to 9 min. or until bacon is crisp, stirring frequently. Drain; discard drippings. Return bacon mixture to pan.
- Stir in flour; cook and stir on medium heat 1 min. Gradually stir in milk; cook 8 min. or until slightly thickened, stirring frequently.
- Add VELVEETA; cook 5 min. or until completely melted, stirring frequently. Stir in beer; cook 2 min. or until heated through, stirring occasionally. Serve topped with parsley.

Nutrition Information

- Calories: 300
- Saturated Fat: 10 g
- Protein: 17 g
- Cholesterol: 60 mg
- Sodium: 1010 mg
- Total Fat: 17 g
- Total Carbohydrate: 18 g
- Sugar: 14 g
- Fiber: 0 g

112. Cheeseburger Soup

Serving: 0 | Prep: 35mins | Cook: | Ready in: 35mins

Ingredients

- 1 lb. extra-lean ground beef
- 1-1/2 cups chopped onions
- 3 cups fat-free reduced-sodium beef broth
- 3/4 lb. red potatoes (about 2), peeled, finely chopped
- 1 cup shredded carrots
- 1 tsp. dill weed
- 1 cup milk
- 1 pkg. (8 oz.) KRAFT Shredded Sharp Cheddar Cheese, divided

Direction

- Brown meat with onions in large saucepan.
- Stir in broth, potatoes, carrots and dill weed; bring to boil. Cover; simmer on medium-low heat 15 to 17 min. or until potatoes are tender, stirring occasionally.
- Add milk and 1-1/2 cups cheese; cook and stir 1 to 2 min. or until cheese is melted. Serve topped with remaining cheese.

Nutrition Information

- Calories: 250
- Saturated Fat: 7 g
- Protein: 21 g
- Total Carbohydrate: 0 g
- Fiber: 2 g
- Sodium: 420 mg
- Sugar: 0 g
- Cholesterol: 65 mg
- Total Fat: 12 g

113. Cheesy Broccoli Noodle Soup

Serving: 8 | Prep: 30mins | Cook: | Ready in: 30mins

Ingredients

- 1 Tbsp. vegetable oil
- 1/2 cup finely chopped onions
- 3 cups water
- 3 chicken bouillon cubes
- 4 oz. thin egg noodles, uncooked
- 3 cups milk
- 1 pkg. (10 oz.) frozen chopped broccoli
- 1/4 lb. (4 oz.) VELVEETA, cut into 1/2-inch cubes
- 1/8 tsp. garlic powder

Direction

- Heat oil in large saucepan on medium-high heat. Add onions; cook and stir 3 to 5 min. or until tender. Add water and bouillon cubes; bring to boil.
- Add noodles; simmer on low heat 4 min., stirring occasionally.
- Add remaining ingredients; bring to boil. Cook on medium-low heat 3 to 5 min. or until VELVEETA is melted and soup is well blended, stirring frequently.

Nutrition Information

- Calories: 170
- Saturated Fat: 3.5 g
- Cholesterol: 30 mg
- Sodium: 600 mg
- Total Carbohydrate: 19 g
- Protein: 9 g
- Total Fat: 7 g
- Fiber: 2 g
- Sugar: 7 g

114. Cheesy Green Chili Soup

Serving: 0 | Prep: 10mins | Cook: 15mins | Ready in: 25mins

Ingredients

- 3 cups chicken broth, divided
- 3/4 cup chopped onion
- 6 poblano chiles, roasted, peeled and deveined

- 1/4 cup BREAKSTONE'S or KNUDSEN Sour Cream
- 2 Tbsp. butter or margarine
- 2 Tbsp. flour
- salt and black pepper
- 1/2 cup KRAFT Shredded Mozzarella Cheese

Direction

- Place 1 cup of the broth, onion, chiles and sour cream in blender container; cover. Blend until smooth.
- Melt butter in medium saucepan on medium heat. Stir in flour. Add chile mixture; mix well. Gradually add the remaining 2 cups broth, stirring until well blended. Reduce heat to medium-low; simmer 10 min., stirring frequently. Season with salt and black pepper to taste.
- Ladle the soup into 4 soup bowls; sprinkle with cheese.

Nutrition Information

- Calories: 190
- Total Fat: 12 g
- Saturated Fat: 7 g
- Cholesterol: 35 mg
- Protein: 9 g
- Sodium: 730 mg
- Fiber: 2 g
- Total Carbohydrate: 0 g
- Sugar: 0 g

115. Cheesy Minestrone Pasta

Serving: 0 | Prep: 25mins | Cook: | Ready in: 25mins

Ingredients

- 2 cups elbow macaroni, uncooked
- 1 small onion, chopped
- 1 pkg. (6 oz.) OSCAR MAYER Baked Cooked Ham, chopped
- 1 large zucchini, chopped
- 1 carrot, peeled, chopped
- 1 can (15 oz.) black beans, rinsed
- 1 can (14.5 oz.) diced tomatoes, undrained
- 1 pkg. (6 oz.) baby spinach leaves
- 4 KRAFT Singles, cut up
- 1/2 cup KRAFT Shredded Low-Moisture Part-Skim Mozzarella Cheese
- 2 Tbsp. KRAFT Grated Parmesan Cheese

Direction

- Cook macaroni as directed on package. Meanwhile, cook and stir onions in Dutch oven or large deep skillet sprayed with cooking spray on medium heat 2 min. Stir in next 6 ingredients; cover. Simmer on medium-low heat 7 min., stirring occasionally.
- Drain macaroni. Add to ingredients in Dutch oven along with the Singles pieces; cook and stir 3 min. or until Singles are melted.
- Serve topped with mozzarella and Parmesan.

Nutrition Information

- Calories: 370
- Total Carbohydrate: 0 g
- Protein: 23 g
- Sugar: 0 g
- Saturated Fat: 4 g
- Cholesterol: 35 mg
- Sodium: 820 mg
- Total Fat: 8 g
- Fiber: 8 g

116. Cheesy Tortilla Soup

Serving: 0 | Prep: 35mins | Cook: | Ready in: 35mins

Ingredients

- 3 Tbsp. butter
- 3 Tbsp. chopped onions
- 3 Tbsp. flour

- 1 can (28 oz.) no-salt-added diced tomatoes, undrained
- 1 can (14.5 oz.) fat-free reduced-sodium chicken broth
- 1 pkg. (1 oz.) TACO BELL® Taco Seasoning Mix
- 2 cups shredded rotisserie chicken
- 2 VELVEETA Fresh Packs (4 oz. each), cut into 1/2-inch cubes
- 1/2 cup tortilla chips (1 oz.), coarsely crushed
- 1 lime, cut into 8 wedges

Direction

- Melt butter in medium saucepan on medium heat. Add onions; cook 2 min. or until crisp-tender, stirring frequently. Stir in flour until blended.
- Add tomatoes, chicken broth and taco seasoning mix; stir. Bring to boil; simmer on medium-low heat 2 min., stirring occasionally. Add chicken and VELVEETA; cook and stir 5 min. or until VELVEETA is completely melted and chicken is heated through.
- Top with crushed chips. Serve with lime wedges.

Nutrition Information

- Calories: 200
- Sugar: 0 g
- Saturated Fat: 6 g
- Total Fat: 11 g
- Total Carbohydrate: 0 g
- Fiber: 1 g
- Cholesterol: 40 mg
- Sodium: 840 mg
- Protein: 8 g

117. Cheesy VELVEETA Salmon & Potato Soup

Serving: 0 | Prep: 20mins | Cook: 50mins | Ready in: 1hours10mins

Ingredients

- 1/2 cup chopped onions
- 1/2 cup sliced zucchini
- 1 small carrot, sliced
- 1 Tbsp. chopped garlic
- 2 Tbsp. olive oil
- 1/2 lb. red potatoes (about 3), cut into 1/2-inch cubes
- 4 cups water
- 1 can (14-3/4 oz.) cream-style corn
- 1 can (12 oz.) fat-free evaporated milk
- 6 oz. VELVEETA, cut into 1/2-inch cubes
- 1/2 tsp. ground ginger
- 1/4 tsp. black pepper
- 3/4 lb. fresh or thawed frozen salmon, cut into 1/2- inch chunks

Direction

- Cook onion, zucchini, carrots and garlic in oil in large saucepan on medium heat 5 to 6 min. or until crisp-tender, stirring occasionally.
- Add potatoes and water; bring to boil. Cook on medium heat 20 to 30 min. or until vegetables are tender. Add corn, milk and VELVEETA; cook 1 to 2 min. or until VELVEETA is melted.
- Add ginger, pepper and fish; simmer on medium-low heat 5 to 7 min. or until fish is done. (Do not let soup come to boil.)

Nutrition Information

- Calories: 230
- Fiber: 1 g
- Protein: 16 g
- Cholesterol: 35 mg
- Total Carbohydrate: 20 g
- Sugar: 11 g
- Total Fat: 10 g
- Saturated Fat: 3.5 g
- Sodium: 460 mg

118. Chicken Corn Chowder

Serving: 3 | Prep: 10mins | Cook: | Ready in: 10mins

Ingredients

- 4 oz. (2/3 of 6-oz. pkg.) OSCAR MAYER CARVING BOARD Flame Grilled Chicken Breast Strips
- 1 can (10-3/4 oz.) condensed cream of potato soup
- 1 can (8 oz.) whole kernel corn, drained
- 1 cup milk

Direction

- Cook ingredients in saucepan on medium heat 5 min. or until heated through, stirring occasionally.

Nutrition Information

- Calories: 200
- Total Fat: 5 g
- Saturated Fat: 2.5 g
- Fiber: 2 g
- Sugar: 6 g
- Sodium: 980 mg
- Cholesterol: 35 mg
- Protein: 15 g
- Total Carbohydrate: 26 g

119. Chicken Pozole

Serving: 0 | Prep: 10mins | Cook: 25mins | Ready in: 35mins

Ingredients

- 1/2 cup KRAFT Zesty Italian Dressing
- 1/2 cup chopped onion
- 6 slices OSCAR MAYER Bacon, chopped
- 5 jalapeño peppers, seeded, chopped
- 2 lb. boneless skinless chicken breasts, cut into 1-inch pieces
- 3 cans (15 oz.) chicken broth
- 2 cans (15 oz.) hominy, drained
- 1 Tbsp. dried epazote leaves
- 2 small zucchini, chopped
- 1/2 cup chopped cilantro
- 4 oz. (1/2 of 8-oz. pkg.) KRAFT Colby Cheese, cubed
- 4 oz. (1/2 of 8-oz. pkg.) KRAFT Monterey Jack Cheese, cubed
- 2 limes, cut into wedges

Direction

- Heat dressing in large saucepan on medium-high heat. Add onion, bacon and peppers; cook 5 to 8 min. or until vegetables are softened and bacon is cooked.
- Add chicken, broth, hominy and epazote. Bring to boil; cover. Reduce heat to simmer; cook 15 min. Add zucchini and cilantro; cook 5 min.
- Place cheese cubes in bottom of bowls; top with stew. Garnish with lime wedges and additional cilantro, if desired.

Nutrition Information

- Calories: 470
- Fiber: 3 g
- Total Fat: 27 g
- Total Carbohydrate: 0 g
- Saturated Fat: 11 g
- Protein: 38 g
- Cholesterol: 110 mg
- Sugar: 0 g
- Sodium: 1330 mg

120. Chicken Tortilla Lime Soup

Serving: 0 | Prep: | Cook: | Ready in:

Ingredients

- 5 flour tortillas (6 inch), cut into thin strips
- 3/4 cup KRAFT Zesty Italian Dressing, divided
- 2 cans (14 oz. each) chicken broth
- 1 can (10 oz.) diced tomatoes and green chilies, undrained
- 1 bay leaf
- 1 lb. boneless skinless chicken breasts, cut into 1/4-inch-wide strips
- 1/4 cup cilantro, chopped
- Juice from 2 medium limes
- 1 cup KRAFT Shredded Cheddar Cheese

Direction

- Preheat oven to 350°F. Toss tortilla strips with 1 Tbsp. of the dressing. Spread onto nonstick baking sheet. Bake 12 to 15 min. or until crisp and golden brown. Cool completely.
- Combine remaining dressing, broth, tomatoes with liquid, bay leaf and pepper in large saucepan. Stir in 1-1/2 cups water. Bring to boil on medium-high heat. Reduce heat to medium-low; simmer 5 min. Add chicken; simmer an additional 5 to 8 min. or until chicken is cooked through. Remove and discard bay leaf. Stir in cilantro and lime juice.
- Ladle into soup bowls just before serving; sprinkle evenly with tortilla strips and cheese. Garnish with dollops of BREAKSTONE'S or KNUDSEN Sour Cream or additional chopped cilantro, if desired.

Nutrition Information

- Calories: 0 g
- Sodium: 0 g
- Sugar: 0 g
- Total Carbohydrate: 0 g
- Total Fat: 0 g
- Protein: 0 g
- Saturated Fat: 0 g
- Fiber: 0 g
- Cholesterol: 0 g

121. Chipotle, Sweet Potato And Black Bean Stew

Serving: 0 | Prep: 40mins | Cook: 40mins | Ready in: 1hours20mins

Ingredients

- 1/2 cup KRAFT Zesty Lime Vinaigrette Dressing, divided
- 1 lb. boneless skinless chicken breasts, cut into bite-size pieces
- 1-1/2 lb. sweet potatoes (about 3), peeled, cut into 1/2-inch pieces
- 1 onion, chopped
- 4 cloves garlic, minced
- 1 carton (32 oz.) fat-free reduced-sodium chicken broth
- 2 canned chipotle peppers in adobo sauce
- 1 can (15.5 oz.) black beans, rinsed, divided
- 1/4 cup BREAKSTONE'S FREE or KNUDSEN Fat Free Sour Cream
- 1/4 cup loosely packed fresh cilantro, chopped

Direction

- Heat 1/4 cup dressing in large saucepan on medium heat. Add chicken; cook 8 to 10 min. or until done, stirring frequently. Spoon chicken into bowl.
- Heat remaining dressing in same saucepan. Add potatoes, onions and garlic; cook 5 min., stirring frequently. Add chicken broth and peppers; mix well. Bring to boil; simmer on medium-low heat 35 to 40 min. or until potatoes are tender. Remove from heat. Stir in 1/2 cup beans.
- Remove 2 cups potato mixture from pan; reserve for later use. Ladle remaining ingredients from saucepan, in batches, into blender; blend until smooth, returning each puréed batch to saucepan.
- Add chicken, reserved potato mixture and remaining beans to soup; stir gently. Cook and stir 2 to 3 min. or until heated through. Serve topped with sour cream and cilantro.

Nutrition Information

- Calories: 220
- Fiber: 6 g
- Sugar: 0 g
- Saturated Fat: 0 g
- Protein: 15 g
- Total Carbohydrate: 0 g
- Cholesterol: 45 mg
- Total Fat: 3 g
- Sodium: 570 mg

122.   Chunky Chicken Vegetable Soup

Serving: 0 | Prep: 25mins | Cook: | Ready in: 25mins

Ingredients

- 1/2 lb. boneless skinless chicken breasts, cut into bite-size pieces
- 1 tsp. oil
- 1 can (14-1/2 oz.) fat-free reduced-sodium chicken broth
- 1-1/2 cups water
- 2 cups mixed fresh vegetables (broccoli florets, chopped red peppers, sliced carrots)
- 1 env. (0.7 oz.) GOOD SEASONS Italian Dressing Mix
- 1/2 cup instant white rice, uncooked
- 2 Tbsp. chopped fresh parsley

Direction

- Cook and stir chicken in hot oil in large saucepan on medium-high heat 5 min. or until done.
- Add broth, water, vegetables and dressing; stir. Bring to boil; cover. Simmer on low heat 5 min.
- Stir in rice and parsley. Remove from heat. Let stand, covered, 5 min.

Nutrition Information

- Calories: 120
- Sugar: 0 g
- Total Carbohydrate: 0 g
- Sodium: 710 mg
- Protein: 12 g
- Cholesterol: 25 mg
- Saturated Fat: 0 g
- Total Fat: 2 g
- Fiber: 1 g

123.   Chunky Veggie & Cannellini Bean Soup

Serving: 0 | Prep: 1hours | Cook: | Ready in: 1hours

Ingredients

- 1/2 cup each chopped onions, carrots and celery
- 1/4 cup KRAFT Balsamic Tomato Basil Vinaigrette Dressing
- 1 lb. smoked spicy sausage (kielbasa or andouille) links, chopped
- 4-1/2 cups water
- 2 cans (15 oz. each) cannellini beans, rinsed
- 2 cans (14 oz. each) fat-free reduced-sodium chicken broth
- 1/2 lb. Yukon gold potatoes (about 2), peeled, chopped
- 1/2 cup (1/2 of 8-oz. tub) PHILADELPHIA Chive & Onion Cream Cheese Spread
- 1/4 cup chopped fresh dill
- 1/4 cup chopped fresh parsley

Direction

- Cook onions, carrots and celery in dressing in large saucepan on medium heat 5 min. or until vegetables are crisp-tender, stirring frequently.
- Add sausage; cook 5 min. or until evenly browned, stirring frequently. Add all remaining ingredients except cream cheese spread, dill and parsley; mix well. Bring to boil; cover. Simmer on medium-low heat 15 min., stirring occasionally.

- Mash carefully with potato masher to break up some of the beans and potatoes; simmer 10 min., stirring occasionally. Gradually add cream cheese spread, stirring after each addition until cream cheese is completely melted and mixture is well blended. Stir in herbs.

Nutrition Information

- Calories: 130
- Cholesterol: 25 mg
- Total Fat: 8 g
- Saturated Fat: 3 g
- Sodium: 520 mg
- Sugar: 1 g
- Protein: 6 g
- Total Carbohydrate: 10 g
- Fiber: 2 g

124. Classic Minestrone Soup

Serving: 0 | Prep: 15mins | Cook: 1hours5mins | Ready in: 1hours20mins

Ingredients

- 2 cans (14.5 oz. each) vegetable broth
- 1 can (28 oz.) diced tomatoes, undrained
- 1 can (15.5 oz.) kidney beans, rinsed
- 1 each celery stalk, zucchini and onion, chopped
- 1 each red potato and carrot, peeled, chopped
- 1/3 cup KRAFT Zesty Italian Dressing
- 1/2 cup small pasta shells, uncooked
- 2 cups tightly packed fresh spinach
- 6 Tbsp. KRAFT Grated Parmesan Cheese

Direction

- Bring all but last 3 ingredients to boil in large saucepan; cover. Simmer on medium-low heat 45 min.
- Stir in pasta and spinach; cook 10 min. or just until pasta is tender.
- Serve topped with cheese.

Nutrition Information

- Calories: 140
- Total Fat: 3.5 g
- Sugar: 0 g
- Protein: 6 g
- Saturated Fat: 1 g
- Sodium: 660 mg
- Total Carbohydrate: 0 g
- Fiber: 5 g
- Cholesterol: 5 mg

125. Cold Cucumber Soup

Serving: 0 | Prep: 25mins | Cook: 4hours | Ready in: 4hours25mins

Ingredients

- 1 onion, chopped
- 1 Tbsp. butter
- 1 can (14.5 oz.) fat-free reduced-sodium chicken broth
- 1 potato, peeled, cubed (about 1 cup)
- 1/4 cup KRAFT Lite Ranch Dressing
- 1/2 cup fat-free milk
- 1 large cucumber, peeled, seeded and chopped

Direction

- Cook and stir onions in butter in large saucepan on medium-high heat 5 min. or until tender. Add broth and potatoes; simmer on low heat 15 to 20 min. or until potatoes are tender. Transfer to blender; blend until smooth. Place in large bowl.
- Add dressing, milk and cucumber to blender; blend until smooth. Add to potato mixture; stir until blended.
- Refrigerate at least 4 hours.

Nutrition Information

- Calories: 90
- Saturated Fat: 2 g
- Protein: 3 g
- Fiber: 2 g
- Total Carbohydrate: 0 g
- Total Fat: 3 g
- Cholesterol: 10 mg
- Sodium: 220 mg
- Sugar: 0 g

126. Corn And Salmon Chowder With Bacon

Serving: 0 | Prep: 10mins | Cook: 40mins | Ready in: 50mins

Ingredients

- 2 tsp. oil
- 1 onion, chopped
- 2 stalks celery, finely chopped
- 2 cloves garlic, minced
- 2 Tbsp. flour
- 3 cups milk
- 3/4 lb. new potatoes (about 6), cut into 1/2-inch cubes
- 1 can (11 oz.) corn with red and green bell peppers, undrained
- 3 sprigs fresh thyme
- 6 oz. VELVEETA, cut into 1/2-inch cubes
- 2 Tbsp. GREY POUPON Dijon Mustard
- 1-1/2 lb. salmon, skin removed, cut into 1-inch pieces
- 6 slices chopped OSCAR MAYER Bacon, cooked
- 30 RITZ Crackers

Direction

- Heat oil in medium saucepan on medium-high heat. Add onions, celery and garlic; cook 5 min. or until crisp-tender, stirring frequently. Stir in flour; cook and stir 1 min. Whisk in milk. Add potatoes, corn and thyme; cover. Simmer 20 min. or until potatoes are tender.
- Stir in VELVEETA and mustard; cover. Simmer on medium-low heat 5 min. or until VELVEETA is melted. Stir in fish; cook 8 min. or until fish flakes easily with fork. Remove and discard thyme sprigs.
- Top chowder with bacon. Serve with crackers.

Nutrition Information

- Calories: 590
- Total Carbohydrate: 43 g
- Sugar: 13 g
- Fiber: 2 g
- Sodium: 1010 mg
- Protein: 40 g
- Cholesterol: 105 mg
- Total Fat: 25 g
- Saturated Fat: 8 g

127. Country Cheese Soup

Serving: 6 | Prep: 20mins | Cook: 20mins | Ready in: 40mins

Ingredients

- 1/3 cup shredded carrot
- 1/3 cup thinly sliced celery
- 2 Tbsp. finely chopped green pepper
- 2 Tbsp. finely chopped onion
- 1/4 cup (1/2 stick) butter or margarine
- 1/3 cup flour
- 1 tsp. salt
- dash black pepper
- 5 cups milk
- 1 pkg. (8 oz.) CRACKER BARREL Sharp Cheddar Cheese, shredded (2 cups)

Direction

- Cook vegetables in butter in large saucepan on medium heat until tender, stirring frequently.
- Add flour and seasonings; mix well. Cook 2 minutes or until bubbly, stirring frequently. Gradually add milk, stirring until well blended. Cook until mixture boils and thickens, stirring constantly. Reduce heat to low; simmer 5 minutes.
- Add cheese; cook until cheese is melted and mixture is heated through, stirring constantly. Do not boil.

Nutrition Information

- Calories: 360
- Sugar: 11 g
- Cholesterol: 75 mg
- Sodium: 790 mg
- Fiber: 1 g
- Saturated Fat: 14 g
- Protein: 16 g
- Total Carbohydrate: 17 g
- Total Fat: 25 g

128. Crab Bisque

Serving: 0 | Prep: 15mins | Cook: 30mins | Ready in: 45mins

Ingredients

- 2 leeks, cut in half lengthwise
- 2 Tbsp. butter or margarine
- 3 cups milk
- 3/4 lb. baking potatoes (about 2), peeled, chopped
- 1 pkg. (8 oz.) imitation crabmeat, rinsed
- 1/2 tsp. dried thyme leaves
- 1/8 tsp. hot pepper sauce
- 1/2 lb. (8 oz.) VELVEETA, cut into 1/2-inch cubes

Direction

- Cut white portion and 1 inch of light green portion of each leek into thin slices. Melt butter in large skillet on medium heat. Add leeks; cook and stir 5 min. or until crisp-tender. Stir in all remaining ingredients except VELVEETA.
- Bring to boil; cover. Simmer on low heat 15 min. or until potatoes are tender.
- Add VELVEETA; cook 5 min. or until VELVEETA is completely melted and mixture is well blended, stirring frequently.

Nutrition Information

- Calories: 300
- Saturated Fat: 9 g
- Protein: 16 g
- Sodium: 970 mg
- Total Fat: 15 g
- Sugar: 11 g
- Fiber: 2 g
- Cholesterol: 55 mg
- Total Carbohydrate: 28 g

129. Cracker Chicken Casserole

Serving: 4 | Prep: 15mins | Cook: 30mins | Ready in: 45mins

Ingredients

- 1 can (10-1/2 oz.) reduced-sodium condensed cream of celery soup
- 2/3 cup milk
- 4 tsp. GREY POUPON Dijon Mustard
- 1/4 tsp. black pepper
- 1-1/2 cups chopped cooked chicken
- 1 pkg. (10 oz.) frozen mixed vegetables (carrots, corn, green beans, peas)
- 1/2 cup chopped onions
- 30 round buttery crackers, crushed (about 1 cup)
- 1 Tbsp. butter, melted

Direction

- Heat oven to 350°F.
- Mix soup, milk, mustard and pepper until blended. Combine next 3 ingredients in large bowl. Add soup mixture; mix lightly.
- Spoon into 2-qt. casserole sprayed with cooking spray.
- Combine cracker crumbs and butter; sprinkle over chicken mixture.
- Bake 25 to 30 min. or until heated through.

Nutrition Information

- Calories: 370
- Saturated Fat: 6 g
- Total Fat: 14 g
- Protein: 21 g
- Sodium: 810 mg
- Sugar: 12 g
- Total Carbohydrate: 39 g
- Cholesterol: 60 mg
- Fiber: 3 g

130. Cream Of Broccoli Soup Recipe

Serving: 0 | Prep: 30mins | Cook: | Ready in: 30mins

Ingredients

- 1/4 cup chopped onions
- 1 Tbsp. butter or margarine
- 1 Tbsp. flour
- 2 cups milk
- 4 oz. (1/2 of 8-oz. pkg.) PHILADELPHIA Cream Cheese, cubed
- 1/2 lb. (8 oz.) VELVEETA, cut into 1/2-inch cubes
- 1 pkg. (10 oz.) frozen chopped broccoli, cooked, drained
- 1/4 tsp. ground nutmeg
- 1/8 tsp. pepper

Direction

- Cook and stir onions in butter in medium saucepan on medium-high heat 3 to 5 min. or until onions are crisp-tender. Whisk in flour until blended.
- Stir in milk; cook on medium heat 2 min., stirring occasionally. Add cream cheese; cook and stir 2 to 3 min. or until melted.
- Add remaining ingredients; mix well. Cook 5 min. or until heated through, stirring occasionally.

Nutrition Information

- Calories: 300
- Total Fat: 21 g
- Fiber: 2 g
- Saturated Fat: 13 g
- Sodium: 760 mg
- Total Carbohydrate: 14 g
- Sugar: 11 g
- Cholesterol: 75 mg
- Protein: 14 g

131. Cream Of Broccoli, Bacon & Potato Soup

Serving: 0 | Prep: 30mins | Cook: 15mins | Ready in: 45mins

Ingredients

- 4 slices OSCAR MAYER Bacon
- 1 onion, chopped
- 1 can (14.5 oz.) fat-free reduced-sodium chicken broth
- 1/2 cup water
- 1 large baking potato (1/2 lb.), peeled, chopped
- 4 cups small broccoli florets
- 1/2 cup KRAFT Shredded Sharp Cheddar Cheese, divided

- 1/3 cup KRAFT Classic Ranch Dressing, divided

Direction

- Cook bacon in large saucepan on medium heat until crisp. Remove bacon from pan, reserving 2 Tbsp. drippings in pan. Drain bacon on paper towels.
- Add onions to reserved drippings; cook and stir 8 min. or until tender. Add broth, water and potatoes; stir. Bring to boil; cover. Simmer on medium-low heat 15 min. or just until potatoes are tender. Stir in broccoli; cook 5 min. or until tender. Stir in 1/4 cup each cheese and dressing.
- Blend soup, in batches, in blender until smooth. Ladle into 4 bowls. Crumble bacon; sprinkle over soup. Top with remaining cheese and dressing.

Nutrition Information

- Calories: 300
- Protein: 9 g
- Saturated Fat: 7 g
- Total Fat: 22 g
- Fiber: 4 g
- Cholesterol: 30 mg
- Sodium: 660 mg
- Total Carbohydrate: 20 g
- Sugar: 5 g

132. Cream Of Mushroom Tortellini Soup

Serving: 7 | Prep: 20mins | Cook: | Ready in: 20mins

Ingredients

- 1 pkg. (16 oz.) frozen cheese tortellini, uncooked
- 3 cups fat-free reduced-sodium chicken broth
- 2 Tbsp. KRAFT Zesty Italian Dressing
- 1/2 lb. sliced fresh mushrooms
- 1 jar (15 oz.) CLASSICO Four Cheese Alfredo Pasta Sauce
- 1 cup frozen peas
- 1 tsp. chopped fresh thyme

Direction

- Cook tortellini as directed on package, substituting broth for the water and eliminating the draining step of the cooked tortellini.
- Meanwhile, heat dressing in large skillet on medium-high heat. Add mushrooms; cook 4 to 5 min. or until evenly browned, stirring frequently.
- Add mushrooms and all remaining ingredients to tortellini; cook on medium heat 3 to 5 min. or until heated through, stirring occasionally.

Nutrition Information

- Calories: 260
- Protein: 10 g
- Sodium: 810 mg
- Sugar: 4 g
- Fiber: 1 g
- Cholesterol: 45 mg
- Total Fat: 11 g
- Saturated Fat: 5 g
- Total Carbohydrate: 32 g

133. Cream Of Potato Chowder

Serving: 0 | Prep: 15mins | Cook: 10mins | Ready in: 25mins

Ingredients

- 1 can (10-3/4 oz.) condensed cream of potato soup
- 1-3/4 cups milk

- 3 OSCAR MAYER Beef Franks, cut into 1/4-inch-thick slices
- 1-1/4 cups frozen peas and carrots
- 1/4 cup frozen corn

Direction

- Mix soup and milk in large saucepan. Stir in remaining ingredients.
- Bring to boil on medium heat; simmer on low 10 min. or until soup is heated through and vegetables are tender, stirring frequently.

Nutrition Information

- Calories: 240
- Protein: 9 g
- Total Fat: 12 g
- Fiber: 3 g
- Total Carbohydrate: 0 g
- Cholesterol: 30 mg
- Sugar: 0 g
- Sodium: 790 mg
- Saturated Fat: 5 g

134. Cream Of Spinach Soup

Serving: 0 | Prep: 20mins | Cook: 20mins | Ready in: 40mins

Ingredients

- 1/2 cup chopped fresh mushrooms
- 1/2 cup chopped onion
- 2 Tbsp. butter or margarine
- 3-1/4 cups milk, divided
- 1/2 tsp. salt
- 1/4 tsp. garlic powder
- dash of pepper
- dash of ground nutmeg
- 2 tsp. potato starch
- 1 pkg. (10 oz.) frozen chopped spinach, thawed, well drained
- 4 oz. (1/2 of 8-oz. pkg.) PHILADELPHIA Cream Cheese, cubed

Direction

- Cook and stir mushrooms and onion in butter in medium saucepan on medium heat until tender. Add 3 cups of the milk and the seasonings. Bring just to boil, stirring frequently.
- Add potato starch to remaining 1/4 cup milk; stir until well blended. Gradually add to hot mixture in saucepan, stirring until well blended. Cook until mixture boils and thickens, stirring constantly. Reduce heat to low; simmer 5 min.
- Stir in remaining ingredients; cook until cream cheese is completely melted and soup is heated through, stirring frequently.

Nutrition Information

- Calories: 290
- Protein: 11 g
- Saturated Fat: 12 g
- Fiber: 2 g
- Sodium: 660 mg
- Cholesterol: 60 mg
- Sugar: 12 g
- Total Carbohydrate: 16 g
- Total Fat: 20 g

135. Creamed Asparagus Soup

Serving: 4 | Prep: 15mins | Cook: 15mins | Ready in: 30mins

Ingredients

- 3 Tbsp. butter
- 1 leek, sliced
- 1 large clove garlic, minced
- 1 lb. fresh asparagus spears, each cut into thirds

- 1 cup fat-free reduced-sodium chicken broth
- 1 cup water
- 1/2 tsp. ground black pepper
- 1/2 cup PHILADELPHIA Chive & Onion Cream Cheese Spread
- 1/4 cup milk

Direction

- Melt butter in medium saucepan on medium heat. Add leeks; cook 5 min. or until tender, stirring occasionally. Stir in garlic; cook and stir 2 min. Add asparagus, broth and water; stir. Simmer on medium-low heat 5 min. or until asparagus is crisp-tender. Stir in pepper.
- Mix cream cheese spread and milk until well blended.
- Process asparagus mixture in food processor until smooth. Pour into 4 soup bowls. Add cream cheese mixture; swirl gently with spoon.

Nutrition Information

- Calories: 200
- Fiber: 3 g
- Total Fat: 15 g
- Cholesterol: 40 mg
- Saturated Fat: 10 g
- Sugar: 4 g
- Sodium: 330 mg
- Total Carbohydrate: 11 g
- Protein: 5 g

136. Creamy Beer Cheese Soup

Serving: 0 | Prep: | Cook: | Ready in:

Ingredients

- 1 Tbsp. butter or margarine
- 1/2 cup finely chopped onions
- 1 clove garlic, minced
- 1 Tbsp. flour
- 1-3/4 cups milk
- 1/2 lb. (8 oz.) VELVEETA, cut into 1/2-inch cubes
- 1/2 cup lager-style beer
- 1/2 tsp. LEA & PERRINS Worcestershire Sauce
- few drops hot pepper sauce

Direction

- Melt butter in large saucepan on medium heat. Add onions and garlic; cook 3 min. or until crisp-tender, stirring frequently. Add flour; mix well. Cook 2 min. or until hot and bubbly, stirring frequently.
- Stir in milk until blended; bring to boil, stirring constantly. Cook and stir 3 to 5 min. or until thickened. Simmer on low heat 5 min., stirring occasionally.
- Add remaining ingredients; mix well. Cook 5 min. or until VELVEETA is completely melted and soup is heated through, stirring constantly.

Nutrition Information

- Calories: 0 g
- Fiber: 0 g
- Protein: 0 g
- Sugar: 0 g
- Total Fat: 0 g
- Saturated Fat: 0 g
- Total Carbohydrate: 0 g
- Sodium: 0 g
- Cholesterol: 0 g

137. Creamy Broccoli & Potato Soup

Serving: 0 | Prep: 20mins | Cook: 15mins | Ready in: 35mins

Ingredients

- 1 Tbsp. oil
- 1 onion, chopped
- 4 cups small broccoli florets, chopped
- 1/2 lb. baking potatoes (about 1 large), peeled, chopped
- 1 can (14 oz.) chicken broth
- 1-1/4 cups water
- 1/4 tsp. black pepper
- 1 tub (8 oz.) PHILADELPHIA Cream Cheese Spread
- 2 Tbsp. milk
- 1 tsp. garlic powder

Direction

- Heat oil in large saucepan on medium heat. Add onions; cook and stir 5 min. or until tender.
- Stir in broccoli, potatoes, broth, water and pepper. Bring to boil; simmer on medium-low heat 15 min. or until vegetables are tender.
- Blend soup, in batches, in blender until smooth. Return to pan. Mix remaining ingredients until blended; whisk into soup. Cook and stir 2 to 3 min. or until heated through.

Nutrition Information

- Calories: 180
- Cholesterol: 25 mg
- Protein: 6 g
- Total Fat: 12 g
- Total Carbohydrate: 0 g
- Sodium: 370 mg
- Fiber: 2 g
- Sugar: 0 g
- Saturated Fat: 6 g

138. Creamy Chicken & Corn Soup

Serving: 0 | Prep: 25mins | Cook: | Ready in: 25mins

Ingredients

- 1/4 cup KRAFT Zesty Italian Dressing
- 1 cup chopped onion s
- 1 jalapeño pepper, finely chopped
- 4 oz. (1/2 of 8-oz. pkg.) PHILADELPHIA Cream Cheese, cubed
- 1 can (14-1/2 oz.) fat-free reduced-sodium chicken broth
- 1 pkt. sazon adobo seasoning with saffron
- 1 can (14.7 oz.) cream-style corn
- 1 cup shredded cooked chicken
- 1 Tbsp. chopped fresh parsley
- RITZ Crackers

Direction

- Heat dressing in medium saucepan on medium-high heat. Add onions and peppers; cook 5 min. or until crisp-tender, stirring frequently. Add cream cheese; cook 5 min. or until cream cheese is completely melted and mixture is well blended, stirring constantly.
- Add broth and adobo seasoning; stir until blended. Stir in corn and chicken; simmer on medium-low heat 10 min. or until heated through, stirring occasionally.
- Sprinkle with parsley. Serve with crackers.

Nutrition Information

- Calories: 370
- Total Carbohydrate: 35 g
- Protein: 16 g
- Total Fat: 20 g
- Saturated Fat: 8 g
- Fiber: 3 g
- Cholesterol: 70 mg
- Sugar: 15 g
- Sodium: 1030 mg

139. Creamy Chicken Tortilla Soup

Serving: 0 | Prep: 45mins | Cook: | Ready in: 45mins

Ingredients

- 1 tsp. oil
- 1 cup chopped red onions
- 1 can (14.5 oz.) fire-roasted diced tomatoes, drained
- 1 can (11 oz.) corn with red and green bell peppers, drained
- 3-1/2 cups fat-free reduced-sodium chicken broth
- 3/4 cup TACO BELL® Hot Sauce
- 2 cups shredded cooked chicken breasts
- 6 oz. Queso Blanco VELVEETA, cut into 1/2-inch cubes
- 3 Tbsp. lime juice
- 1/2 cup crushed tortilla chips

Direction

- Heat oil in large saucepan on medium heat. Add onions; cook 5 to 6 min. or until crisp-tender, stirring frequently.
- Add tomatoes, corn, chicken broth and hot sauce; mix well. Bring to boil; simmer on medium-low heat 15 min., stirring occasionally.
- Add chicken, VELVEETA and lime juice; cook on medium heat 5 min. or until VELVEETA is completely melted, stirring occasionally.
- Serve topped with crushed chips.

Nutrition Information

- Calories: 180
- Fiber: 1 g
- Cholesterol: 40 mg
- Sodium: 770 mg
- Total Carbohydrate: 15 g
- Saturated Fat: 2.5 g
- Sugar: 6 g
- Protein: 15 g
- Total Fat: 6 g

140. Creamy Corn & Frank Chowder

Serving: 0 | Prep: 30mins | Cook: | Ready in: 30mins

Ingredients

- 1 pkg. (16 oz.) OSCAR MAYER Selects Uncured Hardwood Smoked Turkey Franks, cut into 1/2-inch-thick slices
- 1/2 cup chopped green peppers
- 1/2 cup chopped onions
- 2 Tbsp. butter or margarine
- 1 can (14.75 oz.) cream-style corn
- 1/2 lb. (8 oz.) VELVEETA, cut into 1/2-inch cubes
- 1 cup milk
- 1/8 tsp. black pepper

Direction

- Cook and stir franks, green peppers and onions in butter in large saucepan on medium-high heat 5 to 7 min. or until vegetables are crisp-tender, stirring frequently.
- Add remaining ingredients; mix well. Simmer on low heat 10 min. or until VELVEETA is completely melted and mixture is well blended, stirring occasionally.

Nutrition Information

- Calories: 280
- Total Fat: 19 g
- Protein: 13 g
- Cholesterol: 60 mg
- Fiber: 1 g
- Saturated Fat: 8 g
- Sugar: 10 g
- Sodium: 1040 mg
- Total Carbohydrate: 18 g

141. Creamy Italian Sausage And Kale Soup

Serving: 0 | Prep: 35mins | Cook: | Ready in: 35mins

Ingredients

- 1 lb. Italian sausage
- 1 small onion, chopped
- 1 Tbsp. minced garlic
- 2 Tbsp. flour
- 1 cup milk
- 4 oz. (1/2 of 8-oz. pkg.) PHILADELPHIA Cream Cheese, cubed
- 2 cups (about 1/4 of 32-oz. pkg.) ORE-IDA Diced Hash Brown Potatoes
- 1 qt. (4 cups) fat-free reduced-sodium chicken broth
- 6 cups torn stemmed kale leaves

Direction

- Remove casings from sausage if necessary; crumble sausage into medium nonstick saucepan. Cook on medium heat 7 min. or until done, stirring frequently. Remove sausage from pan with slotted spoon; drain on paper towels. Discard all but 2 Tbsp. drippings from pan.
- Add onions and garlic to reserved drippings; cook 3 min., stirring frequently. Stir in flour. Add milk and cream cheese; cook and stir 3 min. or until cream cheese is completely melted and sauce is well blended.
- Add potatoes, chicken broth and sausage; stir. Bring to boil, stirring frequently. Simmer on medium-low heat 15 min., stirring occasionally. Remove from heat. Add kale; cover.
- Let stand 5 to 6 min. or until kale is softened.

Nutrition Information

- Calories: 270
- Fiber: 1 g
- Cholesterol: 50 mg
- Total Fat: 21 g
- Sodium: 580 mg
- Saturated Fat: 9 g
- Total Carbohydrate: 0 g
- Sugar: 0 g
- Protein: 10 g

142. Creamy Mushroom Soup

Serving: 0 | Prep: 30mins | Cook: 15mins | Ready in: 45mins

Ingredients

- 2 Tbsp. butter
- 1-1/2 lb. sliced fresh mushrooms
- 1 onion, chopped
- 2 stalks celery, chopped
- 1/2 lb. baking potatoes (about 2), peeled, cut into 1-inch pieces
- 1 qt. (4 cups) water
- 1 can (14-1/2 oz.) fat-free reduced-sodium chicken broth
- 1/2 tsp. pepper
- 4 oz. (1/2 of 8-oz. pkg.) PHILADELPHIA Neufchatel Cheese, cubed
- 1/4 cup chopped fresh parsley

Direction

- Melt butter in large skillet on medium heat. Add mushrooms, onions and celery; cook 6 to 8 min. or until onions and celery are crisp-tender, stirring occasionally.
- Remove 1 cup vegetable mixture; reserve for later use. Add potatoes, water, broth and pepper to remaining vegetable mixture in skillet; stir. Bring to boil; simmer on medium-low heat 15 min. or until potatoes are tender.
- Add 1/3 of the potato mixture to blender; blend until smooth. Pour into large saucepan. Repeat with remaining potato mixture. Stir in reserved vegetable mixture.

- Whisk in Neufchatel; cook 2 min. or until Neufchatel is completely melted and soup is heated through, stirring frequently. Stir in parsley.

Nutrition Information

- Calories: 90
- Saturated Fat: 3 g
- Sugar: 0 g
- Protein: 4 g
- Total Carbohydrate: 0 g
- Cholesterol: 15 mg
- Total Fat: 5 g
- Sodium: 160 mg
- Fiber: 1 g

143. Creamy Potato Soup

Serving: 0 | Prep: 45mins | Cook: | Ready in: 45mins

Ingredients

- 1/2 cup KRAFT Zesty Italian Dressing
- 16 cloves garlic, minced
- 1/2 cup flour
- 1 lb. baking potato es (about 3), peeled, chopped
- 1-1/2 qt. (6 cups) fat-free reduced-sodium chicken broth
- 3/4 cup BREAKSTONE'S or KNUDSEN Sour Cream
- 6 slices OSCAR MAYER Bacon, cooked, crumbled
- 2 Tbsp. KRAFT Grated Parmesan Cheese

Direction

- Cook dressing and garlic in large saucepan on medium heat 5 min. or until heated through, stirring frequently. Add flour; cook and stir 3 min.
- Add potatoes and chicken broth; stir. Bring to boil; simmer on medium-low heat 20 min. or until potatoes are tender, stirring occasionally. Gradually add sour cream, mixing well after each addition. Cook 5 min., stirring frequently.
- Serve topped with bacon and cheese.

Nutrition Information

- Calories: 190
- Sodium: 760 mg
- Protein: 6 g
- Cholesterol: 25 mg
- Total Carbohydrate: 20 g
- Saturated Fat: 4 g
- Fiber: 2 g
- Sugar: 3 g
- Total Fat: 10 g

144. Creamy Roasted Garlic Cauliflower Soup

Serving: 0 | Prep: 25mins | Cook: 1hours10mins | Ready in: 1hours35mins

Ingredients

- 1 head garlic
- 1 tsp. oil
- 9 slices OSCAR MAYER Bacon, cut into 1/2-inch-thick slices
- 1 small onion, chopped
- 1 lb. baking potatoes (about 3), peeled, chopped
- 4 cups small cauliflower florets, chopped
- 1 qt. (4 cups) fat-free reduced-sodium chicken broth
- 1 cup milk
- 1/4 cup KRAFT Grated Parmesan Cheese
- 1/4 tsp. black pepper

Direction

- Heat oven to 375°F.
- Cut 1/2-inch-thick slice off top of garlic head, exposing tops of all cloves; place, cut side up,

on sheet of foil. Drizzle with oil. Wrap garlic head in foil.
- Bake 40 min. or until garlic is very soft; cool.
- Meanwhile, cook and stir bacon in Dutch oven or small stockpot until crisp. Remove bacon from pan with slotted spoon; drain on paper towels. Discard all but 1 Tbsp. drippings from pan. Add onions to reserved drippings; cook 5 min. or until crisp-tender, stirring frequently.
- Squeeze pulp from garlic cloves into Dutch oven. Add all remaining ingredients; mix well. Bring to boil; simmer on medium-low heat 30 min. or until potatoes are tender, stirring occasionally.
- Blend soup, in small batches, in blender until smooth. Serve topped with bacon.

Nutrition Information

- Calories: 260
- Protein: 15 g
- Sugar: 0 g
- Sodium: 790 mg
- Total Carbohydrate: 0 g
- Cholesterol: 35 mg
- Saturated Fat: 5 g
- Fiber: 2 g
- Total Fat: 14 g

145. Creamy Roasted Red Pepper Tomato Soup

Serving: 0 | Prep: 10mins | Cook: 40mins | Ready in: 50mins

Ingredients

- 4 lb. tomatoes
- 4 large red peppers, chopped and de-seeded
- 4 large yellow peppers, chopped and de-seeded
- 4 large green peppers, chopped and de-seeded
- 3 medium jalapeño peppers, chopped and de-seeded
- 2 large sweet yellow onions, sliced
- 1 head garlic, peeled and roughly chopped
- 1 pkg. (1 lb.) bacon
- 1 cup fresh basil leaves
- sea salt and pepper to taste
- 4 Tbsp. olive oil
- 1/4 cup butter
- 1 pkg. (8 oz.) PHILADELPHIA Cream Cheese, cubed
- 1/4 cup CLASSICO Traditional Basil Pesto Sauce and Spread (for garnish)
- 4 oz. (1/2 of 8-oz. pkg. PHILADELPHIA Cream Cheese, cubed (for garnish)
- 1 cup croutons (for garnish)

Direction

- Preheat oven to 450°F.
- Core and cut tomatoes in half and place in a large oven roasting pan. Add chopped peppers, sliced onions, chopped garlic and uncooked bacon.
- Add 1 cup fresh basil leaves to the roasting pan mixture. Make sure the stems are removed and the leaves have been washed and patted dry. Salt and pepper all items in the roasting pan and toss.
- Pour the olive oil over the items in the roasting pan and toss lightly.
- Place the roasting pan full of veggies, bacon and herbs into an oven on the middle upper rack and bake for approximately 30 minutes until everything is soft and juicy. Cool 10 to 15 minutes.
- Blend veggies in batches in a blender on the liquefy setting. Pour the contents into a large stock pot or soup pan and heat over medium heat.
- Once everything is blended and in the pot, add 1/4 cup butter and the 8 oz. of PHILADELPHIA Cream Cheese and stir until melted and incorporated. Salt and pepper to taste. Adjust the flavoring at this point according to taste, perhaps adding some Italian seasonings or red pepper flakes.

- For the pesto cream sauce garnish, pick up a jar of pesto at the local grocer. Mix 1/4 cup pesto with 4 oz. of cream cheese.
- When serving the soup, garnish with croutons and a dollop of the pesto cream cheese topping. Serve immediately and enjoy!

Nutrition Information

- Calories: 0 g
- Fiber: 0 g
- Sodium: 0 g
- Sugar: 0 g
- Total Carbohydrate: 0 g
- Protein: 0 g
- Total Fat: 0 g
- Saturated Fat: 0 g
- Cholesterol: 0 g

146. Creamy Wild Rice Soup

Serving: 4 | Prep: 50mins | Cook: | Ready in: 50mins

Ingredients

- 1/2 cup wild rice, uncooked
- 4 slices OSCAR MAYER Bacon, chopped
- 1/2 cup finely chopped onions
- 2 carrots, chopped
- 1/4 cup flour
- 4 cups fat-free reduced-sodium chicken broth
- 1/2 cup (1/2 of 8-oz. tub) PHILADELPHIA Cream Cheese Spread
- 1/4 tsp. pepper
- 2 Tbsp. chopped fresh chives

Direction

- Cook rice as directed on package, omitting salt.
- Meanwhile, cook and stir bacon in large saucepan on medium heat until crisp. Remove from pan with slotted spoon, reserving 1 Tbsp. drippings in pan. Drain bacon on paper towels.
- Add onions and carrots to drippings in pan; cook 5 min. or until crisp-tender, stirring occasionally. Stir in flour; cook and stir 1 min. Add broth; stir. Bring to boil on high heat, stirring frequently; simmer on medium-low heat 10 min. or until vegetables are tender, stirring occasionally. Stir in rice, cream cheese spread and pepper. Cook and stir 3 min. or until cream cheese is melted and soup is thickened. Stir in half the bacon. Ladle soup into soup bowls; top with remaining bacon and chives.

Nutrition Information

- Calories: 190
- Total Carbohydrate: 0 g
- Sugar: 0 g
- Protein: 8 g
- Fiber: 2 g
- Total Fat: 9 g
- Saturated Fat: 4 g
- Cholesterol: 25 mg
- Sodium: 670 mg

147. Curry Tomato Soup

Serving: 0 | Prep: 35mins | Cook: | Ready in: 35mins

Ingredients

- 1/4 cup KRAFT Italian Vinaigrette Dressing made with Extra Virgin Olive Oil
- 2 stalks celery, chopped
- 1 carrot, chopped
- 1 onion, chopped
- 3 cups water
- 1 can (28 oz.) crushed tomatoes
- 1 tsp. WYLER'S Instant Bouillon Chicken Flavored Powder
- 1 tsp. each ground coriander and curry powder

Direction

- Heat dressing in large saucepan on medium-high heat. Add celery, carrots and onions; cook and stir 5 min.
- Add water, tomatoes, bouillon powder and dry seasonings; stir. Bring to boil, stirring occasionally. Cover; simmer on medium-low heat 10 min. or until vegetables are tender.
- Pour soup, in batches, into blender; blend until smooth.

Nutrition Information

- Calories: 80
- Protein: 3 g
- Total Carbohydrate: 0 g
- Sodium: 490 mg
- Total Fat: 2 g
- Cholesterol: 0 mg
- Saturated Fat: 0 g
- Fiber: 4 g
- Sugar: 0 g

148. Dijon Roasted Veggie Soup

Serving: 0 | Prep: 25mins | Cook: 45mins | Ready in: 1hours10mins

Ingredients

- 1 medium zucchini
- 2 medium plum tomatoes, halved
- 1 large onion, quartered
- 1 medium red bell pepper, sliced
- 1 cup sliced carrots
- 2 to 3 cloves garlic, peeled
- 5 cups chicken broth
- 1/4 tsp. ground cumin
- 1/4 tsp. crushed red pepper
- 2 cups chopped cooked chicken
- 1/4 cup GREY POUPON Dijon Mustard
- 1/4 cup chopped fresh parsley

Direction

- Preheat oven to 325°F. Cut zucchini lengthwise in half, then cut each piece crosswise in half. Place in 15x10x1-inch baking pan. Add tomatoes, onions, bell peppers, carrots and garlic; mix lightly. Bake 30 to 45 min. or until tender and golden brown; cool.
- Chop vegetables; place in large saucepan. Add chicken broth, cumin and crushed red pepper;mix well. Bring to boil on high heat. Reduce heat to medium-low; simmer, uncovered, 5 min.
- Add chicken and mustard; mix wel. Cook an additional 5 min. or until heated through. Stir in parsley.

Nutrition Information

- Calories: 130
- Cholesterol: 30 mg
- Protein: 15 g
- Saturated Fat: 1 g
- Sodium: 700 mg
- Total Fat: 4.5 g
- Total Carbohydrate: 0 g
- Fiber: 2 g
- Sugar: 0 g

149. Easy Clam Chowder

Serving: 0 | Prep: 15mins | Cook: 30mins | Ready in: 45mins

Ingredients

- 1 small onion, chopped
- 1 stalk celery, chopped
- 2 slices OSCAR MAYER Bacon, cut into 1-inch pieces
- 1 lb. baking potatoes (about 2), peeled, cut into 1/4-inch cubes
- 1-1/2 cups water
- 1 cup milk

- 4 oz. (1/2 of 8-oz. pkg.) PHILADELPHIA Cream Cheese, cubed
- 1 can (6-1/4 oz.) minced clams, undrained

Direction

- Cook and stir onions, celery and bacon in medium saucepan on medium heat 5 min. or until vegetables are crisp-tender. Add potatoes and water; bring to boil. Cook 15 min. or until potatoes are tender.
- Microwave milk and cream cheese in small microwaveable bowl on HIGH 1-1/2 min. or until milk is heated through. Whisk until cream cheese is completely melted and mixture is well blended. Add to potato mixture; stir.
- Stir in clams; cook 2 min. or until heated through, stirring frequently. (Do not let soup come to boil.)

Nutrition Information

- Calories: 230
- Saturated Fat: 6 g
- Total Carbohydrate: 24 g
- Total Fat: 10 g
- Sugar: 4 g
- Fiber: 2 g
- Protein: 11 g
- Cholesterol: 55 mg
- Sodium: 230 mg

150. Easy Clam Chowder Recipe

Serving: 6 | Prep: 40mins | Cook: | Ready in: 40mins

Ingredients

- 2 cans (6-1/2 oz. each) clams, undrained
- 4 slices OSCAR MAYER Bacon, cut into 1-inch pieces
- 3-1/2 cups ORE-IDA Diced Hash Brown Potatoes
- 1 cup chopped onions
- 1/4 cup each chopped green and red bell peppers
- 1 bay leaf
- 2 cups milk
- 1/8 tsp. ground white pepper

Direction

- Drain clams, reserving liquid. Cook and stir bacon in large saucepan on medium heat until crisp. Remove bacon from pan with slotted spoon; drain on paper towels.
- Add potatoes, onions and bell peppers to bacon drippings in pan; cook 4 to 5 min. or until crisp-tender, stirring frequently. Add bay leaf and reserved clam liquid; stir. Bring to boil, stirring frequently. Cover; simmer on medium-low heat 5 min. Remove and discard bay leaf.
- Add milk, white pepper, clams and bacon; mix well. Cook, uncovered, 3 to 5 min. or until heated through, stirring occasionally. (Do not let soup come to boil.)

Nutrition Information

- Calories: 270
- Sodium: 280 mg
- Total Fat: 11 g
- Protein: 19 g
- Fiber: 2 g
- Sugar: 0 g
- Saturated Fat: 5 g
- Cholesterol: 45 mg
- Total Carbohydrate: 0 g

151. Easy Jambalaya Recipe

Serving: 6 | Prep: 30mins | Cook: | Ready in: 30mins

Ingredients

- 2 pkg. (9 oz. each) WEIGHT WATCHERS SMART ONES Santa Fe Rice & Beans
- 1 tsp. canola oil
- 6 oz. boneless skinless chicken breasts, cut into bite-size pieces
- 3 oz. OSCAR MAYER Natural Uncured Turkey Sausage, chopped
- 1 each green and red bell pepper, chopped
- 1 onion, chopped
- 1 stalk celery, chopped
- 1 clove garlic, minced
- 1 tomato, seeded, chopped
- 1 Tbsp. LEA & PERRINS Worcestershire Sauce
- 1 tsp. TACO BELL® Hot Sauce
- 1/2 tsp. dried thyme leaves
- 1/2 tsp. ground red pepper (cayenne)
- 1/4 tsp. ground black pepper

Direction

- Microwave SMART ONES, 1 at a time, as directed on package.
- Meanwhile, heat oil in large skillet on medium heat. Add chicken; cook and stir 6 to 8 min. or until done, adding sausage the last 4 min. Remove from skillet; set aside.
- Spray skillet with cooking spray. Add bell peppers, onions and celery; cook 2 to 3 min. or until crisp-tender, stirring frequently. Add garlic; cook and stir 30 sec. Stir in tomatoes; cook 2 min., stirring frequently.
- Add SMART ONES, chicken mixture and all remaining ingredients; mix lightly. Cook 2 to 3 min. or until heated through, stirring frequently.

Nutrition Information

- Calories: 170
- Cholesterol: 30 mg
- Sodium: 370 mg
- Protein: 13 g
- Saturated Fat: 1.5 g
- Total Carbohydrate: 0 g
- Sugar: 0 g
- Total Fat: 4.5 g
- Fiber: 4 g

152. Easy Layered Cabbage Casserole

Serving: 0 | Prep: 35mins | Cook: 1hours | Ready in: 1hours35mins

Ingredients

- 8 cups shredded cabbage (about 1 large head)
- 2 onions, chopped
- 1/4 cup KRAFT Zesty Italian Dressing
- 1 lb. extra-lean ground beef
- 2 cups instant brown rice, uncooked
- 2 cans (10-3/4 oz. each) reduced-sodium condensed tomato soup
- 2-2/3 cups water

Direction

- Heat oven to 350°F.
- Cook and stir cabbage and onions in dressing in large skillet on medium heat 5 to 10 min. or until tender. Remove from skillet.
- Brown meat in same skillet. Stir in rice, soup and water until blended. Layer 1/3 of the cabbage mixture and half the meat mixture in 13x9-inch baking dish sprayed with cooking spray. Repeat layers; top with remaining cabbage mixture. Cover.
- Bake 1 hour.

Nutrition Information

- Calories: 240
- Saturated Fat: 1.5 g
- Total Fat: 5 g
- Protein: 14 g
- Sodium: 330 mg
- Total Carbohydrate: 0 g
- Cholesterol: 30 mg
- Fiber: 5 g
- Sugar: 0 g

153. Easy Seafood Gumbo

Serving: 0 | Prep: 30mins | Cook: | Ready in: 30mins

Ingredients

- 1/4 cup butter
- 1/4 cup flour
- 1/2 cup each chopped celery, green peppers and onions
- 3 cloves garlic, minced
- 6-1/2 oz. (1/2 of 13-oz. pkg.) OSCAR MAYER Natural Uncured Turkey Sausage, sliced
- 1 can (14-1/2 oz.) diced tomatoes, drained
- 1 can (14-1/2 oz.) fat-free reduced-sodium chicken broth
- 2 tsp. LEA & PERRINS Worcestershire Sauce
- 1/2 tsp. Cajun seasoning
- 1 lb. uncooked deveined peeled medium shrimp
- 3 cups hot cooked long-grain white rice

Direction

- Melt butter in Dutch oven on medium heat. Stir in flour; cook 5 to 6 min. or until golden brown, stirring constantly. Add celery, green peppers and onions; cook 2 to 3 min. or until crisp-tender, stirring frequently.
- Add sausage, tomatoes, chicken broth, Worcestershire sauce and Cajun seasoning; stir until blended. Bring to boil; cover. Simmer on medium-low heat 5 min., stirring occasionally.
- Stir in shrimp; cook 4 to 5 min. or just until tender, stirring frequently.
- Serve over rice.

Nutrition Information

- Calories: 290
- Saturated Fat: 6 g
- Protein: 15 g
- Total Carbohydrate: 30 g
- Cholesterol: 105 mg
- Sugar: 3 g
- Fiber: 2 g
- Sodium: 750 mg
- Total Fat: 12 g

154. Easy Vegetable Soup

Serving: 0 | Prep: 20mins | Cook: 30mins | Ready in: 50mins

Ingredients

- 1/2 cup chopped onion
- 2 tsp. margarine or butter
- 1 qt. (4 cups) chicken broth
- 2 medium carrots, peeled, sliced and halved (about 1 cup)
- 2 medium potatoes, peeled, chopped
- 1 cup cut green beans
- 1 Tbsp. chopped fresh parsley
- 1 tsp. dried tarragon leaves
- 1/4 tsp. ground black pepper
- saltine crackers

Direction

- Cook onion in margarine in large saucepan on medium-high heat until tender.
- Add chicken broth, carrots, potatoes, green beans, parsley, tarragon and pepper.
- Bring to boil. Reduce heat to medium-low; simmer 20 min. or until vegetables are tender. Serve hot with crackers.

Nutrition Information

- Calories: 140
- Fiber: 2 g
- Protein: 5 g
- Sugar: 0 g
- Cholesterol: 0 mg
- Sodium: 630 mg
- Total Carbohydrate: 0 g

- Saturated Fat: 0.5 g
- Total Fat: 3 g

155. Fast Black Bean Soup

Serving: 2 | Prep: 10mins | Cook: | Ready in: 10mins

Ingredients

- 1 cup fat-free reduced-sodium chicken broth
- 1/4 cup TACO BELL® Thick & Chunky Medium Salsa
- 1 can (15 oz.) no-salt-added black beans, rinsed
- 2 oz. VELVEETA, cut into 1/2-inch cubes

Direction

- Blend all ingredients except VELVEETA in blender until smooth.
- Pour into medium saucepan; cook on medium heat 5 min. or until heated through, stirring occasionally.
- Add VELVEETA; cook 1 min. or until melted, stirring constantly.

Nutrition Information

- Calories: 290
- Cholesterol: 20 mg
- Sugar: 5 g
- Sodium: 810 mg
- Protein: 18 g
- Total Carbohydrate: 40 g
- Saturated Fat: 4 g
- Total Fat: 6 g
- Fiber: 13 g

156. Fisherman's Chowder

Serving: 0 | Prep: 45mins | Cook: | Ready in: 45mins

Ingredients

- 6 slices OSCAR MAYER Bacon, cut into 1/2-inch pieces
- 1 large onion, chopped
- 2 stalks celery, chopped
- 1 large carrot, chopped
- 2 cups fat-free reduced-sodium chicken broth
- 1 large white potato (1/2 lb.), chopped
- 1/2 cup (1/2 of 8-oz. tub) PHILADELPHIA Cream Cheese Spread
- 2 cups milk
- 1 pkg. (12 oz.) frozen cod fillets, thawed, drained and cut into 2-inch pieces

Direction

- Cook and stir bacon in large saucepan until crisp. Use slotted spoon to remove bacon from pan; drain on paper towels. Discard all but 1 Tbsp. drippings from pan.
- Add next 3 ingredients to reserved drippings in pan; cook on medium heat 12 to 14 min. or until vegetables are crisp-tender, stirring occasionally. Add broth and potatoes; stir. Bring to boil; cover. Simmer 10 to 12 min. or until potatoes are tender.
- Add cream cheese spread; cook, uncovered, 2 to 3 min. or until melted, stirring frequently. Add milk, fish and bacon; stir. Bring to boil, stirring frequently. Cook 3 to 4 min. or until fish flakes easily with fork.

Nutrition Information

- Calories: 180
- Fiber: 1 g
- Cholesterol: 40 mg
- Sugar: 5 g
- Protein: 13 g
- Sodium: 330 mg
- Saturated Fat: 4 g
- Total Carbohydrate: 12 g
- Total Fat: 9 g

157. French Onion Soup With Bacon

Serving: 0 | Prep: 1hours | Cook: | Ready in: 1hours

Ingredients

- 4 slices OSCAR MAYER Bacon, cut into 1/2-inch pieces
- 3 large Spanish onions, thinly sliced, separated into rings
- 2 cans (14-1/2 oz. each) fat-free reduced-sodium beef broth
- 1/2 tsp. black pepper
- 1/4 tsp. dried thyme leaves
- 5 slices Italian bread, toasted
- 1 cup KRAFT Shredded Italian* Five Cheese with a TOUCH OF PHILADELPHIA
- 2 Tbsp. KRAFT Grated Parmesan Cheese

Direction

- Cook and stir bacon in large saucepan on medium heat until crisp. Remove bacon from pan with slotted spoon; drain on paper towels. Discard all but 2 Tbsp. drippings from pan.
- Add onions to reserved drippings in pan; cook 20 min. or until golden brown, stirring frequently. Add broth, pepper and thyme; stir. Simmer 15 min. Remove from heat; stir in bacon.
- Heat broiler. Ladle soup into 5 ovenproof bowls; top with remaining ingredients.
- Broil, 4 inches from heat, 2 to 3 min. or until cheeses are melted and golden brown.

Nutrition Information

- Calories: 260
- Saturated Fat: 6 g
- Sodium: 750 mg
- Fiber: 2 g
- Sugar: 7 g
- Total Carbohydrate: 20 g
- Protein: 14 g
- Total Fat: 15 g
- Cholesterol: 30 mg

158. Hearty French Onion Soup Recipe

Serving: 0 | Prep: 40mins | Cook: | Ready in: 40mins

Ingredients

- 2 Tbsp. butter or margarine
- 2 Tbsp. oil
- 3 large onions, sliced, separated into rings
- 3 cans (14-1/2 oz. each) fat-free reduced-sodium beef broth
- 1 Tbsp. A.1. Original Sauce
- 1 cup seasoned croutons
- 1 cup KRAFT Shredded Low-Moisture Part-Skim Mozzarella Cheese

Direction

- Heat butter and oil in large saucepan on medium heat. Add onions; cook 20 min. or until golden brown, stirring frequently.
- Add broth and A.1.; stir. Bring to boil; simmer on medium-low heat 5 min.
- Heat broiler. Ladle soup into 6 ovenproof bowls; top with croutons and cheese. Broil 2 to 3 min. or until cheese is melted.

Nutrition Information

- Calories: 210
- Sugar: 0 g
- Total Fat: 14 g
- Cholesterol: 20 mg
- Sodium: 620 mg
- Fiber: 2 g
- Saturated Fat: 6 g
- Total Carbohydrate: 0 g
- Protein: 10 g

159. Hearty Golden Chowder

Serving: 0 | Prep: 20mins | Cook: 30mins | Ready in: 50mins

Ingredients

- 2 cups cold water
- 2 cups chopped potatoes
- 1/2 cup sliced carrots
- 1/2 cup sliced celery
- 1/4 cup chopped onion
- 1 Tbsp. chopped fresh chives
- 1 tsp. salt
- dash pepper
- 1/4 cup (1/2 stick) butter or margarine
- 1/4 cup flour
- 2 cups milk
- 2 cups KRAFT Shredded Sharp Cheddar Cheese

Direction

- Bring water, vegetables, chives and seasonings to boil in medium saucepan on high heat. Reduce heat to low; cover. Simmer 10 minutes. Do not drain.
- Melt butter in large saucepan on low heat. Stir in flour. Cook 2 minutes or until bubbly. Gradually add milk, stirring until well blended. Cook on medium heat until mixture boils and thickens, stirring constantly. Add cheese; cook until melted, stirring constantly.
- Add vegetable mixture; cook until heated through. Do not boil.

Nutrition Information

- Calories: 320
- Sodium: 750 mg
- Total Fat: 22 g
- Saturated Fat: 12 g
- Cholesterol: 65 mg
- Fiber: 2 g
- Protein: 12 g
- Total Carbohydrate: 20 g
- Sugar: 6 g

160. Hearty Italian Chicken Chowder

Serving: 0 | Prep: 10mins | Cook: 15mins | Ready in: 25mins

Ingredients

- 1/4 cup KRAFT Lite Zesty Italian Dressing
- 1/2 lb. boneless skinless chicken breasts, chopped
- 1 can (14-1/2 oz.) stewed tomatoes, undrained
- 1 cup fat-free reduced-sodium chicken broth
- 1 zucchini, chopped
- 1/2 cup elbow macaroni, uncooked
- 1 tsp. dried basil leaves
- 1/2 cup KRAFT 2% Milk Shredded Mozzarella Cheese

Direction

- Heat dressing in large saucepan on medium heat. Add chicken; cook 3 min., stirring once.
- Add tomatoes, broth, zucchini, macaroni and basil. Bring to boil on high heat.
- Simmer on medium heat 8 min. or until macaroni is tender. Sprinkle with cheese.

Nutrition Information

- Calories: 390
- Saturated Fat: 4 g
- Protein: 40 g
- Sugar: 0 g
- Sodium: 1220 mg
- Cholesterol: 80 mg
- Total Fat: 10 g
- Fiber: 4 g
- Total Carbohydrate: 0 g

161. Hearty Mushroom Beef Barley Soup

Serving: 0 | Prep: 40mins | Cook: 1hours5mins | Ready in: 1hours45mins

Ingredients

- 8 slices OSCAR MAYER Bacon, cut into 1-inch pieces
- 1 lb. mixed mushrooms (button, cremini, shiitake), sliced
- 1/4 cup KRAFT Zesty Italian Dressing
- 2 Tbsp. A.1. Original Sauce
- 1/2 lb. boneless beef chuck steak, cut into 1/2-inch pieces
- 1 large onion, chopped
- 2 carrots, chopped
- 4 cloves garlic, minced
- 1 qt. (4 cups) water
- 2 cans (14.5 oz. each) fat-free reduced-sodium beef broth
- 3/4 cup barley, uncooked

Direction

- Cook and stir bacon in Dutch oven or stockpot on medium heat until crisp. Remove bacon from pan with slotted spoon; drain on paper towels. Discard all but 2 Tbsp. drippings from pan.
- Add mushrooms to drippings in pan; cook on medium-high heat 5 min. or until mushrooms start to release their liquid. Simmer on low heat 15 min. or until mushrooms are golden brown and all liquid is cooked off.
- Add dressing, A.1., beef, onions and carrots; cook and stir 5 min. or until onions are crisp-tender, adding garlic for the last minute.
- Stir in water, broth, barley and bacon. Bring to boil; cover. Simmer on low heat 50 min. or until barley is tender.

Nutrition Information

- Calories: 180
- Cholesterol: 25 mg
- Total Carbohydrate: 16 g
- Sugar: 5 g
- Total Fat: 8 g
- Sodium: 420 mg
- Protein: 13 g
- Saturated Fat: 2.5 g
- Fiber: 4 g

162. Hearty Vegetable Beef Soup

Serving: 8 | Prep: 30mins | Cook: 1hours30mins | Ready in: 2hours

Ingredients

- 1 boneless beef chuck eye roast (2 lb.), trimmed, cut into 8 pieces
- 2-1/2 qt. (10 cups) fat-free reduced-sodium beef broth
- 3 carrots, cut into 4x1/4-inch pieces
- 1 onion, chopped
- 2 jalapeño peppers, seeded, finely chopped
- 1/2 tsp. crushed red pepper
- 1/4 cup KRAFT Zesty Italian Dressing
- 1 lb. red potato (about 3), peeled, cut into 4x1/4-inch pieces
- 2 turnips, cut into wedges
- 1 can (15 oz.) hominy, drained
- 1 cup cooked barley
- 1 pkg. (10 oz.) frozen peas
- 1/4 cup A.1. Original Sauce
- 1/2 cup chopped fresh mint

Direction

- Place meat in stockpot. Add broth; bring to boil on medium-high heat. Cover; simmer on low heat 1 hour, skimming surface occasionally.
- Cook carrots, onions, jalapeño peppers and crushed red pepper in dressing in large skillet on medium heat 10 min., stirring occasionally. Add to ingredients in stockpot; stir. Add all remaining ingredients except mint; stir.

Simmer on medium-low heat 20 min. or just until potatoes are tender. (Do not overcook.)
- Spoon 1 piece of meat in each of 8 bowls. Ladle broth and vegetables over meat. Sprinkle with mint.

Nutrition Information

- Calories: 310
- Total Fat: 10 g
- Saturated Fat: 3 g
- Sodium: 970 mg
- Fiber: 6 g
- Sugar: 0 g
- Total Carbohydrate: 0 g
- Protein: 25 g
- Cholesterol: 50 mg

163. Homemade Chicken Soup With Rice

Serving: 10 | Prep: 20mins | Cook: 1hours40mins | Ready in: 2hours

Ingredients

- 1-1/2 lb. bone-in chicken breasts
- 5 cups water, divided
- 1/4 tsp. pepper
- 1 cup chopped onions
- 1 cup chopped celery
- 2 chicken bouillon cubes
- 1 cup chopped carrots
- 1 cup chopped potatoes
- 1-1/2 cups small broccoli florets
- 1 cup instant white rice, uncooked
- 1/2 lb. (8 oz.) VELVEETA, cut into 1/2-inch cubes

Direction

- Place chicken, 4 cups (1 qt.) water and pepper in large Dutch oven. Bring to boil; cover. Simmer on low heat 1 hour. Remove chicken from pot. Discard skin and bones. Cut chicken into bite-size pieces; return to pot.
- Add remaining water, onions, celery and bouillon. Bring to boil. Simmer on low heat 10 min., stirring occasionally. Add carrots and potatoes; simmer 20 min.; stirring occasionally.
- Add broccoli and rice; simmer 10 min. Add VELVEETA; cook 5 min. or until VELVEETA is melted.

Nutrition Information

- Calories: 180
- Protein: 16 g
- Saturated Fat: 3.5 g
- Sodium: 540 mg
- Sugar: 4 g
- Total Fat: 6 g
- Total Carbohydrate: 16 g
- Fiber: 2 g
- Cholesterol: 45 mg

164. Italian Pasta E Fagioli

Serving: 0 | Prep: 35mins | Cook: | Ready in: 35mins

Ingredients

- 1 jar (24 oz.) CLASSICO Tomato and Basil Pasta Sauce
- 2 cups water
- 4 large cloves garlic, minced
- 4 cups wide egg noodles, uncooked
- 1/2 cup (1/2 of 8-oz. tub) PHILADELPHIA Cream Cheese Spread
- 1 pkg. (6 oz.) baby spinach leaves
- 1 can (15 oz.) cannellini beans, rinsed
- 3 Tbsp. chopped fresh basil
- 1 cup KRAFT Shredded Italian* Five Cheese with a TOUCH OF PHILADELPHIA
- 3 Tbsp. KRAFT Grated Parmesan Cheese

Direction

- Bring pasta sauce, water and garlic to boil in large skillet. Stir in noodles; cover.
- Cook on medium-low heat 10 to 12 min. or just until noodles are tender, stirring occasionally. Add cream cheese spread; cook 3 to 5 min. or until melted, stirring frequently.
- Stir in spinach, beans and basil; cover. Cook 5 min. or until heated through, stirring occasionally. Top with remaining cheeses; cook, covered, 3 to 5 min. or until melted, stirring occasionally.

Nutrition Information

- Calories: 340
- Sodium: 710 mg
- Total Carbohydrate: 0 g
- Fiber: 6 g
- Protein: 16 g
- Total Fat: 14 g
- Sugar: 0 g
- Saturated Fat: 7 g
- Cholesterol: 60 mg

165. Italian Style Gumbo Recipe

Serving: 0 | Prep: 45mins | Cook: | Ready in: 45mins

Ingredients

- 1 cup long-grain white rice, uncooked
- 3 Tbsp. butter
- 3 Tbsp. flour
- 1/2 cup KRAFT Grated Parmesan Cheese, divided
- 3/4 lb. Italian sausage, crumbled
- 3 stalks celery, sliced
- 1 green pepper, chopped
- 1 small onion, chopped
- 1 can (14.5 oz.) diced tomatoes with basil, garlic and oregano, undrained
- 1 can (14.5 oz.) fat-free reduced-sodium chicken broth
- 1/2 lb. frozen uncooked cleaned medium shrimp, thawed

Direction

- Cook rice as directed on package, omitting salt.
- Meanwhile, melt butter in large saucepan on medium heat. Stir in flour and 1/4 cup cheese; cook and stir 5 min. or until mixture comes to boil. Add sausage, celery, peppers and onions; cook 15 min., stirring frequently. Stir in tomatoes, chicken broth and shrimp; cook 10 min. or until mixture is heated through and shrimp are done, stirring occasionally.
- Spoon shrimp mixture over rice; top with remaining cheese.

Nutrition Information

- Calories: 270
- Total Carbohydrate: 25 g
- Protein: 14 g
- Saturated Fat: 6 g
- Cholesterol: 65 mg
- Sodium: 590 mg
- Fiber: 1 g
- Total Fat: 12 g
- Sugar: 4 g

166. Kale & Barley Soup

Serving: 0 | Prep: 40mins | Cook: | Ready in: 40mins

Ingredients

- 4 slices OSCAR MAYER Bacon, cut into 1/4-inch-thick slices
- 1 cup chopped onions
- 1 cup chopped carrots
- 1 Tbsp. minced garlic
- 1 qt. (4 cups) fat-free reduced-sodium chicken broth

- 1 cup OLIVO by CLASSICO Traditional Pasta Sauce
- 1/2 cup quick-cooking barley
- 4 cups loosely packed chopped stemmed kale
- 1 can (15 oz.) cannellini beans, rinsed

Direction

- Cook bacon, onions and carrots in Dutch oven on medium heat 12 min. or until bacon is almost done and vegetables are tender, stirring occasionally. Add garlic; cook and stir 2 min.
- Stir in chicken broth, pasta sauce and barley. Bring just to boil; simmer on medium-low heat 10 min., stirring occasionally.
- Add kale and beans; stir. Cook on medium heat 10 min., stirring occasionally.

Nutrition Information

- Calories: 180
- Sugar: 7 g
- Total Fat: 3 g
- Saturated Fat: 0.5 g
- Cholesterol: 5 mg
- Sodium: 550 mg
- Total Carbohydrate: 30 g
- Fiber: 8 g
- Protein: 8 g

167. Kale And Farro Soup

Serving: 0 | Prep: 25mins | Cook: 35mins | Ready in: 1hours

Ingredients

- 1/2 cup KRAFT Italian Roasted Red Pepper Dressing
- 1 cup chopped onions
- 2 portobello mushrooms, chopped
- 2 qt. (8 cups) fat-free reduced-sodium chicken broth
- 1 can (14.5 oz.) no-salt-added diced tomatoes, undrained
- 4 cups tightly packed stemmed kale, chopped
- 2 cups pearled farro, uncooked
- 2 large carrots, chopped
- 2 stalks celery, chopped
- 1/2 cup KRAFT Grated Parmesan Cheese

Direction

- Heat dressing in large saucepan on medium heat. Add onions and mushrooms; cook 6 to 8 min. or until mushrooms release their liquid and are evenly browned, stirring occasionally.
- Add all remaining ingredients except cheese; stir. Bring to boil; simmer on medium-low heat 30 to 35 min. or until farro and kale are tender, stirring occasionally.
- Serve topped with cheese.

Nutrition Information

- Calories: 230
- Total Carbohydrate: 0 g
- Sugar: 0 g
- Cholesterol: 5 mg
- Protein: 11 g
- Total Fat: 3.5 g
- Fiber: 7 g
- Saturated Fat: 1 g
- Sodium: 590 mg

168. La Ceiba Conch Soup

Serving: 0 | Prep: 20mins | Cook: 35mins | Ready in: 55mins

Ingredients

- 1/2 cup (1/2 stick) butter or margarine
- 2 lb. yuca (cassava), peeled, chopped
- 2 medium carrots, peeled, chopped
- 2 medium onions, chopped
- 1 medium green pepper, chopped

- 3 cloves garlic, minced
- 4 cups chicken broth
- 1 can (13.4 oz.) coconut milk
- 2 green bananas, sliced
- 1 lb. conch meat, cut into bite-size pieces
- 1/2 cup chopped cilantro

Direction

- Melt butter in large saucepan on medium heat. Add yuca, carrots, onions, peppers and garlic; mix well. Cook 10 min., stirring frequently.
- Add chicken broth and coconut milk; bring to boil. Simmer 15 min., stirring occasionaly. Add bananas; mix well. Cook 5 min. or until bananas are soft, stirring frequently.
- Stir in conch meat and cilantro; cook an additional 5 min. or until conch meat is cooked through, stirring occasionally.

Nutrition Information

- Calories: 320
- Saturated Fat: 11 g
- Sodium: 390 mg
- Fiber: 3 g
- Sugar: 0 g
- Total Carbohydrate: 0 g
- Cholesterol: 45 mg
- Total Fat: 16 g
- Protein: 14 g

169. Lasagna Soup

Serving: 0 | Prep: 15mins | Cook: 10mins | Ready in: 25mins

Ingredients

- 1 Tbsp. oil
- 4 cloves garlic, minced
- 2 cans (14-1/2 oz. each) fat-free reduced-sodium chicken broth
- 1 can (15 oz.) tomato sauce
- 1 can (14.5 oz.) petite diced tomatoes, undrained
- 3 cups wide egg noodles, uncooked
- 3 Tbsp. chopped fresh basil, divided
- 3/4 cup POLLY-O Original Ricotta Cheese
- 1-1/4 cups KRAFT Shredded Italian* Five Cheese with a TOUCH OF PHILADELPHIA, divided
- 3 Tbsp. KRAFT Grated Parmesan Cheese, divided

Direction

- Heat oil in large saucepan on medium heat. Add garlic; cook and stir 1 min. or until fragrant. Add broth, tomato sauce and diced tomatoes; stir. Bring to boil on medium-high heat. Add noodles; simmer on medium heat 10 min. or until tender. Stir in 2 Tbsp. basil.
- Mix ricotta, 1/2 cup shredded cheese, 2 Tbsp. Parmesan and remaining basil until blended. Combine remaining shredded cheese and Parmesan.
- Top each serving of soup with 2 Tbsp. of the ricotta mixture. Sprinkle with shredded cheese mixture.

Nutrition Information

- Calories: 210
- Protein: 12 g
- Total Carbohydrate: 18 g
- Fiber: 2 g
- Total Fat: 10 g
- Cholesterol: 40 mg
- Sodium: 730 mg
- Sugar: 5 g
- Saturated Fat: 5 g

170. Lentil Soup

Serving: 0 | Prep: 10mins | Cook: 40mins | Ready in: 50mins

Ingredients

- 6 slices OSCAR MAYER Bacon, chopped
- 1 small onion, chopped
- 1 clove garlic, minced
- 3 cans (14-1/2 oz. each) fat-free reduced-sodium chicken broth
- 1/2 lb. dry lentils, sorted, washed
- 1/2 lb. red potato (1 large potato), chopped
- 3 small carrots (1/4 lb.), chopped
- 3 OSCAR MAYER Wieners, cut into 1/4-inch-thick slices
- 1/2 cup BREAKSTONE'S or KNUDSEN Sour Cream

Direction

- Cook bacon and onions in large saucepan 8 to 10 min. or until bacon is crisp and onions are crisp-tender, stirring occasionally. Add garlic; cook 1 min.
- Add next 5 ingredients; stir. Bring to boil; simmer on low heat 25 to 30 min. or until lentils and vegetables are tender.
- Serve topped with sour cream.

Nutrition Information

- Calories: 340
- Total Carbohydrate: 0 g
- Protein: 18 g
- Cholesterol: 40 mg
- Sodium: 730 mg
- Total Fat: 19 g
- Saturated Fat: 8 g
- Fiber: 10 g
- Sugar: 0 g

171. Lima Bean Soup

Serving: 0 | Prep: 10mins | Cook: 1hours5mins | Ready in: 1hours15mins

Ingredients

- 1/4 cup KRAFT Zesty Italian Dressing
- 1 can (14.5 oz) diced tomatoes with garlic and olive oil, undrained
- 1 large onion, chopped
- 2 cloves garlic, minced
- 1 lb. dried lima beans
- 1/2 cup fresh cilantro leaves
- 1-3/4 qt. (7 cups) water
- 40 RITZ Crackers

Direction

- Heat dressing in large saucepan on medium heat. Add tomatoes, onions and garlic; cook 4 min. Stir in beans and cilantro; cook 1 min.
- Add water; bring to boil. Cover. Cook on low heat 1 hour or until beans are tender.
- Serve with crackers.

Nutrition Information

- Calories: 320
- Total Fat: 7 g
- Fiber: 12 g
- Sodium: 450 mg
- Saturated Fat: 1.5 g
- Protein: 14 g
- Sugar: 0 g
- Cholesterol: 0 mg
- Total Carbohydrate: 0 g

172. Luscious Potato, Leek & Bacon Soup

Serving: 0 | Prep: 30mins | Cook: | Ready in: 30mins

Ingredients

- 8 slices OSCAR MAYER Selects Uncured Turkey Bacon, chopped
- 3 cups vegetable broth
- 2 large leeks (1 lb.), white and light green parts only, thinly sliced

- 1 lb. baking potatoes (about 3), peeled, chopped
- dash white pepper
- 1/2 cup milk

Direction

- Cook bacon in medium skillet on medium-high heat 5 min. or until bacon is lightly browned, stirring occasionally.
- Meanwhile, bring broth to boil in medium saucepan. Add leeks, potatoes and pepper; simmer 10 min. or until potatoes are tender. Remove from heat.
- Reserve 1/4 cup bacon. Add remaining bacon and milk to soup; blend, in small batches, in blender until smooth; pour into bowl. Top with reserved bacon.

Nutrition Information

- Calories: 150
- Total Fat: 5 g
- Fiber: 2 g
- Sugar: 0 g
- Saturated Fat: 1.5 g
- Cholesterol: 20 mg
- Sodium: 700 mg
- Protein: 5 g
- Total Carbohydrate: 0 g

173. Mac & Grilled Cheese Tomato Soup

Serving: 6 | Prep: 30mins | Cook: | Ready in: 30mins

Ingredients

- 1 pkg. (14.5 oz.) KRAFT Macaroni & Cheese Dinner
- 2 Tbsp. butter, divided
- 1 onion, chopped
- 1 can (14.5 oz.) fat-free reduced-sodium chicken broth
- 1 cup water
- 1 can (28 oz.) no-salt-added diced tomatoes, undrained
- 4 slices white bread
- 4 KRAFT Singles
- 1/4 cup chopped fresh basil

Direction

- Prepare Dinner as directed on package. Meanwhile, melt 2 tsp. butter in large saucepan on medium heat. Add onions; cook and stir 5 min. Stir in broth, water and tomatoes. Bring to boil; simmer on medium-low heat 10 min. or until onions are tender.
- Blend tomato mixture, in small batches, in blender until smooth, returning each puréed batch to saucepan. Keep warm until ready to serve.
- Fill bread slices with Singles to make 2 sandwiches. Spread outsides of sandwiches with remaining butter. Cook in skillet on medium heat 3 min. on each side or until Singles are melted and sandwiches are golden brown on both sides. Cut each sandwich into 12 pieces.
- Spoon Dinner into 6 bowls; top with basil, soup and grilled cheese "croutons."

Nutrition Information

- Calories: 560
- Protein: 16 g
- Fiber: 4 g
- Cholesterol: 35 mg
- Sugar: 14 g
- Saturated Fat: 9 g
- Total Fat: 26 g
- Sodium: 1200 mg
- Total Carbohydrate: 65 g

174. Mac 'N Double Cheese Soup

Serving: 0 | Prep: 5mins | Cook: 25mins | Ready in: 30mins

Ingredients

- 3 cups water
- 2 cups milk
- 1 pkg. (14 oz.) KRAFT Deluxe Macaroni & Cheese Dinner
- 2 cups frozen vegetable blend
- 1/2 lb. (8 oz.) VELVEETA, cut into 1/2-inch cubes

Direction

- Bring water and milk to boil in large saucepan.
- Stir in Macaroni and vegetable blend. Return to boil; simmer on medium-low heat 12 to 14 min. or until macaroni is tender.
- Add VELVEETA and Cheese Sauce from pouch; cook until VELVEETA is completely melted and mixture is well blended, stirring constantly.

Nutrition Information

- Calories: 280
- Sugar: 8 g
- Cholesterol: 30 mg
- Total Fat: 12 g
- Protein: 13 g
- Fiber: 2 g
- Sodium: 890 mg
- Total Carbohydrate: 30 g
- Saturated Fat: 6 g

175. Manhattan Clam Chowder

Serving: 8 | Prep: 45mins | Cook: 15mins | Ready in: 1hours

Ingredients

- 4 cups water
- 18 fresh hard-shell clams, washed
- 4 slices OSCAR MAYER Bacon
- 1 cup chopped onions
- 1 cup chopped celery
- 1/2 cup each chopped green and red bell pepper
- 1/4 cup chopped carrots
- 1 can (14.5 oz.) diced tomatoes, undrained
- 2 cups ORE-IDA Diced Hash Brown Potatoes, thawed
- 1 cup fat-free reduced-sodium vegetable broth
- 1/2 tsp. dried thyme leaves, crushed
- 1/4 tsp. ground red pepper (cayenne)
- 2 Tbsp. chopped fresh parsley

Direction

- Bring water and clams to boil in large saucepan on medium-high heat; cover. Cook 10 to 15 min. or until clams open. Strain clam liquid through a sieve lined with double layer of paper towels or cheesecloth; reserve 1-1/2 cups clam liquid. Remove clams from shells; set aside. Rinse pan. Add bacon; cook until crisp. Remove bacon from pan, reserving 1 Tbsp. drippings in pan. Drain bacon on paper towels; crumble.
- Add onions, celery, bell peppers and carrots to reserved bacon drippings in pan; cook 3 to 5 min. or until tender. Stir in reserved clam juice, tomatoes, potatoes, vegetable broth, thyme and ground red pepper. Bring to boil; cover. Simmer on low heat 20 to 25 min. or until vegetables are tender, stirring occasionally.
- Stir in clams. Return to boil; cook 1 to 2 min. or until heated through. Serve topped with crumbled bacon and parsley.

Nutrition Information

- Calories: 90
- Total Carbohydrate: 13 g
- Sodium: 230 mg

- Total Fat: 3.5 g
- Sugar: 4 g
- Saturated Fat: 1 g
- Fiber: 3 g
- Cholesterol: 10 mg
- Protein: 4 g

176. Marvelous Minestrone

Serving: 6 | Prep: 25mins | Cook: | Ready in: 25mins

Ingredients

- 2 cans (14-1/2 oz. each) fat-free reduced-sodium chicken broth
- 1 can (15 oz.) chickpeas (garbanzo beans), rinsed
- 1 can (14-1/2 oz.) diced tomatoes, undrained
- 2 cups frozen Italian-style vegetable blend
- 1/2 cup elbow macaroni, uncooked
- 1/4 cup KRAFT Zesty Italian Dressing
- 1/4 cup KRAFT Grated Parmesan Cheese

Direction

- Bring all ingredients except cheese to boil in large saucepan.
- Simmer on medium-low heat 6 to 8 min. or until macaroni is tender.
- Serve topped with cheese.

Nutrition Information

- Calories: 180
- Total Fat: 5 g
- Saturated Fat: 1.5 g
- Protein: 9 g
- Total Carbohydrate: 0 g
- Sodium: 620 mg
- Cholesterol: 5 mg
- Fiber: 6 g
- Sugar: 0 g

177. Mediterranean Sun Dried Tomato Lentil Soup

Serving: 0 | Prep: 30mins | Cook: | Ready in: 30mins

Ingredients

- 3 Tbsp. KRAFT Sun Dried Tomato Vinaigrette Dressing made with Extra Virgin Olive Oil
- 1 onion, chopped
- 2 cloves garlic, minced
- 2 carrots, peeled, chopped
- 2 cans (15 oz. each) lentils, rinsed
- 2 tsp. ground cumin
- 1 tsp. ground ginger
- 1/2 tsp. each crushed red pepper and ground black pepper
- 1 can (28 oz.) crushed tomatoes, undrained
- 3 cups low-sodium tomato juice
- 1 cup chopped baby kale
- 2 Tbsp. fresh lemon juice

Direction

- Heat dressing in large saucepan on medium heat. Add onions and garlic; cook 3 to 5 min. or until crisp-tender, stirring frequently. Add carrots, lentils and dry seasonings; mix well. Cook 2 min., stirring frequently.
- Stir in crushed tomatoes, then tomato juice; bring to boil, stirring frequently. Simmer on medium-low heat 10 min., stirring occasionally and adding kale for the last 2 min.
- Remove from heat. Stir in lemon juice.

Nutrition Information

- Calories: 160
- Total Carbohydrate: 0 g
- Total Fat: 1.5 g
- Saturated Fat: 0 g
- Sugar: 0 g
- Protein: 10 g
- Sodium: 250 mg
- Fiber: 9 g

- Cholesterol: 0 mg
- Sugar: 0 g
- Protein: 23 g
- Total Fat: 7 g
- Sodium: 860 mg
- Total Carbohydrate: 0 g
- Cholesterol: 100 mg
- Saturated Fat: 2 g

178. Mediterranean Style Seafood Chowder

Serving: 10 | Prep: 25mins | Cook: | Ready in: 25mins

Ingredients

- 2 cups small pasta shells, uncooked
- 2 Tbsp. olive oil
- 1 each green and red pepper, cut into thin strips
- 2 stalks celery, sliced
- 1 onion, chopped
- 1 lb. uncooked deveined peeled medium shrimp
- 1 lb. bay scallops
- 1 cup clam juice
- 1 can (6.5 oz.) minced clams, undrained
- 1 jar (24 oz.) CLASSICO Vodka Sauce Pasta Sauce
- 1 Tbsp. CLASSICO Traditional Basil Pesto Sauce and Spread

Direction

- Cook pasta as directed on package, omitting salt.
- Meanwhile, heat oil in large saucepan on medium heat. Add vegetables; cook 5 min. or until crisp-tender, stirring frequently. Add shrimp and scallops; cook 2 to 3 min. or just until shrimp turn pink and scallops are opaque, stirring occasionally. Add remaining ingredients; stir. Simmer on medium-low heat 2 to 3 min. or until heated through, stirring occasionally.
- Drain pasta. Add to chowder; stir.

Nutrition Information

- Calories: 260
- Fiber: 2 g

179. Mexican Soup With Tortilla Chips

Serving: 8 | Prep: 25mins | Cook: | Ready in: 25mins

Ingredients

- 1 lb. lean ground beef
- 2 cans (14-1/2 oz. each) beef broth
- 1 jar (16 oz.) TACO BELL® Thick & Chunky Salsa
- 1 can (7 oz.) corn, undrained
- 1 cup tortilla chips (1 oz.), crushed
- 1 cup KRAFT Mexican Style Finely Shredded Four Cheese

Direction

- Brown meat in large saucepan; drain.
- Add broth, salsa and corn; stir. Bring to boil; simmer on low heat 5 min. or until heated through.
- Serve topped with crushed chips and cheese.

Nutrition Information

- Calories: 200
- Saturated Fat: 4.5 g
- Fiber: 1 g
- Cholesterol: 45 mg
- Protein: 17 g
- Sodium: 940 mg
- Total Carbohydrate: 12 g
- Total Fat: 10 g
- Sugar: 3 g

180. Midwest Chowder

Serving: 0 | Prep: 45mins | Cook: | Ready in: 45mins

Ingredients

- 1 lb. baking potatoes (about 3), peeled, finely chopped
- 1 carrot, chopped
- 1 stalk celery chopped
- 1/4 cup chopped onions
- 2 cups water
- 1/4 cup butter or margarine
- 1/4 cup flour
- 2 cups milk
- 1-1/4 cups shredded CRACKER BARREL Sharp Cheddar Cheese
- 1 can (14.75 oz.) cream-style corn

Direction

- Bring vegetables and water to boil in saucepan on high heat. Cover; simmer on low heat 10 min., stirring occasionally. Remove from heat. (Do not drain.) Set aside.
- Melt butter in separate large saucepan on low heat. Stir in flour; cook and stir 2 min. or until bubbly. Gradually stir in milk until blended. Bring to boil on medium heat, stirring frequently; cook 1 to 2 min. or until thickened, stirring constantly. Simmer on low heat 5 min.
- Add cheese; cook and stir 2 min. or until melted. Add corn and undrained cooked vegetables; cook 5 min. or until heated through, stirring occasionally. (Do not boil.)

Nutrition Information

- Calories: 250
- Cholesterol: 40 mg
- Fiber: 2 g
- Total Carbohydrate: 26 g
- Saturated Fat: 8 g
- Sodium: 320 mg
- Protein: 8 g
- Total Fat: 13 g
- Sugar: 5 g

181. Minestrone Soup

Serving: 0 | Prep: 15mins | Cook: 6hours15mins | Ready in: 6hours30mins

Ingredients

- 1/4 cup KRAFT Zesty Italian Dressing
- 1 onion, chopped
- 1 stalk celery, chopped
- 1 carrot, peeled, chopped
- 1 can (19 oz.) red kidney beans, rinsed
- 1 can (14-1/2 oz.) diced tomatoes, undrained
- 2 cans (14-1/2 oz. each) vegetable broth
- 2 cups water
- 1 tsp. dried Italian seasoning
- 1-1/2 cups small pasta shells, uncooked
- 1/2 cup KRAFT Grated Parmesan Cheese

Direction

- Heat dressing in large nonstick skillet on medium-high heat. Add onions, celery and carrots; cook 2 min. or until crisp-tender, stirring occasionally. Pour into slow cooker. Add beans, tomatoes, broth, water and seasoning; stir. Cover with lid.
- Cook on LOW 6 hours (or on HIGH 3 hours).
- Stir in macaroni; cook 10 to 15 min. or until macaroni is tender. Top with cheese just before serving.

Nutrition Information

- Calories: 200
- Sodium: 770 mg
- Protein: 10 g
- Total Fat: 4.5 g
- Cholesterol: 5 mg
- Saturated Fat: 1.5 g
- Fiber: 5 g

- Total Carbohydrate: 0 g
- Sugar: 0 g

182. Minestrone Soup With Poblano Chile

Serving: 0 | Prep: 10mins | Cook: 30mins | Ready in: 40mins

Ingredients

- 1 pkg. (32 oz.) low sodium chicken broth
- 1 can (14 oz.) no-salt-added diced tomatoes
- 1 small white onion, chopped
- 2 cloves garlic, minced
- 1 cup of butternut squash diced and cooked
- 1 stalk celery, diced
- 1 medium carrot, diced
- 1 cup ditalini pasta
- 1 can (15 oz.) of cannellini beans low sodium, drained
- 2 Tbsp. of OSCAR MAYER Real Bacon Bits
- 1 cup of roasted, peeled and deveined diced poblano chile peppers
- 1 tsp. dried oregano leaves
- season to taste
- 1/4 cup KRAFT Shredded Parmesan Cheese
- fresh basil to decorate

Direction

- In a medium saucepan, add the chicken broth, tomatoes, onion, garlic, butternut squash, celery and carrot. Cook over medium-high heat for 20 minutes. Once it begins to boil add the pasta and cannellini beans. The pasta should be ready in 10 minutes. Add bacon, poblano peppers and of course sprinkle oregano and pepper.
- You can place the Minestrone in mini "pans" bowls for your guests. When you are serving don't forget to sprinkle each bowl with Parmesan cheese and fresh basil.

Nutrition Information

- Calories: 0 g
- Protein: 0 g
- Fiber: 0 g
- Sodium: 0 g
- Total Fat: 0 g
- Sugar: 0 g
- Saturated Fat: 0 g
- Cholesterol: 0 g
- Total Carbohydrate: 0 g

183. Mom's Cheesy Potato Chowder With Bacon Bits

Serving: 0 | Prep: 20mins | Cook: | Ready in: 20mins

Ingredients

- 1 can (10-3/4 oz.) condensed cream of potato soup
- 3 cups milk
- 2 Tbsp. finely chopped onion
- 2 cups ORE-IDA Diced Hash Brown Potatoes
- 1 cup KRAFT Shredded Cheddar Cheese
- 2 slices OSCAR MAYER Center Cut Bacon, cooked, crumbled
- 2 green onions, thinly sliced

Direction

- Mix soup, milk and onion in large saucepan until blended. Stir in hash browns.
- Bring to boil on high heat, stirring occasionally; simmer on medium-low heat 10 min., stirring frequently.
- Serve topped with cheese, bacon and green onions.

Nutrition Information

- Calories: 210
- Total Carbohydrate: 0 g
- Cholesterol: 30 mg

- Total Fat: 10 g
- Sugar: 0 g
- Protein: 10 g
- Sodium: 480 mg
- Fiber: 1 g
- Saturated Fat: 6 g

184. Nana's Cheese Soup

Serving: 14 | Prep: 25mins | Cook: | Ready in: 25mins

Ingredients

- 3 lb. red potatoes (about 9), peeled, chopped
- 4 cups water
- 1 can (12 oz.) evaporated milk
- 2 cups 2% milk
- 4 cups chopped broccoli
- 3 Tbsp. chopped onions
- 3/4 lb. (12 oz.) VELVEETA, cut into 1/2-inch cubes
- 6 oz. OSCAR MAYER CARVING BOARD Slow Cooked Ham, chopped

Direction

- Cook potatoes, water and evaporated milk in Dutch oven 10 min. or until potatoes are tender.
- Add 2% milk, broccoli and onions; cook on medium heat 5 min. or until broccoli is tender, stirring frequently.
- Stir in VELVEETA and ham; cook on low heat 5 min. or until VELVEETA is completely melted and soup is heated through, stirring constantly.

Nutrition Information

- Calories: 220
- Total Carbohydrate: 26 g
- Sodium: 520 mg
- Fiber: 2 g
- Total Fat: 8 g

- Cholesterol: 30 mg
- Sugar: 8 g
- Protein: 11 g
- Saturated Fat: 5 g

185. New England Chowder

Serving: 0 | Prep: | Cook: | Ready in:

Ingredients

- 1/4 cup butter, divided
- 2 cups oyster crackers
- 1 Tbsp. seafood seasoning, divided
- 1 cup chopped onions
- 2 stalks celery, chopped
- 3 Tbsp. dry sherry
- 1-1/2 lb. red potatoes (about 5), peeled, cut into 1/2-inch chunks
- 3 cups fat-free reduced-sodium chicken broth
- 3 cans (6.5 oz. each) minced clams, drained
- 2 Tbsp. LEA & PERRINS Worcestershire Sauce
- 1 pkg. (8 oz.) PHILADELPHIA Cream Cheese, cubed

Direction

- Heat oven to 350°F.
- Melt 1 Tbsp. butter. Drizzle over crackers in medium bowl. Add 1 tsp. seafood seasoning; mix lightly. Spread onto rimmed baking sheet sprayed with cooking spray. Bake 10 min. or until lightly browned.
- Meanwhile, melt remaining butter in large saucepan. Add onions and celery; cook 5 min. or until crisp-tender, stirring frequently. Stir in sherry; cook and stir 30 sec. Add potatoes and chicken broth; stir. Bring to boil; simmer on medium-low heat 10 min. or until potatoes are tender, stirring occasionally. Remove 2 cups soup from saucepan. Blend in blender or food processor or until smooth. Return to saucepan.
- Add clams, Worcestershire sauce and remaining seafood seasoning; stir. Simmer 10

min., stirring occasionally. Add cream cheese; cook and stir 2 to 3 min. or until melted.
- Serve topped with seasoned oyster crackers.

Nutrition Information

- Calories: 0 g
- Total Carbohydrate: 0 g
- Saturated Fat: 0 g
- Sugar: 0 g
- Protein: 0 g
- Sodium: 0 g
- Fiber: 0 g
- Cholesterol: 0 g
- Total Fat: 0 g

186. New England Clam Chowder

Serving: 0 | Prep: 45mins | Cook: | Ready in: 45mins

Ingredients

- 4 slices OSCAR MAYER Bacon, chopped
- 1 yellow onion, chopped
- 2 stalks celery, chopped
- 1/2 tsp. dried thyme leaves
- 1 lb. baking potatoes (about 2), peeled, cut into 1/4-inch cubes
- 1-1/2 cups water
- 1 cup milk
- 4 oz. (1/2 of 8-oz. pkg.) PHILADELPHIA Cream Cheese, cubed
- 2 cans (6-1/4 oz. each) minced clams, undrained
- 1 green onion, thinly sliced

Direction

- Cook and stir bacon in medium saucepan on medium heat until crisp. Remove bacon from pan with slotted spoon, reserving 1 Tbsp. dripping in saucepan. Drain bacon on paper towels. Add yellow onions, celery and thyme to drippings in pan; cook and stir 5 min. or until vegetables are crisp-tender. Add potatoes, water and 2 Tbsp. bacon; bring to boil. Cook 15 min. or until potatoes are tender, stirring occasionally.
- Microwave milk and cream cheese in small microwaveable bowl on HIGH 1-1/2 min. or until milk is heated through. Whisk until cream cheese is completely melted and mixture is well blended. Add to potato mixture; stir.
- Stir in clams; cook 2 min. or until heated through, stirring frequently. (Do not boil.) Sprinkle with remaining bacon and green onions.

Nutrition Information

- Calories: 250
- Sodium: 290 mg
- Saturated Fat: 6 g
- Total Fat: 12 g
- Fiber: 2 g
- Sugar: 5 g
- Protein: 15 g
- Total Carbohydrate: 21 g
- Cholesterol: 55 mg

187. No Cream Creamy Broccoli Soup

Serving: 0 | Prep: 50mins | Cook: | Ready in: 50mins

Ingredients

- 2 carrots, chopped
- 2 stalks celery, chopped
- 1 onion, chopped
- 3 Tbsp. oil
- 2 cans (14-1/2 oz. each) fat-free reduced-sodium chicken broth
- 1/2 tsp. pepper
- 4-1/2 cups small broccoli florets
- 1/2 cup long-grain white rice, uncooked

- 2 cups milk
- 1/4 cup KRAFT Grated Parmesan Cheese

Direction

- Cook and stir carrots, celery and onions in hot oil in large saucepan on medium-high heat 5 min. Add broth and pepper; stir. Bring to boil.
- Stir in broccoli and rice; simmer on medium-low heat 15 to 20 min. or until vegetables and rice are tender, stirring occasionally.
- Add soup, in batches, to blender or food processor; blend until puréed. Return each batch to saucepan. Add milk and cheese; cook 3 to 5 min. or until heated through, stirring occasionally.

Nutrition Information

- Calories: 150
- Saturated Fat: 2 g
- Protein: 6 g
- Sugar: 0 g
- Total Fat: 8 g
- Sodium: 320 mg
- Total Carbohydrate: 0 g
- Fiber: 4 g
- Cholesterol: 10 mg

188. ORE IDA Loaded Potato Soup Recipe

Serving: 8 | Prep: 15mins | Cook: 10mins | Ready in: 25mins

Ingredients

- 1 pkg. (24 oz.) ORE-IDA STEAM N' MASH Cut Russet Potatoes
- 2 cups CLASSICO Creamy Alfredo Pasta Sauce
- 2 cups frozen broccoli florets, coarsely chopped
- 2 cups milk
- 1 tsp. dried Italian seasoning
- 1 tsp. garlic powder
- 1 cup KRAFT Shredded Cheddar Cheese
- 1/2 cup crumbled cooked OSCAR MAYER Bacon
- 1 green onion, sliced

Direction

- Microwave potatoes as directed on package. (Do not mash.)
- Cook pasta sauce, broccoli, milk and seasonings in medium saucepan on medium heat 4 to 5 min. or until heated through, stirring frequently. Add potatoes; stir. Simmer on medium-low heat 5 min., stirring frequently.
- Serve soup topped with remaining ingredients.

Nutrition Information

- Calories: 250
- Sugar: 5 g
- Sodium: 870 mg
- Saturated Fat: 7 g
- Total Carbohydrate: 22 g
- Cholesterol: 60 mg
- Total Fat: 13 g
- Fiber: 3 g
- Protein: 12 g

189. Old Fashioned Potato Soup

Serving: 0 | Prep: 40mins | Cook: 25mins | Ready in: 1hours5mins

Ingredients

- 5 slices OSCAR MAYER Bacon, chopped into 1/4-inch-thick strips
- 1 cup each chopped carrots, celery and yellow onions

- 2 Tbsp. flour
- 1-1/2 cups milk
- 4 oz. (1/2 of 8-oz pkg.) PHILADELPHIA Cream Cheese, cubed
- 3/4 lb. baking potatoes (about 2), peeled, cut into 1/2-inch pieces
- 3 cups fat-free reduced-sodium chicken broth
- 3 green onions, chopped

Direction

- Cook and stir bacon in medium saucepan until crisp. Remove bacon from pan with slotted spoon; drain on paper towels. Discard all but 2 Tbsp. drippings from pan.
- Add carrots, celery and yellow onions to reserved drippings; cook on medium heat 5 min. or until vegetables are crisp-tender, stirring frequently. Add flour; cook and stir 1 min. Gradually stir in milk; cook 3 min. or until vegetable mixture is slightly thickened, stirring constantly. Add cream cheese; cook on medium-low heat 2 to 3 min. or until completely melted.
- Add potatoes and chicken broth; stir. Bring to boil on medium heat; cover. Simmer on medium-low heat 20 to 25 min. or until potatoes are tender, stirring occasionally.
- Serve topped with bacon and green onions.

Nutrition Information

- Calories: 290
- Sodium: 790 mg
- Total Fat: 17 g
- Cholesterol: 50 mg
- Fiber: 2 g
- Sugar: 7 g
- Protein: 14 g
- Saturated Fat: 8 g
- Total Carbohydrate: 22 g

190. PHILADELPHIA® Corn Chowder

Serving: 0 | Prep: 15mins | Cook: 10mins | Ready in: 25mins

Ingredients

- 1/3 cup chopped green pepper
- 1/4 cup chopped onion
- 2 Tbsp. butter or margarine
- 4 oz. (1/2 of 8-oz. pkg.) PHILADELPHIA Cream Cheese, cubed
- 1 cup milk
- 1 cup water
- 1 WYLER'S Instant Bouillon Chicken Flavored Cube
- 1 can (14.75 oz.) cream-style corn
- dash of black pepper

Direction

- Cook and stir green pepper and onion in butter in medium skillet on medium heat until tender.
- Add cream cheese and milk. Reduce heat to low; cook until cream cheese is completely melted, stirring frequently. Remove from heat; set aside.
- Bring water to boil in medium saucepan on medium-high heat. Add bouillon; stir until dissolved. Reduce heat to low. Gradually stir in cream cheese mixture. Add remaining ingredients; mix well. Cook until heated through, stirring frequently. (Do not boil.)

Nutrition Information

- Calories: 260
- Fiber: 2 g
- Total Fat: 17 g
- Protein: 6 g
- Sugar: 8 g
- Saturated Fat: 10 g
- Cholesterol: 50 mg
- Total Carbohydrate: 25 g
- Sodium: 860 mg

191. Plantain Garlic Soup

Serving: 0 | Prep: 15mins | Cook: 20mins | Ready in: 35mins

Ingredients

- 2-1/2 qt. (10 cups) water
- 2 lb. green plantains, ends trimmed, peeled
- 2 cloves garlic, minced
- 2-1/2 cups milk
- 1 tsp. salt
- 1-1/2 cups KRAFT Shredded Mozzarella Cheese
- 1/2 cup BREAKSTONE'S or KNUDSEN Sour Cream
- 1/2 cup chopped cilantro

Direction

- Bring water to boil in large saucepan. Add plantains; cover. Cook 15 min. Drain plantains, reserving 1-1/4 qt. (5 cups) of the cooking water.
- Cut plantains into 2-inch chunks; place in food processor or blender container. Add garlic and the reserved cooking water; cover. Process until smooth.
- Return plantain mixture to saucepan. Add milk and salt; mix well. Bring to boil, stirring frequently to prevent burning. Reduce heat to low. Add cheese and sour cream; cook until cheese is completely melted and mixture is well blended, stirring frequently. Sprinkle with the cilantro.

Nutrition Information

- Calories: 220
- Sodium: 490 mg
- Protein: 9 g
- Fiber: 2 g
- Total Carbohydrate: 28 g
- Sugar: 15 g
- Saturated Fat: 5 g
- Cholesterol: 30 mg
- Total Fat: 8 g

192. Potato Cheese Soup

Serving: 0 | Prep: 25mins | Cook: 18mins | Ready in: 43mins

Ingredients

- 2 Tbsp. butter or margarine
- 1/4 cup chopped red onions
- 1-1/2 lb. red potatoes (about 5), peeled, cubed
- 1 can (14-1/2 oz.) fat-free reduced-sodium chicken broth
- 1 can (5 oz.) evaporated milk
- 1 cup water, divided
- 1 Tbsp. flour
- 6 oz. VELVEETA, cut into 1/2-inch cubes

Direction

- Melt butter in large saucepan on medium heat. Add onions; cook and stir 5 min. or until crisp-tender.
- Add potatoes, chicken broth, milk and 1/2 cup water; cook on medium heat 15 to 18 min. or until potatoes are tender. Mix flour and remaining water until blended. Add to soup; cook and stir until thickened.
- Add VELVEETA; cook 5 min. or until VELVEETA is melted and soup is well blended, stirring constantly.

Nutrition Information

- Calories: 180
- Fiber: 2 g
- Sugar: 5 g
- Total Fat: 8 g
- Sodium: 430 mg
- Total Carbohydrate: 20 g
- Protein: 6 g

- Cholesterol: 25 mg
- Saturated Fat: 5 g

193. Princess Fiona's Royal Swamp Soup

Serving: 8 | Prep: 15mins | Cook: 10mins | Ready in: 25mins

Ingredients

- 1 lb. ground beef
- 2 cans (14-1/2 oz. each) beef broth
- 1 jar (16 oz.) TACO BELL® Thick & Chunky Salsa
- 1 can (7 oz.) whole kernel corn, undrained
- 1 cup tortilla chips, crushed
- 1 cup KRAFT Mexican Style Shredded Cheese

Direction

- Brown meat in large saucepan; drain.
- Add broth, salsa and corn; mix well. Bring to boil. Reduce heat to low; simmer 5 minutes or until heated through, stirring occasionally.
- Serve topped with the crushed chips and cheese.

Nutrition Information

- Calories: 230
- Cholesterol: 45 mg
- Sodium: 940 mg
- Fiber: 2 g
- Sugar: 4 g
- Saturated Fat: 6 g
- Total Fat: 13 g
- Total Carbohydrate: 13 g
- Protein: 16 g

194. Quick Chicken Jambalaya

Serving: 0 | Prep: 40mins | Cook: | Ready in: 40mins

Ingredients

- 4 slices OSCAR MAYER Bacon, chopped
- 1 green pepper, chopped
- 1 large onion, chopped
- 1 stalk celery, finely chopped
- 1 pkg. (16 oz.) OSCAR MAYER Selects Uncured Angus Beef Franks, cut into 1/2-inch pieces
- 2 cups instant white rice, uncooked
- 1-1/2 cups chopped cooked chicken
- 1-1/2 cups water
- 1/2 cup KRAFT Original Barbecue Sauce
- 1 can (14-1/2 oz.) diced tomatoes, undrained

Direction

- Cook bacon in large skillet until crisp. Add vegetables; cook 3 to 5 min or until crisp-tender.
- Add remaining ingredients; stir. Bring to boil; cover. Simmer on low heat 12 to 14 min. or until rice is cooked, stirring occasionally.

Nutrition Information

- Calories: 420
- Protein: 18 g
- Total Carbohydrate: 0 g
- Total Fat: 25 g
- Cholesterol: 70 mg
- Sodium: 830 mg
- Fiber: 2 g
- Saturated Fat: 10 g
- Sugar: 0 g

195. Quick Chicken Minestrone

Serving: 0 | Prep: 20mins | Cook: | Ready in: 20mins

Ingredients

- 2 cups water
- 2 cups frozen Italian-style vegetable blend
- 2 cans (14.5 oz. each) diced tomatoes with basil, garlic and oregano, undrained
- 6 oz. boneless skinless chicken breasts, cut into bite-size pieces
- 1 cup rotini pasta, uncooked
- 1 env. (0.7 oz.) GOOD SEASONS Italian Dressing Mix
- 1/4 cup KRAFT Grated Parmesan Cheese

Direction

- Bring all ingredients except cheese to boil in large saucepan, stirring occasionally.
- Simmer on medium-low heat 10 min. or until chicken is done and pasta is tender, stirring occasionally.
- Serve topped with remaining cheese.

Nutrition Information

- Calories: 110
- Cholesterol: 15 mg
- Protein: 8 g
- Sugar: 0 g
- Total Fat: 2 g
- Sodium: 920 mg
- Saturated Fat: 1 g
- Total Carbohydrate: 0 g
- Fiber: 1 g

196. Ravioli & Italian Sausage Soup With Parmesan

Serving: 0 | Prep: 30mins | Cook: | Ready in: 30mins

Ingredients

- 1/2 lb. Italian sausage, casing removed
- 1 clove garlic, minced
- 3-1/2 cups fat-free reduced-sodium chicken broth
- 2 cups water
- 1 pkg. (9 oz.) frozen cheese ravioli
- 1 can (15 oz.) chickpeas (garbanzo beans), rinsed
- 1 can (14-1/2 oz.)) can stewed tomatoes, undrained
- 3 Tbsp. GREY POUPON Dijon Mustard
- 1/2 tsp. dried oregano leaves
- 1/4 tsp. ground black pepper
- 1 cup torn fresh spinach leaves
- 1/4 cup KRAFT Grated Parmesan Cheese

Direction

- Cook and stir sausage and garlic in 4-qt. heavy saucepan on medium heat 5 min. or until sausage is done. Drain sausage; cover to keep warm.
- Add broth and water to same saucepan; bring to boil. Add ravioli; cook 4 to 5 min. or until tender. Stir in sausage, beans, tomatoes, mustard, oregano and pepper; cook 5 min. or until heated through.
- Add spinach; cook 1 min. or until wilted. Serve topped with cheese.

Nutrition Information

- Calories: 210
- Cholesterol: 25 mg
- Sodium: 750 mg
- Total Carbohydrate: 23 g
- Fiber: 4 g
- Sugar: 4 g
- Saturated Fat: 3 g
- Total Fat: 8 g
- Protein: 12 g

197. Refreshing Gazpacho

Serving: 0 | Prep: 15mins | Cook: 1hours | Ready in: 1hours15mins

Ingredients

- 3 cups chopped honeydew melon, divided
- 1/2 cup KRAFT Zesty Italian Dressing
- 2 cucumbers, peeled, cut lengthwise in half and seeded
- 10 plum tomatoes
- 2 serrano chiles, stemmed
- 2 cloves garlic
- 1 tsp. dried oregano leaves

Direction

- Reserve 1 cup melon. Blend half the remaining melon with half of each of the remaining ingredients in blender until smooth; pour into large bowl. Repeat with all remaining ingredients except reserved melon.
- Refrigerate 1 hour. Meanwhile, finely chop reserved melon; refrigerate until ready to use.
- Pour gazpacho into 8 serving bowls; top with chopped melon.

Nutrition Information

- Calories: 80
- Saturated Fat: 0 g
- Total Carbohydrate: 0 g
- Sugar: 0 g
- Cholesterol: 0 mg
- Fiber: 2 g
- Total Fat: 3.5 g
- Protein: 1 g
- Sodium: 170 mg

198. Roasted Corn & Poblano Soup

Serving: 0 | Prep: 50mins | Cook: | Ready in: 50mins

Ingredients

- 4 large ears corn on the cob, divided
- 1/4 cup KRAFT Zesty Italian Dressing
- 1 small onion, chopped
- 2 cloves garlic, minced
- 1-1/2 qt. (6 cups) water
- 3/4 lb. red potatoes (about 2), peeled, cut into 1/4-inch cubes
- 2 cubes chicken bouillon
- 1 large poblano chile, roasted, peeled, seeded and cut into thin strips
- 1/2 cup BREAKSTONE'S or KNUDSEN Sour Cream

Direction

- Cut corn from 3 of the cobs. Heat dressing in large saucepan. Add onions and garlic, cook and stir 5 min. Add water, potatoes, bouillon and corn kernels; stir. Bring to boil; cover. Simmer on medium-low heat 15 min. or until potatoes are tender, stirring occasionally.
- Meanwhile, cook remaining ear of corn directly over gas flame 8 to 10 min. or until tender, turning constantly. Cut corn from cob; set aside.
- Blend potato mixture, in batches, in blender until smooth; strain into bowl. Discard drained solids. Stir peppers and reserved corn into strained soup; ladle into soup bowls. Top with sour cream and reserved roasted corn.

Nutrition Information

- Calories: 150
- Cholesterol: 10 mg
- Fiber: 3 g
- Sugar: 0 g
- Total Carbohydrate: 0 g
- Total Fat: 5 g
- Protein: 4 g
- Saturated Fat: 2 g
- Sodium: 360 mg

199. Roasted Poblano Tomato Soup

Serving: 0 | Prep: 30mins | Cook: | Ready in: 30mins

Ingredients

- 2 cans (10-3/4 oz. each) condensed tomato soup
- 2 poblano chiles, roasted, stemmed and seeded
- 2 soup cans water
- 2 corn tortillas (6 inch), thinly sliced
- 2 Tbsp. KRAFT Zesty Italian Dressing
- 1/4 cup BREAKSTONE'S or KNUDSEN Sour Cream

Direction

- Blend soup and chiles in blender until smooth; pour into saucepan. Stir in water. Bring to boil on medium heat; simmer on low 5 min. or until heated through.
- Cook tortilla strips and dressing in skillet on medium heat 5 min. or until crisp, stirring frequently.
- Serve soup topped with sour cream and tortilla strips.

Nutrition Information

- Calories: 140
- Saturated Fat: 2 g
- Total Carbohydrate: 24 g
- Total Fat: 5 g
- Cholesterol: 10 mg
- Protein: 3 g
- Sugar: 11 g
- Fiber: 3 g
- Sodium: 750 mg

200. Roasted Root Vegetable Soup

Serving: 0 | Prep: 20mins | Cook: 1hours5mins | Ready in: 1hours25mins

Ingredients

- 1 large parsnip, peeled, thinly sliced
- 2 large carrots, peeled, thinly sliced
- 1 large red pepper, cut into 1/2-inch chunks
- 1 large sweet potato, peeled, cut into 1/2-inch chunks
- 1/4 cup KRAFT Lite House Italian Dressing
- 2-1/2 cups fat-free reduced-sodium chicken broth, divided
- 1 can (15 oz.) cannellini beans, rinsed
- 1/2 tsp. freshly ground black pepper
- 1 cup KRAFT 2% Milk Shredded Italian* Three Cheese Blend
- 1/4 cup chopped fresh basil

Direction

- Heat oven to 375°F.
- Spread vegetables onto bottom of 15x10x1-inch pan. Drizzle with dressing; toss to evenly coat vegetables. Bake 40 to 45 min. or until tender, stirring after 20 min.
- Add 1/2 cup broth and 1-1/2 cups vegetables to blender; blend until smooth. Pour into large saucepan. Add remaining broth, remaining vegetables, beans and black pepper. Bring to boil on high heat; simmer on medium-low heat 10 min., stirring occasionally.
- Serve topped with cheese and basil.

Nutrition Information

- Calories: 260
- Saturated Fat: 3 g
- Sodium: 800 mg
- Protein: 15 g
- Cholesterol: 15 mg
- Fiber: 10 g
- Total Fat: 5 g
- Total Carbohydrate: 0 g

- Sugar: 0 g

201. Salmon Vegetable Chowder

Serving: 6 | Prep: 35mins | Cook: | Ready in: 35mins

Ingredients

- 1 Tbsp. butter
- 1 small onion, chopped
- 2 stalks celery, sliced
- 1 cup fat-free reduced-sodium chicken broth
- 1/4 lb. red potato (about 1), peeled, chopped
- 1/2 cup chopped zucchini
- 1/8 tsp. ground red pepper (cayenne)
- 2 cups milk
- 1 cup frozen roasted corn
- 1 can (14.75 oz.) red salmon, drained, flaked
- 1 Tbsp. chopped fresh chives

Direction

- Melt butter in large saucepan on medium heat. Add onions and celery; cook and stir 3 min.
- Add broth, potato, zucchini and red pepper; stir. Bring to boil; cover. Simmer 10 to 12 min. or until potatoes are tender, stirring occasionally.
- Stir in milk, corn and salmon; simmer 5 min. Serve sprinkled with chives.

Nutrition Information

- Calories: 190
- Sugar: 0 g
- Sodium: 220 mg
- Total Carbohydrate: 0 g
- Fiber: 2 g
- Total Fat: 7 g
- Cholesterol: 45 mg
- Protein: 19 g
- Saturated Fat: 3 g

202. Santa Fe Chicken Enchilada Stew

Serving: 0 | Prep: 30mins | Cook: | Ready in: 30mins

Ingredients

- 4 corn tortillas (6 inch), cut into strips
- 1 tsp. oil
- 1 tub (8 oz.) PHILADELPHIA Cream Cheese Spread
- 1 cup plus 2 Tbsp. milk, divided
- 2 Tbsp. (about 1/2 of 1-oz. pkg.) TACO BELL® Taco Seasoning Mix
- 1 lb. boneless skinless chicken breasts, cut into bite-size pieces
- 1 can (15 oz.) black beans, rinsed
- 1 can (11 oz.) corn with red and green bell peppers, drained
- 1 can (14.5 oz.) diced tomatoes, drained
- 1/4 cup chopped fresh cilantro

Direction

- Heat oven to 400°F.
- Toss tortilla strips with oil; spread into single layer on rimmed baking sheet. Bake 10 to 12 min. or until crisp, stirring occasionally.
- Meanwhile, mix cream cheese spread, 2 Tbsp. milk and taco seasoning until blended. Cook chicken in large saucepan sprayed with cooking spray on medium-high heat 8 to 10 min. or until done, stirring frequently. Stir in cream cheese mixture, remaining milk, beans, corn and tomatoes; simmer on medium-low heat 6 to 8 min. or until heated through, stirring frequently.
- Serve topped with tortilla strips and cilantro.

Nutrition Information

- Calories: 360
- Fiber: 7 g
- Sugar: 0 g
- Sodium: 620 mg

- Protein: 27 g
- Saturated Fat: 7 g
- Total Carbohydrate: 0 g
- Total Fat: 14 g
- Cholesterol: 75 mg

203. Santa Fe Soup

Serving: 8 | Prep: 30mins | Cook: | Ready in: 30mins

Ingredients

- 1 lb. lean ground beef
- 3/4 cup chopped green peppers
- 1/2 cup chopped onions
- 1 jalapeño pepper, chopped
- 1 can (15-1/2 oz.) hominy, undrained
- 1 can (15 oz.) reduced-sodium kidney beans, undrained
- 1 can (14-1/2 oz.) no-salt-added stewed tomatoes, undrained
- 1 can (10 oz.) diced tomatoes and green chiles, undrained
- 1/2 lb. (8 oz.) VELVEETA, cut into 1/2-inch cubes

Direction

- Brown meat with peppers and onions in large saucepan on medium heat; drain.
- Add remaining ingredients; cook on medium heat 10 min. or until VELVEETA is melted and mixture is thoroughly heated, stirring frequently.

Nutrition Information

- Calories: 280
- Sodium: 910 mg
- Fiber: 6 g
- Protein: 20 g
- Total Carbohydrate: 0 g
- Sugar: 0 g
- Cholesterol: 55 mg

- Total Fat: 11 g
- Saturated Fat: 6 g

204. Savory Seafood Chowder

Serving: 0 | Prep: 30mins | Cook: | Ready in: 30mins

Ingredients

- 2 Tbsp. olive oil
- 1 small onion, finely chopped
- 3 cloves garlic, minced
- 2 cans (14.5 oz. each) no-salt-added diced tomatoes with basil, garlic and oregano, undrained
- 1/2 cup plus 3 Tbsp. dry white wine, divided
- 1 lb. cod fillets, cut into 1-inch pieces
- 1/2 lb. bay scallops
- 1/2 lb. uncooked deveined peeled medium shrimp
- 1 pkg. (8 oz.) PHILADELPHIA Neufchatel Cheese, softened
- 2 Tbsp. chopped fresh basil

Direction

- Heat oil in large saucepan on medium heat. Add onions and garlic; cook and stir 5 min. or until onions are crisp-tender.
- Stir in tomatoes and 1/2 cup wine. Bring to boil, stirring frequently. Add cod; stir. Simmer on medium-low heat 6 min. Add scallops and shrimp; stir. Simmer 4 min. or until shrimp turn pink, scallops turn opaque and cod flakes easily with fork, stirring occasionally.
- Whisk Neufchatel and remaining wine until blended. Add to chowder along with the basil; mix well. Cook and stir 2 to 3 min. or until heated through.

Nutrition Information

- Calories: 250
- Fiber: 2 g

- Cholesterol: 105 mg
- Total Carbohydrate: 10 g
- Protein: 24 g
- Total Fat: 10 g
- Saturated Fat: 4.5 g
- Sugar: 4 g
- Sodium: 340 mg

205. Shrimp Corn Chowder

Serving: 6 | Prep: 15mins | Cook: 40mins | Ready in: 55mins

Ingredients

- 4 Tbsp. butter
- 2 cups chopped scallions, green tops only
- 2 pkg. (8 oz. each) PHILADELPHIA Cream Cheese, cubed
- 1 Tbsp. seafood seasoning
- 4 cups shrimp stock or fish stock
- 3 cups half-and-half, warmed
- 3 cups diced red potatoes (1/4 inch), skin on
- 2 lb. large shrimp (see note)
- 2 cans (15.25 oz. each) no-salt-added corn, drained
- 1 can (10-3/4 oz.) condensed cream of potato soup

Direction

- In a large stockpot, over medium-high heat, melt butter until it just begins to bubble. Now toss in the chopped scallions and continue cooking on medium-high heat until the scallions are wilted. Add both packages of cream cheese, blending with a wooden spoon until the cream cheese has melted completely. Now blend in the seafood seasoning.
- Pour shrimp stock into the cream cheese mixture, blending together with a wire whisk until smooth. Blend in the warmed half-and-half. Allow the mixture to simmer, stirring occasionally with a wooden spoon, until there is steam rising from the pot. Add the diced potatoes, keeping the heat on medium-high. Stir occasionally, allowing the potatoes to cook 25 min. or until fork-tender.
- Once potatoes are tender, add the steamed shrimp (see Tip); stir. Add drained corn and cream of potato soup; stir until blended. Reduce heat to low and simmer for 10 min., stirring frequently with a wooden spoon so soup does not scorch.

Nutrition Information

- Calories: 0 g
- Total Carbohydrate: 0 g
- Saturated Fat: 0 g
- Total Fat: 0 g
- Cholesterol: 0 g
- Sodium: 0 g
- Fiber: 0 g
- Sugar: 0 g
- Protein: 0 g

206. Slow Cooker Beef & Potato Vegetable Soup

Serving: 14 | Prep: 20mins | Cook: 8hours | Ready in: 8hours20mins

Ingredients

- 2 lb. stew beef, cut into ½ inch chunks
- 2 Tbsp. steak seasoning
- 2 Tbsp. flour
- 1 tsp. vegetable oil
- 6 cups beef broth
- 2 cans (10 oz.) tomatoes with habanero peppers
- 2 russet potatoes, peeled and cut in ½-inch chunks
- 1 green pepper, deseeded, cut into 1/4-1/2-inch chunks
- 1 poblano chile, seeded, cut into 1/2-inch pieces
- 1/2 sweet onion, diced

- 3 stalks celery, chopped in ½-in pieces
- 4 carrots, , cut into ¼-inch pieces
- 3 cloves garlic, minced
- 1/4 cup A.1. Original Sauce
- 1 tsp. red pepper flakes
- 1/2 tsp. black pepper
- 1 cup KRAFT Shredded Cheddar Cheese

Direction

- Gently pound beef pieces with a meat tenderizer. Mix together steak seasoning and flour. Toss beef in mixture to coat.
- Heat vegetable oil in frying pan over med-high heat. Brown beef. Set aside.
- Add beef and remaining ingredients to slow cooker. Stir to mix. Cover and cook on low 8-10 hours.

Nutrition Information

- Calories: 0 g
- Total Fat: 0 g
- Sugar: 0 g
- Saturated Fat: 0 g
- Total Carbohydrate: 0 g
- Protein: 0 g
- Sodium: 0 g
- Fiber: 0 g
- Cholesterol: 0 g

207. Slow Cooked Winter Vegetable Soup

Serving: 0 | Prep: 20mins | Cook: 5hours | Ready in: 5hours20mins

Ingredients

- 1 large sweet potato (12 oz.), peeled, cut into 1/2-inch chunks
- 1 red potato (8 oz.), peeled, cut into 1/2-inch chunks
- 2 carrots, peeled, sliced
- 1 large red pepper, coarsely chopped
- 1 can (15 oz.) cannellini beans, rinsed
- 2 cans (14-1/2 oz. each) fat-free reduced-sodium chicken broth
- 1/4 cup KRAFT Tuscan House Italian Dressing
- 1/4 cup chopped fresh parsley
- 1/2 tsp. ground black pepper
- 1 cup KRAFT Shredded Italian* Five Cheese Blend

Direction

- Place vegetables and beans in slow cooker. Add broth and dressing; cover with lid. Cook on LOW 5 to 6 hours (or on HIGH 3 to 4 hours).
- Remove 1-1/2 cups vegetables with slotted spoon; place in blender. Use ladle to remove 3/4 cup broth; add to blender. Blend until smooth; return to slow cooker. Stir in parsley and black pepper.
- Serve topped with cheese.

Nutrition Information

- Calories: 200
- Sugar: 0 g
- Saturated Fat: 2.5 g
- Cholesterol: 10 mg
- Sodium: 460 mg
- Protein: 9 g
- Fiber: 6 g
- Total Fat: 7 g
- Total Carbohydrate: 0 g

208. Slow Cooker Bean And Barley Soup

Serving: 0 | Prep: 20mins | Cook: 8hours | Ready in: 8hours20mins

Ingredients

- 1/2 lb. sliced fresh cremini mushrooms
- 1 cup each sliced carrots and celery
- 1/2 cup chopped onions
- 1/2 cup pearl barley, uncooked
- 3 cloves garlic, minced
- 1/2 tsp. cracked black pepper
- 1 can (15.5 oz.) no-salt-added no-salt-added white kidney beans, rinsed
- 1 can (14.5 oz.) diced tomatoes with basil, garlic and oregano, undrained
- 1 qt. (4 cups) no-salt-added vegetable stock
- 1/4 cup KRAFT Sun Dried Tomato Vinaigrette Dressing
- 2 Tbsp. LEA & PERRINS Worcestershire Sauce
- 1/2 cup KRAFT Shredded Parmesan Cheese

Direction

- Combine all ingredients except cheese in slow cooker sprayed with cooking spray; cover with lid.
- Cook on LOW 8 hours (or on HIGH 4 hours).
- Serve topped with cheese.

Nutrition Information

- Calories: 160
- Cholesterol: 5 mg
- Total Carbohydrate: 0 g
- Fiber: 7 g
- Total Fat: 3 g
- Protein: 7 g
- Saturated Fat: 1 g
- Sodium: 460 mg
- Sugar: 0 g

209. Slow Cooker Cheesy Potato Soup With Bacon

Serving: 0 | Prep: 20mins | Cook: 7hours | Ready in: 7hours20mins

Ingredients

- 4 cups chicken broth
- 6 cups potatoes, peeled and cut into ½-inch cubes
- 2 celery stalks, diced
- 1 cup chopped onion
- 1 tsp. black pepper
- 1-1/2 cups chopped OSCAR MAYER Fully Cooked Bacon
- 1 cup light cream
- 1 cup VELVEETA, cut into small cubes
- 1 cup KRAFT Shredded Mild Cheddar Cheese
- 6 oz. plain Greek yogurt
- 4 Tbsp. cornstarch
- 1/2 cup cold water

Direction

- PLACE chicken broth, potatoes, celery, onion and pepper into slow cooker. Cook on low for approximately 6 hours until vegetables are tender.
- ADD bacon to the slow cooker.
- COMBINE cream, VELVEETA cubes, cheese and yogurt in a saucepan on the stove. Cook over low to medium heat until hot.
- POUR cheese mixture into slow cooker, stirring constantly.
- COMBINE cornstarch and cold water in a separate bowl, mixing well. Slowly add to slow cooker. Cook 30 more minutes are serve.

Nutrition Information

- Calories: 0 g
- Fiber: 0 g
- Cholesterol: 0 g
- Sodium: 0 g
- Total Carbohydrate: 0 g
- Sugar: 0 g
- Total Fat: 0 g
- Saturated Fat: 0 g
- Protein: 0 g

210. Slow Cooker Chicken Enchilada Soup

Serving: 0 | Prep: 10mins | Cook: 8hours | Ready in: 8hours10mins

Ingredients

- 1 lb. chicken, cooked
- 1 can (15 oz.) whole peeled tomatoes
- 1 can (10 oz.) enchilada sauce (mild red sauce)
- 1 can (4 oz.) chopped green chili peppers
- 1 tsp. garlic powder
- 2 cups water
- 2 cups chicken broth
- 1 tsp. chili powder
- 1 tsp. salt
- 1/4 tsp. black pepper
- 1/4 tsp. dried basil leaves
- 1 pkg. (10 oz.) frozen corn
- 1 Tbsp. chopped fresh cilantro
- 1 cup KRAFT Mexican Style Finely Shredded Four Cheese
- 7 corn tortillas
- olive oil

Direction

- PLACE all of the ingredients (besides the corn tortillas, olive oil, and cheese) into the slow cooker.
- COOK on low for 6-8 hours.
- AFTER the 6-8 hours take a potato masher and mash up the tomatoes. This should also shred the chicken, but if you would like the pieces smaller you can shred the chicken inside the crock pot.
- PREHEAT the oven to 350°F. Rub olive oil on both sides of the corn tortillas (add salt if desired) and cut into thin strips. Place on a baking sheet for about 10 minutes.

Nutrition Information

- Calories: 0 g
- Cholesterol: 0 g
- Protein: 0 g
- Sodium: 0 g
- Total Carbohydrate: 0 g
- Fiber: 0 g
- Total Fat: 0 g
- Saturated Fat: 0 g
- Sugar: 0 g

211. Slow Cooker Chicken And Broccoli Cheese Soup

Serving: 0 | Prep: 15mins | Cook: 6hours30mins | Ready in: 6hours45mins

Ingredients

- 1 lb. boneless skinless chicken breasts, cut into 1-inch pieces
- 1/4 cup flour
- 1/2 tsp. garlic powder
- 1 cup sliced carrots
- 1 small onion, chopped
- 1 can (14-1/2 oz.) fat-free reduced-sodium chicken broth
- 1 Tbsp. LEA & PERRINS Worcestershire Sauce
- 2 cups small broccoli florets
- 1 pkg. (4 oz.) VELVEETA Fresh Packs, cut into 1/2-inch cubes
- 1/3 cup KRAFT Finely Shredded Sharp Cheddar Cheese

Direction

- Toss chicken with flour and garlic powder in slow cooker sprayed with cooking spray.
- Add all remaining ingredients except broccoli, VELVEETA and shredded cheese; cover with lid.
- Cook on LOW 6 to 8 hours (or on HIGH 3 to 4 hours).
- Stir in broccoli and VELVEETA; cook, covered, on HIGH 30 min.
- Top with shredded cheese before serving.

Nutrition Information

- Calories: 250
- Cholesterol: 85 mg
- Total Fat: 8 g
- Sodium: 620 mg
- Protein: 27 g
- Total Carbohydrate: 0 g
- Sugar: 0 g
- Fiber: 3 g
- Saturated Fat: 4 g

212. Slow Cooker Chicken And Wild Rice Soup

Serving: 0 | Prep: 15mins | Cook: 6hours30mins | Ready in: 6hours45mins

Ingredients

- 1 lb. boneless skinless chicken breasts, cut into bite-size pieces
- 1/2 cup wild rice, uncooked
- 1 cup each chopped celery and onions
- 1 cup shredded carrots
- 3 cans (14.5 oz. each) fat-free reduced-sodium chicken broth
- 1/4 cup flour
- 1/2 cup whipping cream
- 2 Tbsp. lite soy sauce
- 1 cup PLANTERS Sliced Almonds, toasted
- 4 oz. (1/2 of 8-oz. pkg.) PHILADELPHIA Cream Cheese, softened

Direction

- Place chicken in slow cooker lined with Reynolds Kitchens™ Slow Cooker Liner; top with rice and vegetables. Add broth; cover with lid.
- Cook on LOW 6 to 7 hours (or on HIGH 3 to 4 hours).
- Whisk flour, cream and soy sauce in medium bowl until blended. Ladle 1 cup liquid from slow cooker into flour mixture; mix well. Return to slow cooker; mix well. Stir in nuts. Cook, covered, on HIGH 20 min.
- Add cream cheese; stir. Cook, covered, 10 min.; stir before serving.

Nutrition Information

- Calories: 280
- Total Carbohydrate: 16 g
- Sodium: 450 mg
- Sugar: 3 g
- Total Fat: 16 g
- Saturated Fat: 6 g
- Fiber: 3 g
- Cholesterol: 65 mg
- Protein: 17 g

213. Slow Cooker Creamy Lentil Soup

Serving: 0 | Prep: 15mins | Cook: 7hours | Ready in: 7hours15mins

Ingredients

- 2 Tbsp. butter
- 1 large onion, chopped
- 1 qt. (4 cups) water
- 2 cans (14.5 oz. each) fat-free reduced-sodium chicken broth
- 1/4 cup KRAFT Asian Toasted Sesame Dressing
- 1 lb. dry lentils, rinsed
- 1 can (6 oz.) tomato paste
- 1/2 tsp. ground cumin
- 1/4 tsp. ground red pepper (cayenne)
- 4 oz. (1/2 of 8-oz. pkg.) PHILADELPHIA Cream Cheese, cubed, softened

Direction

- Melt butter in medium skillet on medium heat. Add onions; cook 8 min. or until tender, stirring frequently. Add to slow cooker.
- Stir in all remaining ingredients except cream cheese; cover with lid. Cook on LOW 7 to 8

hours (or on HIGH 3 to 4 hours) until lentils are tender.
- Add cream cheese; whisk until cream cheese is completely melted and soup is well blended.

Nutrition Information

- Calories: 250
- Sodium: 420 mg
- Total Carbohydrate: 34 g
- Saturated Fat: 4 g
- Protein: 14 g
- Cholesterol: 20 mg
- Fiber: 15 g
- Total Fat: 8 g
- Sugar: 5 g

214. Slow Cooker Cuban Black Bean Soup

Serving: 0 | Prep: 30mins | Cook: 11hours | Ready in: 11hours30mins

Ingredients

- 1/4 cup KRAFT Italian Vinaigrette Dressing made with Extra Virgin Olive Oil
- 1 each green and red pepper, finely chopped
- 1 white onion, finely chopped
- 1 can (14.5 oz.) petite diced tomatoes, drained
- 8 cloves garlic, minced
- 1 tsp. ground cumin
- 1 tsp. dried oregano leaves
- 1 lb. dried black beans, soaked (See tip.)
- 1-1/2 qt. (6 cups) fat-free reduced-sodium chicken broth
- 1 pkg. (7-1/2 oz.) OSCAR MAYER CARVING BOARD Slow Cooked Ham, chopped
- 2 bay leaves

Direction

- Heat dressing in large skillet on medium heat. Add peppers and onions; cook 5 to 6 min. or until vegetables are crisp-tender, stirring frequently. Stir in tomatoes, garlic, cumin and oregano; cook 5 min., stirring occasionally. Add to slow cooker. Stir in beans, broth, ham and bay leaves; cover with lid.
- Cook on LOW 10 hours (or on HIGH 5 hours). Remove and discard bay leaves.
- Blend half the soup, in small batches, in blender until smooth. Return each blended batch to remaining soup in slow cooker; stir.

Nutrition Information

- Calories: 180
- Sodium: 510 mg
- Cholesterol: 10 mg
- Saturated Fat: 0 g
- Protein: 13 g
- Total Carbohydrate: 0 g
- Fiber: 7 g
- Total Fat: 1.5 g
- Sugar: 0 g

215. Slow Cooker French Onion Soup

Serving: 0 | Prep: 20mins | Cook: 7hours | Ready in: 7hours20mins

Ingredients

- 2 lb. onions, sliced, separated into rings
- 2 Tbsp. brown sugar
- 2 Tbsp. KRAFT Balsamic Vinaigrette Dressing
- 1 Tbsp. LEA & PERRINS Worcestershire Sauce
- 1-1/2 qt. (6 cups) fat-free reduced-sodium beef broth
- 2 cups water
- 1 bottle (12 oz.) non-alcoholic beer
- 1 Tbsp. chopped fresh thyme
- 20 French bread slices (1/2 inch thick), toasted
- 1-1/2 cups KRAFT Shredded Swiss Cheese

Direction

- Combine first 4 ingredients in slow cooker sprayed with cooking spray; cover with lid. Cook on HIGH 1 hour, stirring after 30 min.
- Reduce heat to LOW. Add broth, water, beer and thyme to slow cooker; stir. Cook, covered, on LOW 6 to 8 hours (or on HIGH 4 hours).
- Heat broiler. Ladle soup into 10 ovenproof bowls; top with toast slices and cheese.
- Broil, 6 inches from heat, 3 to 5 min. or until cheese is melted and golden brown.

Nutrition Information

- Calories: 190
- Cholesterol: 15 mg
- Sugar: 10 g
- Total Fat: 7 g
- Saturated Fat: 3.5 g
- Protein: 10 g
- Total Carbohydrate: 26 g
- Sodium: 470 mg
- Fiber: 2 g

216. Slow Cooker Jambalaya Stuffed Peppers

Serving: 6 | Prep: 15mins | Cook: 6hours | Ready in: 6hours15mins

Ingredients

- 3 large peppers (1 each green, red and yellow)
- 6-1/2 oz. (1/2 of 13-oz. pkg.) OSCAR MAYER Natural Uncured Turkey Sausage, chopped
- 1 can (15.5 oz.) red beans, rinsed
- 3/4 cup TACO BELL® Thick & Chunky Medium Salsa
- 1/2 cup long-grain white rice, uncooked
- 1 tsp. Creole seasoning
- 2 Tbsp. chopped fresh parsley

Direction

- Cut tops off peppers; reserve tops for another use, or discard along with the pepper membranes and seeds.
- Combine sausage, beans, salsa, rice and seasoning; spoon into pepper shells. Stand in slow cooker; cover with lid.
- Cook on LOW 6 to 8 hours (or on HIGH 2-1/2 to 3-1/2 hours).
- Sprinkle with parsley. Cut in half to serve.

Nutrition Information

- Calories: 170
- Sugar: 0 g
- Cholesterol: 25 mg
- Sodium: 620 mg
- Fiber: 4 g
- Total Fat: 3 g
- Protein: 9 g
- Saturated Fat: 1 g
- Total Carbohydrate: 0 g

217. Slow Cooker Lemon Chicken And Orzo Soup

Serving: 0 | Prep: 15mins | Cook: 4hours30mins | Ready in: 4hours45mins

Ingredients

- 2 cups shredded rotisserie chicken
- 3 green onions, chopped
- 1 qt. (4 cups) fat-free reduced-sodium chicken broth
- 1 jar (18 oz.) HEINZ HomeStyle Classic Chicken Gravy
- juice from 2 lemons
- 1 cup orzo pasta, uncooked
- 4 oz. (1/2 of 8-oz. pkg.) PHILADELPHIA Cream Cheese, cubed, softened
- 2 Tbsp. chopped fresh dill
- 2 cups tightly packed baby spinach leaves

Direction

- Place chicken in slow cooker sprayed with cooking spray; top with onions. Add chicken broth, gravy and lemon juice; cover with lid.
- Cook on LOW 4 hours (or on HIGH 2 hours).
- Stir in orzo; cook, covered, on HIGH 30 min.
- Add cream cheese, dill and spinach; stir until cream cheese is completely melted.

Nutrition Information

- Calories: 260
- Fiber: 2 g
- Protein: 12 g
- Saturated Fat: 5 g
- Total Fat: 11 g
- Total Carbohydrate: 28 g
- Sodium: 620 mg
- Sugar: 2 g
- Cholesterol: 35 mg

218. Slow Cooker Loaded Baked Potato Soup

Serving: 0 | Prep: 40mins | Cook: 4hours | Ready in: 4hours40mins

Ingredients

- 8 slices OSCAR MAYER Bacon, cut into 1/2-inch pieces
- 1 onion, finely chopped
- 2 Tbsp. flour
- 1 carton (32 oz.) fat-free reduced-sodium chicken broth, divided
- 1 pkg. (24 oz.) ORE-IDA STEAM N' MASH Cut Russet Potatoes
- 1 pkg. (8 oz.) KRAFT Shredded Triple Cheddar Cheese with a TOUCH OF PHILADELPHIA, divided
- 1/2 cup milk
- 1/2 cup BREAKSTONE'S or KNUDSEN Sour Cream
- 1/4 cup chopped fresh chives

Direction

- Cook and stir bacon in large Skillet on medium heat until crisp. Remove bacon from Skillet with slotted spoon, reserving 2 Tbsp. drippings in Skillet. Drain bacon on paper towels; refrigerate until ready to use.
- Add onions to drippings in Skillet; cook and stir 5 min. or until crisp-tender. Stir in flour; cook and stir 1 min. Add 1 cup broth; cook and stir 2 min. or until sauce comes to boil and thickens. Pour into Slow Cooker. Stir in remaining broth. Add potatoes; cover with lid. Cook on LOW 4 to 5 hours (or HIGH 2 to 3 hours).
- Use slotted spoon to transfer 4 cups potatoes to medium bowl; mash until smooth. Add 1-1/2 cups cheese to remaining mixture in Slow Cooker; stir until melted. Stir in mashed potatoes and milk; cook, covered, 5 min. or until heated through.
- Place bacon on paper towel-covered microwaveable plate. Microwave on HIGH 20 to 30 sec. or until heated through. Serve soup topped with bacon, remaining cheese, sour cream and chives.

Nutrition Information

- Calories: 290
- Fiber: 3 g
- Cholesterol: 50 mg
- Total Fat: 19 g
- Sodium: 790 mg
- Total Carbohydrate: 19 g
- Sugar: 3 g
- Protein: 12 g
- Saturated Fat: 10 g

219. Slow Cooker Pot Roast

Serving: 10 | Prep: 10mins | Cook: 8hours | Ready in: 8hours10mins

Ingredients

- 1/2 cup A.1. Original Sauce
- 1/2 cup water
- 1 pkg. (0.9 oz.) onion-mushroom soup mix
- 1 boneless beef chuck eye roast (2-1/2 lb.)
- 1 lb. red new potatoes
- 1 pkg. (16 oz.) baby carrots
- 1 onion, thickly sliced

Direction

- Mix first 3 ingredients until blended.
- Place meat in slow cooker; top with vegetables and sauce. Cover with lid.
- Cook on LOW 8 to 9 hours (or on HIGH 6 to 7 hours).

Nutrition Information

- Calories: 270
- Sodium: 490 mg
- Total Carbohydrate: 0 g
- Fiber: 3 g
- Saturated Fat: 3 g
- Sugar: 0 g
- Cholesterol: 95 mg
- Protein: 32 g
- Total Fat: 8 g

220. Slow Cooker Southwest Wedding Soup

Serving: 0 | Prep: 15mins | Cook: 3hours | Ready in: 3hours15mins

Ingredients

- 1-1/4 qt. (5 cups) water
- 1 Tbsp. taco seasoning mix
- 1 tsp. WYLER'S Instant Bouillon Chicken Flavored Powder
- 1 can (14.5 oz.) diced tomatoes, drained
- 1 onion, chopped
- 1 carrot, chopped
- 26 frozen Italian-style mini meatballs (about 1/2 of 26-oz. pkg.)
- 1/2 cup orzo pasta, uncooked
- 1 cup KRAFT Mexican Style Finely Shredded Four Cheese

Direction

- Whisk water, taco seasoning mix and bouillon in slow cooker until blended.
- Add tomatoes, onions and carrots; mix well. Stir in meatballs; cover with lid.
- Cook on LOW 3 to 4 hours (or on HIGH 1 to 2 hours), adding pasta for the last 30 min. of the cooking time.
- Serve topped with cheese.

Nutrition Information

- Calories: 240
- Protein: 11 g
- Total Carbohydrate: 0 g
- Saturated Fat: 6 g
- Cholesterol: 15 mg
- Sodium: 590 mg
- Sugar: 0 g
- Total Fat: 14 g
- Fiber: 2 g

221. Slow Cooker Split Pea Soup

Serving: 0 | Prep: 15mins | Cook: 8hours | Ready in: 8hours15mins

Ingredients

- 2 cans (14.5 oz. each) fat-free reduced-sodium chicken broth
- 2 cups water
- 1/2 cup KRAFT Lite House Italian Dressing
- 1 lb. dried split peas, rinsed
- 4 carrots, peeled, sliced

- 1 onion, chopped
- 2 oz. OSCAR MAYER CARVING BOARD Slow Cooked Ham, finely chopped
- 2 bay leaves

Direction

- Bring first 3 ingredients to boil in saucepan. Place remaining ingredients in slow cooker. Add broth mixture; cover with lid.
- Cook on LOW 8 to 10 hours (or on HIGH 4 to 5 hours); stir.
- Discard bay leaves. Ladle 1 cup soup into shallow bowl; use fork to mash vegetables in bowl. Pour into soup in slow cooker; mix well.

Nutrition Information

- Calories: 210
- Sodium: 360 mg
- Fiber: 13 g
- Saturated Fat: 0 g
- Sugar: 0 g
- Cholesterol: 3.164 mg
- Protein: 14 g
- Total Carbohydrate: 0 g
- Total Fat: 1.5 g

222. Slow Cooker Tomato Soup With Croutons

Serving: 8 | Prep: 25mins | Cook: 6mins | Ready in: 31mins

Ingredients

- 4 Tbsp. butter
- 2 large onions, peeled and sliced
- 1 pt. cherry tomatoes, cleaned and halved
- 1 can (28 oz.) crushed tomatoes
- 6 cups chicken or vegetable stock
- 4 oz. (1/2 8 oz. pkg.) PHILADELPHIA Cream Cheese, softened
- 2 Tbsp. unsalted butter or margarine
- 4 slices bread
- 4 slices KRAFT Singles

Direction

- Add butter to the bottom of your slow cooker and turn it on high. In a few minutes, the butter will melt. At this point, add the onions and cherry tomatoes and toss to coat in the butter. Let this mixture cook for one hour on high.
- Carefully remove the lid of your slow cooker and add to it the crushed tomatoes and stock. Cover and cook either on HIGH for 3-4 hours or on LOW for 6-8 hours.
- Let soup cool slightly, then blend until smooth in your blender. Return soup to slow cooker.
- Stir in cream cheese and put the top back on the slow cooker for another 10-15 minutes, or until the cream cheese has melted in. Season as needed.
- Fill bread slices with Singles, spread outside of sandwich with butter. Cook in skillet on medium heat 3 min. on each side or until Singles are melted and sandwich is golden brown on both sides. Cut into quarters.
- Serve soup with Grilled Cheese Croutons!

Nutrition Information

- Calories: 270
- Saturated Fat: 10 g
- Fiber: 4 g
- Cholesterol: 45 mg
- Total Carbohydrate: 0 g
- Protein: 7 g
- Sugar: 0 g
- Total Fat: 16 g
- Sodium: 670 mg

223. Southwest Cheese Soup

Serving: 0 | Prep: 25mins | Cook: | Ready in: 25mins

Ingredients

- 1/2 lb. (8 oz.) VELVEETA, cut into 1/2-inch cubes
- 1 can (15 oz.) whole kernel corn, drained
- 1 can (15 oz.) black beans, rinsed
- 1 can (14-1/2 oz.) diced tomatoes and green chiles, undrained
- 1 cup milk
- 1/4 cup BREAKSTONE'S or KNUDSEN Sour Cream

Direction

- Mix all ingredients except sour cream in large saucepan.
- Cook on medium heat 20 min. or until VELVEETA is melted and soup is heated through, stirring frequently.
- Serve topped with sour cream.

Nutrition Information

- Calories: 260
- Total Fat: 11 g
- Sodium: 970 mg
- Protein: 13 g
- Sugar: 9 g
- Cholesterol: 35 mg
- Total Carbohydrate: 28 g
- Fiber: 6 g
- Saturated Fat: 7 g

224. Southwest Chicken And Rice Soup

Serving: 0 | Prep: 5mins | Cook: 5mins | Ready in: 10mins

Ingredients

- 1 can (10.5 oz.) reduced-fat reduced-sodium condensed chicken with rice soup
- 1 soup can water
- 1/4 cup TACO BELL® Thick & Chunky Salsa
- 6 Tbsp. KRAFT Shredded Cheddar Cheese

Direction

- Heat soup as directed on label with water.
- Stir in salsa. Top each serving with 2 Tbsp. cheese.

Nutrition Information

- Calories: 110
- Cholesterol: 20 mg
- Total Fat: 6 g
- Saturated Fat: 3.5 g
- Total Carbohydrate: 8 g
- Sodium: 400 mg
- Fiber: 1 g
- Sugar: 0.9767 g
- Protein: 5 g

225. Southwest Creamy Tomato Soup

Serving: 6 | Prep: 20mins | Cook: | Ready in: 20mins

Ingredients

- 2 cans (14.5 oz. each) diced tomatoes with green peppers and onions, undrained
- 1/4 cup chopped fresh cilantro
- 2 Tbsp. chopped canned chipotle peppers in adobo sauce
- 1 Tbsp. ground cumin
- 1 Tbsp. garlic powder
- 2 Tbsp. honey
- 1 cup BREAKSTONE'S or KNUDSEN Sour Cream

Direction

- Bring all ingredients except sour cream to boil in saucepan on medium heat, stirring frequently.

- Simmer on medium-low heat 10 min., stirring occasionally. Remove from heat.
- Stir in sour cream.

Nutrition Information

- Calories: 150
- Total Fat: 8 g
- Protein: 3 g
- Cholesterol: 30 mg
- Total Carbohydrate: 17 g
- Saturated Fat: 4.5 g
- Sodium: 380 mg
- Fiber: 3 g
- Sugar: 12 g

226. Southwest Slow Cooker Chicken Ramen Soup

Serving: 0 | Prep: 20mins | Cook: 6hours | Ready in: 6hours20mins

Ingredients

- 1 pkg. (1 oz.) TACO BELL® Taco Seasoning Mix
- 1 lb. boneless skinless chicken breasts
- 1-1/2 cups TACO BELL® Thick & Chunky Medium Salsa
- 1 can (15.5 oz.) black beans, rinsed
- 1 cup each chopped carrots and red peppers
- 5 cups fat-free reduced-sodium chicken broth
- 1 pkg. (3.4 oz.) chicken-flavored ramen noodle soup mix
- 1/2 cup chopped fresh cilantro
- 1-1/2 cups (8 oz.) KRAFT Mexican Style Shredded Four Cheese with a TOUCH OF PHILADELPHIA, divided

Direction

- Sprinkle taco seasoning evenly onto both sides of chicken breasts; place in slow cooker sprayed with cooking spray. Top with salsa, beans, carrots and peppers. Pour chicken broth over ingredients in slow cooker; cover with lid. Cook on LOW 6 to 7 hours (or on HIGH 3 to 4 hours).
- Remove chicken from slow cooker; set aside. Discard Seasoning Packet from soup mix. Break apart Ramen Noodles; stir into remaining ingredients in slow cooker. Cook, covered, 10 min. or until noodles are tender. Meanwhile, shred chicken.
- Return chicken to soup. Add cilantro and 1 cup cheese; stir. Ladle soup into serving bowls; top with remaining cheese.

Nutrition Information

- Calories: 170
- Sugar: 4 g
- Fiber: 4 g
- Saturated Fat: 3.5 g
- Protein: 13 g
- Total Carbohydrate: 14 g
- Cholesterol: 40 mg
- Sodium: 960 mg
- Total Fat: 7 g

227. Spicy Mixed Bean Taco Soup

Serving: 0 | Prep: 25mins | Cook: | Ready in: 25mins

Ingredients

- 1 Tbsp. oil
- 1 lb. lean ground chicken
- 1 onion, chopped
- 1 red bell pepper, chopped
- 2 cans (15.5 oz. each) no-salt-added pinto beans, rinsed
- 1 can (15.5 oz.) no-salt-added black beans, rinsed
- 1 can (14.5 oz.) diced tomatoes and green chiles, undrained
- 1 can (14.25 oz.) corn, undrained

- 1-1/2 cups fat-free reduced-sodium chicken broth
- 1 can (8 oz.) tomato sauce
- 2 tsp. chili powder
- 2 tsp. ground cumin
- 1 tsp. paprika
- 1/4 tsp. crushed red pepper
- 1-1/2 cups KRAFT 2% Milk Shredded Cheddar Cheese

Direction

- Heat oil in large saucepan on medium-high heat. Add chicken, onions and bell peppers; cook 5 min. or until chicken is done, stirring frequently.
- Add all remaining ingredients except cheese; stir, carefully breaking up tomatoes with back of spoon. Bring to boil; simmer on medium-low heat 10 min., stirring occasionally.
- Serve topped with cheese.

Nutrition Information

- Calories: 210
- Cholesterol: 35 mg
- Sodium: 510 mg
- Saturated Fat: 2.5 g
- Total Fat: 8 g
- Protein: 15 g
- Total Carbohydrate: 0 g
- Fiber: 6 g
- Sugar: 0 g

228. Spicy Southwest Corn Cheese Soup

Serving: 0 | Prep: 15mins | Cook: 10mins | Ready in: 25mins

Ingredients

- 1 pkg. (10 oz.) frozen whole kernel corn, thawed, drained
- 1 clove garlic, minced
- 1 Tbsp. butter or margarine
- 1/2 lb. (8 oz.) VELVEETA, cut up
- 1 can (4 oz.) chopped green chiles, undrained
- 3/4 cup chicken broth
- 3/4 cup milk
- 2 Tbsp. chopped cilantro
- 1/2 cup crushed tortilla chips (about 6 chips)

Direction

- Cook and stir corn and garlic in butter in large saucepan on medium-high heat until garlic is tender. Reduce heat to medium.
- Add all remaining ingredients except chips; cook until VELVEETA is completely melted and soup is heated through, stirring occasionally.
- Serve topped with the crushed chips.

Nutrition Information

- Calories: 320
- Protein: 14 g
- Sugar: 9 g
- Sodium: 1210 mg
- Fiber: 3 g
- Saturated Fat: 10 g
- Cholesterol: 55 mg
- Total Carbohydrate: 28 g
- Total Fat: 18 g

229. Spring Pea Soup

Serving: 0 | Prep: 5mins | Cook: 15mins | Ready in: 20mins

Ingredients

- 1/2 cup KRAFT Lite House Italian Dressing
- 2 cups cubed peeled potatoes (1 inch)
- 2 pkg. (9 oz. each) frozen peas and pearl onions
- 2 cans (14 oz. each) low sodium chicken broth

- 1/2 cup BREAKSTONE'S Reduced Fat or KNUDSEN Light Sour Cream
- 2 Tbsp. chopped fresh mint

Direction

- Mix all ingredients except sour cream in large saucepan. Bring to boil on medium-high heat. Reduce heat to medium-low; simmer 15 min. or until vegetables are tender.
- Transfer vegetable mixture to blender container in small batches; cover. Blend until smooth; pour into medium bowl. Repeat until all of the vegetable mixture is pureed. Stir in sour cream.
- Serve warm sprinkled with mint.

Nutrition Information

- Calories: 110
- Saturated Fat: 1.5 g
- Sodium: 200 mg
- Fiber: 1 g
- Sugar: 0 g
- Protein: 3 g
- Cholesterol: 10 mg
- Total Carbohydrate: 0 g
- Total Fat: 5 g

230. Squash Soup

Serving: 0 | Prep: 20mins | Cook: 20mins | Ready in: 40mins

Ingredients

- 1 large acorn squash (1-1/2 lb.)
- 1 can (14-1/2 oz.) fat-free reduced-sodium chicken broth
- 1 cup sliced carrots
- 1/3 cup chopped onions
- 1/4 tsp. dried basil leaves, crushed
- 1/4 cup MIRACLE WHIP Dressing

Direction

- Prick squash several times with fork. Microwave whole squash on HIGH 2 min. Cut squash in half lengthwise; remove seeds. Place squash, cut-sides up, in shallow microwaveable dish. Cover loosely. Microwave on HIGH 8 to 10 min. or until tender, turning dish every 4 min. Let stand 5 min. Scoop out squash into medium saucepan; mash.
- Add all remaining ingredients except dressing; bring to boil. Cover. Simmer on medium heat 12 to 15 min. or until carrots and onions are tender, stirring occasionally.
- Whisk in dressing until blended. Cook until heated through, stirring occasionally.

Nutrition Information

- Calories: 120
- Cholesterol: 5 mg
- Sodium: 310 mg
- Fiber: 3 g
- Protein: 1 g
- Total Carbohydrate: 0 g
- Sugar: 0 g
- Total Fat: 5 g
- Saturated Fat: 1 g

231. Sweet Potato And Black Bean Soup

Serving: 0 | Prep: 30mins | Cook: 15mins | Ready in: 45mins

Ingredients

- 1/4 cup KRAFT Balsamic Vinaigrette Dressing
- 2-1/4 lb. sweet potatoes (about 5), peeled, cubed
- 1 large onion, chopped
- 3 cloves garlic, minced
- 1-1/2 tsp. ground cumin
- 1/4 tsp. crushed red pepper
- 1/8 tsp. black pepper

- 2-1/2 cups fat-free reduced-sodium chicken broth
- 2 cans (15.5 oz. each) black beans, rinsed
- 1/3 cup BREAKSTONE'S or KNUDSEN Sour Cream
- 2 Tbsp. chopped fresh cilantro

Direction

- Heat dressing in large saucepan on medium heat. Add potatoes, onions, garlic, cumin, crushed pepper and black pepper; cook 3 to 5 min. or until onions are crisp-tender, stirring frequently.
- Stir in broth. Bring to boil; cover. Simmer on medium-low heat 10 to 15 min. or until potatoes are tender. Remove from heat.
- Blend soup, in small batches, in blender or food process until smooth. Return to pan. Add beans; mix well. Cook on medium heat 5 min. or until heated through, stirring occasionally.
- Serve topped with sour cream and cilantro.

Nutrition Information

- Calories: 250
- Protein: 11 g
- Total Fat: 6 g
- Total Carbohydrate: 0 g
- Fiber: 11 g
- Sugar: 0 g
- Cholesterol: 10 mg
- Saturated Fat: 2 g
- Sodium: 470 mg

232. Taco Soup

Serving: 0 | Prep: 25mins | Cook: | Ready in: 25mins

Ingredients

- 1 lb. extra-lean ground beef
- 1 onion, chopped
- 3 cans (15.5 oz. each) mild chili beans
- 1 can (14.5 oz.) whole tomatoes, undrained
- 1 can (14.25 oz.) corn, undrained
- 1 can (8 oz.) tomato sauce
- 1 pkg. (1 oz.) TACO BELL® Taco Seasoning Mix
- 1-1/2 cups water
- 1-1/2 cups KRAFT 2% Milk Shredded Cheddar Cheese

Direction

- Brown meat with onions in large saucepan; drain. Return meat mixture to pan.
- Add all remaining ingredients except cheese; stir, breaking up tomatoes with spoon. Bring to boil; simmer on medium-low heat 5 min., stirring occasionally.
- Top with cheese.

Nutrition Information

- Calories: 250
- Total Fat: 6 g
- Saturated Fat: 2.5 g
- Sugar: 4 g
- Fiber: 9 g
- Cholesterol: 30 mg
- Total Carbohydrate: 30 g
- Protein: 17 g
- Sodium: 900 mg

233. Tasty Tuna Casserole

Serving: 0 | Prep: 15mins | Cook: 30mins | Ready in: 45mins

Ingredients

- 1 pkg. (7-1/4 oz.) KRAFT Macaroni & Cheese Dinner
- 1 can (10-3/4 oz.) condensed cream of celery soup
- 1/2 cup milk
- 1 can (5 oz.) tuna, drained

- 1/2 cup chopped red peppers
- 1 green onion, sliced
- 1 cup crushed potato chips

Direction

- Heat oven to 350°F.
- Prepare Dinner as directed on package. Stir in soup, milk, tuna, peppers and onions.
- Spoon into 2-qt. casserole; top with crushed chips.
- Bake 30 min. or until heated through.

Nutrition Information

- Calories: 320
- Saturated Fat: 3.5 g
- Cholesterol: 20 mg
- Fiber: 2 g
- Sodium: 900 mg
- Sugar: 0 g
- Total Fat: 14 g
- Protein: 12 g
- Total Carbohydrate: 0 g

234. Tex Mex Minestrone Recipe

Serving: 0 | Prep: 5mins | Cook: 25mins | Ready in: 30mins

Ingredients

- 1/2 lb. lean ground beef
- 1-1/2 cups water
- 1 large tomato, chopped
- 1 cup (1/2 of 15-oz. can) black beans, rinsed
- 1/2 cup fat-free reduced-sodium beef broth
- 1/4 cup small shell macaroni, uncooked
- 1/4 cup KRAFT Zesty Italian Dressing
- 1/2 tsp. ground cumin
- 1/2 cup KRAFT Mexican Style Finely Shredded Four Cheese

Direction

- Brown meat in large saucepan; drain.
- Add all remaining ingredients except cheese; mix well. Bring to boil; simmer on medium-low heat 8 min. or until pasta is tender, stirring occasionally.
- Serve topped with cheese.

Nutrition Information

- Calories: 270
- Fiber: 5 g
- Sugar: 3 g
- Protein: 19 g
- Total Carbohydrate: 19 g
- Saturated Fat: 5 g
- Cholesterol: 45 mg
- Total Fat: 13 g
- Sodium: 340 mg

235. Tex Mex Soup

Serving: 0 | Prep: 10mins | Cook: 17mins | Ready in: 27mins

Ingredients

- 1 cup chopped onion
- 1 large fresh jalapeño pepper, seeded, finely chopped
- 1 Tbsp. minced garlic
- 1 tsp. ground cumin
- 1 Tbsp. olive oil
- 1 qt. (4 cups) water
- 2 cups frozen BOCA Veggie Ground Crumbles
- 1 can (15 oz.) black beans, undrained
- 1 cup frozen corn
- 1 avocado, chopped
- 1/4 cup chopped fresh cilantro
- 1 lime, cut into 6 wedges

Direction

- Cook onions, peppers, garlic and cumin in hot oil in large saucepan on medium heat 5 min. or until vegetables are crisp-tender, stirring frequently.
- Add water and crumbles; stir. Bring to boil. Stir in beans and corn; cook 2 min. or until heated through.
- Ladle into bowls; top with avocados and cilantro. Squeeze lime wedge over each bowl of soup.

Nutrition Information

- Calories: 220
- Cholesterol: 0 mg
- Saturated Fat: 1 g
- Fiber: 10 g
- Sodium: 440 mg
- Protein: 13 g
- Total Carbohydrate: 0 g
- Sugar: 0 g
- Total Fat: 8 g

236. Three Onion French Onion Soup

Serving: 0 | Prep: 45mins | Cook: 1hours | Ready in: 1hours45mins

Ingredients

- 2 Tbsp. each butter and olive oil
- 1 lb. each red onions, sweet onions and yellow onions, cut lengthwise in half, then crosswise into thin slices
- 3 cloves garlic, minced
- 4 sprigs fresh thyme
- 1/4 cup dry sherry
- 1-3/4 qt. (7 cups) fat-free reduced-sodium beef broth
- 2 Tbsp. LEA & PERRINS Worcestershire Sauce
- 1 Tbsp. HEINZ Apple Cider Vinegar
- 2 bay leaves
- 16 French bread slices (1/2 inch thick), toasted
- 1 pkg. (8 oz.) KRAFT Shredded Italian* Five Cheese Blend

Direction

- Melt butter with oil in Dutch oven on medium-high heat. Add onions; cook 10 min. or until tender, stirring frequently. Simmer on medium-low heat 1 hour or until onions are golden brown, stirring occasionally and adding garlic and thyme for the last 5 min.
- Stir in sherry; cook and stir on medium-high heat 1 min. Add beef broth, Worcestershire sauce, vinegar and bay leaves; stir. Bring to boil, stirring occasionally. Cover, simmer on medium-low heat 20 min., stirring occasionally. Remove and discard thyme sprigs and bay leaves.
- Heat broiler. Ladle soup into 8 ovenproof bowls; top with toast slices and cheese.
- Broil, 4 inches from heat, 3 to 5 min. or until cheese is melted and golden brown.

Nutrition Information

- Calories: 240
- Total Fat: 9 g
- Protein: 13 g
- Fiber: 4 g
- Sugar: 0 g
- Total Carbohydrate: 0 g
- Saturated Fat: 6 g
- Cholesterol: 25 mg
- Sodium: 750 mg

237. Tomato Bisque

Serving: 0 | Prep: 10mins | Cook: | Ready in: 10mins

Ingredients

- 1 can (10-3/4 oz.) condensed tomato soup
- 3 oz. PHILADELPHIA Cream Cheese, cubed
- dash black pepper

Direction

- Prepare soup with water in saucepan as directed on label.
- Add cream cheese; cook 2 to 3 min. or until completely melted, stirring constantly.
- Sprinkle with pepper.

Nutrition Information

- Calories: 170
- Cholesterol: 30 mg
- Sugar: 9 g
- Fiber: 0.8625 g
- Saturated Fat: 6 g
- Protein: 3 g
- Total Fat: 11 g
- Total Carbohydrate: 15 g
- Sodium: 450 mg

238. Tomato Soup With Chipotle Peppers

Serving: 0 | Prep: 10mins | Cook: 25mins | Ready in: 35mins

Ingredients

- 1 onion, chopped
- 2 Tbsp. olive oil
- 2 cans (14-1/2 oz. each) diced tomatoes, undrained
- 2 carrots, chopped
- 1 can (14 oz.) fat-free reduced-sodium chicken broth
- 1/4 cup KRAFT Lite Thousand Island Dressing
- 1 Tbsp. chopped chipotle peppers in adobo sauce

Direction

- Cook and stir onions in hot oil in large skillet until crisp-tender.

- Add tomatoes, carrots and broth; mix well. Bring to boil on medium-high heat; simmer on medium-low 15 min. or until vegetables are tender, stirring occasionally.
- Blend vegetable mixture, in small batches; in blender until smooth, blending dressing and chipotle peppers with the last batch. Serve warm or chilled.

Nutrition Information

- Calories: 140
- Total Carbohydrate: 0 g
- Saturated Fat: 1 g
- Cholesterol: 0 mg
- Sugar: 0 g
- Fiber: 4 g
- Total Fat: 6 g
- Sodium: 560 mg
- Protein: 4 g

239. Tomato Soup With Grilled Cheese

Serving: 6 | Prep: 45mins | Cook: | Ready in: 45mins

Ingredients

- 1 tsp. oil
- 1 onion, finely chopped
- 1 small carrot, finely chopped
- 1 stalk celery, finely chopped
- 2 cups fat-free reduced-sodium chicken broth
- 1 cup water
- 1 can (28 oz.) diced tomatoes, undrained
- 1/4 tsp. black pepper
- 4 oz. (1/2 of 8-oz. pkg.) PHILADELPHIA Cream Cheese, cubed
- 1/4 cup plus 2 Tbsp. chopped fresh basil, divided

Direction

- Heat oil in large saucepan on medium-high heat. Add onions, carrots and celery; cook and stir 5 min. Stir in broth and water. Bring to boil; cover. Simmer 10 min. or until vegetables are tender.
- Add tomatoes and pepper; stir. Return to boil. Simmer 5 min. Stir in cream cheese and 1/4 cup basil. Remove from heat. Use immersion blender to blend soup until smooth. Return to heat; cover. Keep warm on low heat while you prepare America's Favorite Grilled Cheese Sandwiches.
- Cut each sandwich into 6 pieces. Ladle soup into 6 bowls; sprinkle with remaining basil. Top each soup bowl with 2 sandwich pieces. Serve immediately.

Nutrition Information

- Calories: 220
- Cholesterol: 40 mg
- Sodium: 640 mg
- Sugar: 8 g
- Total Fat: 13 g
- Saturated Fat: 7 g
- Fiber: 3 g
- Protein: 7 g
- Total Carbohydrate: 19 g

240. Tortilla Soup

Serving: 0 | Prep: 20mins | Cook: 20mins | Ready in: 40mins

Ingredients

- 2 Tbsp. KRAFT Zesty Italian Dressing
- 2 cloves garlic, minced
- 2 cans (14-1/2 oz. each) fat-free reduced-sodium chicken broth
- 1-1/2 cups water
- 6 small boneless skinless chicken breasts (1-1/2 lb.)
- 1 can (15 oz.) tomato sauce
- 4 cups tortilla chips (about 6 oz.), coarsely crushed
- 1/2 cup KRAFT Shredded Cheddar & Monterey Jack Cheeses
- 1/3 cup BREAKSTONE'S or KNUDSEN Sour Cream
- 1 large avocado, chopped
- 2 Tbsp. chopped fresh cilantro

Direction

- Cook dressing and garlic in large saucepan on medium-high heat 1 min., stirring occasionally. Stir in broth and water. Add chicken. Bring liquid to boil; simmer on medium-low heat 20 min. or until chicken is done (165°F). Remove chicken from pan, reserving liquid in pan; set chicken aside. Pour reserved liquid through fine-mesh strainer into bowl. Discard strained solids; return liquid to saucepan.
- Shred chicken; add to liquid in pan. Stir in tomato sauce; cook on medium-high heat 5 min. or until heated through, stirring occasionally.
- Serve chicken mixture topped with remaining ingredients.

Nutrition Information

- Calories: 320
- Fiber: 4 g
- Cholesterol: 65 mg
- Total Carbohydrate: 21 g
- Sugar: 3 g
- Protein: 23 g
- Total Fat: 16 g
- Sodium: 680 mg
- Saturated Fat: 4.5 g

241. Turkey Jambalaya

Serving: 0 | Prep: 15mins | Cook: 20mins | Ready in: 35mins

Ingredients

- 1 cup chopped celery
- 1 cup chopped green pepper
- 1 cup chopped onion
- 1 lb. Mexican chorizo, cut into small chunks
- 1 tsp. oil
- 2 cans (14-1/2 oz. each) stewed tomatoes, undrained
- 1-1/2 cups water
- 2 cups chopped cooked turkey
- 1 Tbsp. Cajun seasoning
- 3 cups instant white rice, uncooked

Direction

- Cook and stir celery, green pepper, onion and chorizo in hot oil in large skillet on medium-high heat 5 minutes or until chorizo is cooked through.
- Add tomatoes with their liquid, the water, turkey and seasoning; mix well. Bring to boil.
- Stir in rice. Reduce heat to low; cover. Simmer 5 minutes. Remove from heat. Let stand, covered, 5 minutes. Mix lightly before serving.

Nutrition Information

- Calories: 640
- Total Fat: 33 g
- Total Carbohydrate: 50 g
- Fiber: 3 g
- Sugar: 6 g
- Protein: 37 g
- Sodium: 1300 mg
- Saturated Fat: 12 g
- Cholesterol: 100 mg

242. Turkey Pozole Soup

Serving: 0 | Prep: 30mins | Cook: 2hours | Ready in: 2hours30mins

Ingredients

- Carcass from cooked 14-lb. turkey, cut up
- 2 onions, divided
- 1 large carrot, cut into chunks
- 1 large celery stalk, cut into chunks
- 2 bay leaves
- 2 cloves garlic, peeled
- 4-1/2 qt. water
- 1 chicken bouillon cube
- 3 cups shredded cooked turkey
- 2 cans (28 oz. each) hominy, drained
- 2 tsp. dried Mexican oregano, crushed
- 1 cup green salsa
- 8 slices OSCAR MAYER Bacon, cut into 1-inch pieces
- 9 radishes, thinly sliced
- 1 cup shredded lettuce

Direction

- Place turkey carcass in 8-qt. stockpot. Chop 1 onion; set aside. Cut remaining onion into quarters; add to stockpot with carrots, celery, bay leaves, garlic and water. Bring to boil. Simmer on low heat 2 hours, skimming surface as needed and cooking the bacon in skillet until crisp after 1-3/4 hours. Transfer bacon to paper towels; drain, reserving drippings in skillet. Add chopped onions to drippings in skillet; cook and stir 5 min. or until crisp-tender.
- Strain turkey broth; discard strained solids. Return broth to pot. Stir in bacon, chopped onions and all remaining ingredients except radishes and lettuce. Bring to boil; simmer on medium-low heat 15 min.
- Serve soup topped with radishes and lettuce.

Nutrition Information

- Calories: 150
- Total Fat: 6 g
- Sodium: 870 mg
- Protein: 13 g
- Saturated Fat: 2 g
- Total Carbohydrate: 11 g
- Sugar: 0 g

- Cholesterol: 25 mg
- Fiber: 2 g

243. VELVEETA Jambalaya Skillet

Serving: 0 | Prep: 20mins | Cook: |Ready in: 20mins

Ingredients

- 1 pkg. (12 oz.) OSCAR MAYER Natural Uncured Beef Sausage, sliced
- 1 green pepper, chopped
- 2-1/4 cups water
- 1 pkg. (14.3 oz.) VELVEETA CHEESY SKILLETS Dinner Kit Jambalaya

Direction

- Cook and stir sausage and peppers in large nonstick skillet on medium heat 5 to 7 min. or until sausage is lightly browned and peppers are crisp-tender. Add water, Seasoning Mix and Pasta; stir. Bring to boil; cover.
- Simmer on medium-low heat 11 to 13 min. or until pasta is tender and most the water is absorbed, stirring occasionally. Remove from heat.
- Stir in VELVEETA Cheese Sauce.

Nutrition Information

- Calories: 490
- Sodium: 1170 mg
- Saturated Fat: 9 g
- Total Fat: 28 g
- Total Carbohydrate: 42 g
- Cholesterol: 45 mg
- Fiber: 3 g
- Sugar: 6 g
- Protein: 17 g

244. VELVEETA® Cheesy Broccoli Soup

Serving: 0 | Prep: 25mins | Cook: |Ready in: 25mins

Ingredients

- 2 Tbsp. butter or margarine
- 1/4 cup chopped onions
- 2 Tbsp. flour
- 2-1/2 cups milk
- 3/4 lb. (12 oz.) VELVEETA, cut into 1/2-inch cubes
- 1 pkg. (10 oz.) frozen chopped broccoli, thawed, drained
- 1/8 tsp. pepper

Direction

- Melt butter in large saucepan on medium heat. Add onions; cook and stir 5 min. or until crisp-tender. Add flour; cook 1 min. or until bubbly, stirring constantly.
- Stir in milk. Bring to boil; simmer on medium-low heat 1 min.
- Add remaining ingredients; stir. Cook 5 to 8 min. or until VELVEETA is completely melted and soup is heated through, stirring occasionally.

Nutrition Information

- Calories: 250
- Total Fat: 14 g
- Total Carbohydrate: 16 g
- Protein: 13 g
- Saturated Fat: 9 g
- Sugar: 10 g
- Cholesterol: 50 mg
- Sodium: 890 mg
- Fiber: 2 g

245. VELVEETA® Easy Spicy Chicken Spaghetti

Serving: 0 | Prep: | Cook: | Ready in:

Ingredients

- 1/2 lb. spaghetti, uncooked
- 1 lb. boneless skinless chicken breasts, cut into bite-size pieces
- 2 (4 oz. each) VELVEETA Fresh Packs, cut into 1/2-inch cubes
- 1 can (10-3/4 oz.) 98%-fat-free condensed cream of chicken soup
- 1 can (10 oz.) RO*TEL Diced Tomatoes & Green Chilies, undrained
- 1 can (4 oz.) mushroom pieces and stems, drained
- 2 Tbsp. milk

Direction

- Heat oven to 350°F.
- Cook spaghetti as directed on package, omitting salt.
- Meanwhile, cook and stir chicken in large skillet sprayed with cooking spray on medium-high heat 8 to 10 min. or until done. Add remaining ingredients; cook and stir 5 min. or until VELVEETA is completely melted and mixture is well blended.
- Drain spaghetti. Add to chicken mixture; mix lightly. Spoon into 9-inch square pan sprayed with cooking spray.
- Bake 30 to 35 min. or until heated through.

Nutrition Information

- Calories: 0 g
- Sugar: 0 g
- Sodium: 0 g
- Fiber: 0 g
- Saturated Fat: 0 g
- Protein: 0 g
- Cholesterol: 0 g
- Total Carbohydrate: 0 g
- Total Fat: 0 g

246. Vegetable And Cheese Chowder

Serving: 0 | Prep: 15mins | Cook: 40mins | Ready in: 55mins

Ingredients

- 1/4 cup (1/2 stick) butter or margarine
- 1 medium green pepper, chopped
- 1 cup sliced carrots
- 1 medium baking potato, chopped
- 1/4 cup chopped onions
- 5 Tbsp. flour
- 2 cans (14-1/2 oz. each) chicken broth
- 8 KRAFT DELI DELUXE Process American Cheese Slices, chopped
- 2 cups milk
- 1 pkg. (10 oz.) frozen green peas, 10 oz
- 1/8 tsp. ground white pepper

Direction

- Melt butter in 3-qt. saucepan on medium heat. Add green peppers, carrots, potatoes and onions; cook 20 min. or until vegetables are tender, stirring occasionally.
- Add flour; cook and stir 1 min. Gradually add broth, stirring until well blended after each addition. Bring to boil, stirring constantly. Reduce heat to medium.
- Add cheese; stir until completely melted. Gradually add milk, stirring until well blended after each addition. Stir in peas. Cook until heated through, stirring occasionally. Season with the white pepper.

Nutrition Information

- Calories: 330
- Protein: 15 g
- Fiber: 4 g
- Sodium: 1060 mg

- Total Carbohydrate: 0 g
- Total Fat: 19 g
- Sugar: 0 g
- Cholesterol: 55 mg
- Saturated Fat: 10 g

247. Vegetables And Corn Dumpling Soup

Serving: 0 | Prep: 50mins | Cook: | Ready in: 50mins

Ingredients

- 1 cup masa harina
- 2/3 cup water
- 1 egg
- 1/2 cup KRAFT Shredded Low-Moisture Part-Skim Mozzarella Cheese
- 1 Tbsp. oil
- 1 red pepper, chopped
- 1 small onion, chopped
- 1 clove garlic, minced
- 3 cans (14 oz. each) fat-free reduced-sodium vegetable broth
- 1 pkt. seasoning with coriander and annatto
- 1 pkg. (5 oz.) baby spinach leaves
- 1/3 cup BREAKSTONE'S or KNUDSEN Sour Cream

Direction

- Mix first 3 ingredients until blended. Stir in cheese. Shape into 24 balls; make small indentation in center of each with your thumb.
- Heat oil in Dutch oven on medium heat. Add dumplings, in batches; cook 2 min. or until golden brown, stirring occasionally. Remove from pan; set aside.
- Add peppers and onions to pan; cook and stir 5 min. Stir in garlic; cook 1 min. Add broth and seasoning; bring to boil. Add dumplings; cover. Simmer on medium-low heat 8 min. or until dumplings are done. Stir in spinach; cook, covered, 3 min.
- Serve topped with sour cream.

Nutrition Information

- Calories: 200
- Saturated Fat: 3 g
- Cholesterol: 45 mg
- Protein: 7 g
- Total Carbohydrate: 0 g
- Sodium: 280 mg
- Fiber: 3 g
- Sugar: 0 g
- Total Fat: 8 g

248. Vegetarian Slow Cooker Minestrone

Serving: 0 | Prep: 10mins | Cook: 7hours30mins | Ready in: 7hours40mins

Ingredients

- 1 cup dried navy beans, rinsed
- 4 carrots, sliced
- 4 cloves garlic, minced
- 1-1/4 qt. (5 cups) reduced-sodium vegetable broth
- 3/4 cup ditalini pasta, uncooked
- 3/4 cup CLASSICO Traditional Basil Pesto Sauce and Spread
- 1 pkg. (5 oz.) baby spinach leaves
- Juice from 1 lemon
- 1/3 cup KRAFT Grated Parmesan Cheese

Direction

- Place beans, carrots and garlic in slow cooker sprayed with cooking spray. Add broth; stir. Cover with lid.
- Cook on LOW 7 to 8 hours (or on HIGH 3-1/2 to 4 hours).
- Stir in pasta and pesto sauce; cook, covered, on LOW 30 min. (or on HIGH 15 min.).
- Add spinach and lemon juice; stir. Serve topped with cheese.

Nutrition Information

- Calories: 270
- Total Fat: 10 g
- Fiber: 9 g
- Protein: 10 g
- Sugar: 0 g
- Cholesterol: 5 mg
- Total Carbohydrate: 0 g
- Saturated Fat: 2 g
- Sodium: 430 mg

249. Velvety Vegetable Cheese Soup

Serving: 0 | Prep: 25mins | Cook: | Ready in: 25mins

Ingredients

- 1 pkg. (16 oz.) frozen broccoli, cauliflower and carrot blend
- 2 cans (14-1/2 oz. each) fat-free reduced-sodium chicken broth
- 3/4 lb. (12 oz.) VELVEETA, cut into 1/2-inch cubes

Direction

- Bring vegetables and broth to boil in large covered saucepan on medium-high heat; simmer on low heat 10 min. or until vegetables are tender. Remove from heat.
- Mash vegetables to desired consistency.
- Stir in VELVEETA; cook 5 min. or until VELVEETA is completely melted and soup is heated through, stirring frequently.

Nutrition Information

- Calories: 190
- Cholesterol: 35 mg
- Sugar: 6 g
- Saturated Fat: 7 g
- Total Carbohydrate: 10 g
- Total Fat: 11 g
- Fiber: 2 g
- Sodium: 1030 mg
- Protein: 11 g

250. Western Bean And Burger Soup

Serving: 0 | Prep: 35mins | Cook: | Ready in: 35mins

Ingredients

- 1 can (15 oz.) black beans, drained
- 1 can (14-1/2 oz.) diced tomatoes and green chiles, undrained
- 1 pkg. (12 oz.) frozen BOCA Veggie Ground Crumbles
- 3 cups water
- 1 cup frozen corn
- 1 small onion, chopped
- 3 cloves garlic, minced
- 1 Tbsp. ground cumin
- 1/2 tsp. hot pepper sauce

Direction

- Bring ingredients to boil in large saucepan on medium-high heat; cover.
- Simmer on low heat 15 min. or until crumbles are cooked through (160ºF), stirring occasionally.

Nutrition Information

- Calories: 140
- Fiber: 7 g
- Protein: 14 g
- Sodium: 430 mg
- Saturated Fat: 0 g
- Total Carbohydrate: 0 g
- Total Fat: 0.5 g
- Cholesterol: 0 mg
- Sugar: 0 g

Index

A

Ale 4,62

Almond 14,116

Apple 53,128

Asparagus 4,74

B

Bacon 4,5,32,54,55,59,60,62,66,70,72,79,81,82,83,86,87,89,91,94,96,100,102,103,106,114,119,131

Baking 31

Barley 4,5,55,56,89,91,113

Basil 15,68,80,90,98,134

Beans 84

Beef 3,4,5,12,19,38,55,56,74,89,106,112,132

Beer 4,75

Biscuits 3,27

Brisket 4,56

Broccoli 3,4,5,26,29,58,59,61,63,72,75,102,115,132

Burger 6,135

Butter 3,4,11,26,60

C

Cabbage 3,4,30,84

Caramel 4,60

Carrot 4,60,61

Cauliflower 4,79

Cheddar 3,4,7,8,9,10,11,12,14,18,19,24,26,27,31,32,36,38,40,45,50,54,59,61,62,63,67,70,72,88,99,100,103,113,114,115,119,122,124,126,130

Cheese 3,4,5,6,7,8,9,10,11,12,14,15,16,17,18,19,20,21,22,23,24,25,26,27,28,29,31,32,33,34,35,36,38,39,40,41,42,43,44,45,46,47,48,50,54,57,58,59,61,62,63,64,66,67,68,69,70,72,73,74,75,76,78,79,80,81,83,86,87,88,90,91,92,93,95,96,97,98,99,100,101,102,103,104,105,106,107,109,110,111,112,113,114,115,116,117,118,119,120,121,122,123,124,126,127,128,129,130,132,133,134,135

Chicken 3,4,5,13,24,25,26,27,28,29,30,31,32,33,34,35,36,37,38,39,40,41,42,43,44,45,46,47,49,50,66,68,71,76,77,81,88,90,104,106,110,115,116,118,120,122,123,133

Chipotle 3,4,5,15,44,67,129

Chips 5,98

Chorizo 3,17

Cider 53,128

Crab 4,71

Crackers 70,76,94

Cream 3,4,5,8,11,12,14,17,20,22,24,25,26,27,28,31,32,35,40,41,45,54,57,60,61,64,67,68,72,73,74,75,76,77,78,79,80,81,83,86,90,94,101,102,103,104,105,108,109,110,112,116,118,119,121,122,125,126,128,129,130,134

Crumble 10,17,18,21,22,46,53,56,73,127,135

Cucumber 4,69

Curry 4,81

D

Dumplings 3,35

F

Fat 7,8,9,10,11,12,13,14,15,16,17,18,19,20,21,22,23,24,25,26,27,28,29,30,31,32,33,34,35,36,37,38,39,40,41,42,43,44,45,46,47,48,49,50,51,52,53,54,55,56,57,58,59,60,61,62,63,64,65,66,67,68,69,70,71,72,73,74,75,76,77,78,79,80,81,82,83,84,85,86,87,88,89,90,91,92,93,94,95,96,97,98,99,100,101,10

2,103,104,105,106,107,108,109,110,111,112,113,114,115,116,117,118,119,120,121,122,123,124,125,126,127,128,129,130,131,132,133,134,135

Fish 4,86

French bread 117,128

G

Garlic 4,5,79,105

Gin 3,36

Gravy 118

H

Ham 4,28,52,53,57,64,101,117,121

Heart 3,4,30,31,87,88,89

Honey 20,28

J

Jam 4,5,51,52,53,83,106,118,130,132

K

Kale 4,5,78,91,92

Ketchup 7,56

L

Leek 4,5,57,94

Lemon 5,118

Lime 4,66,67

M

Macaroni 7,23,40,45,57,58,95,96,126

Matzo 29

Meat 3,18

Milk 7,11,12,18,22,24,26,33,36,38,40,41,45,54,88,109,124,126

Mozzarella 64,87,88,105,134

Mushroom 4,73,78,89

Mustard 8,28,53,70,71,82,107

N

Noodles 123

Nut 7,8,9,10,11,12,13,14,15,16,17,18,19,20,21,22,23,24,25,26,27,28,29,30,31,32,33,34,35,36,37,38,39,40,41,42,43,44,45,46,47,48,49,50,51,52,53,54,55,56,57,58,59,60,61,62,63,64,65,66,67,68,69,70,71,72,73,74,75,76,77,78,79,80,81,82,83,84,85,86,87,88,89,90,91,92,93,94,95,96,97,98,99,100,101,102,103,104,105,106,107,108,109,110,111,112,113,114,115,116,117,118,119,120,121,122,123,124,125,126,127,128,129,130,131,132,133,134,135

O

Oil 11,25,49,60,81,97,117

Olive 11,25,60,81,97,117

Onion 4,5,35,68,75,87,117,128

P

Parmesan 5,16,34,64,69,79,87,90,91,92,93,97,99,100,103,107,114,134

Parsnip 4,60

Pasta 4,5,15,64,73,90,92,98,103,132

Pepper 3,4,5,14,80,92,118,129

Pesto 80,98,134

Pie 3,30,31

Plantain 5,105

Pork 3,17,45

Potato 3,4,5,21,32,54,59,65,67,72,73,75,78,79,83,94,96,100,103,105,112,114,119,125

Q

Quinoa 3,15

R

Rice 4,5,58,81,84,90,116,122

Ricotta 93

S

Salmon 4,5,65,70,110

Salsa 3,7,11,12,16,18,19,22,25,27,31,33,37,39,40,41,45,47,86,98,106,118,122,123

Salt 80

Sausage 4,5,51,52,55,78,84,85,107,118,132

Savory 5,28,111

Seafood 4,5,85,98,111

Seasoning 21,33,65,110,123,126,132

Soup 1,3,4,5,6,7,26,27,29,30,31,32,33,34,36,37,38,41,46,51,52,53,54,55,56,57,58,59,60,61,62,63,64,65,66,68,69,70,72,73,74,75,76,77,78,79,80,81,82,85,86,87,89,90,91,92,93,94,95,96,97,98,99,100,101,102,103,105,106,107,108,109,111,112,113,114,115,116,117,118,119,120,121,122,123,124,125,126,127,128,129,130,131,132,134,135

Spaghetti 4,5,50,133

Spinach 4,74

Squash 3,4,5,11,26,60,125

Steak 3,9,17

Stew 4,5,67,110

Stuffing 28,32,35

Sugar 7,8,9,10,11,12,13,14,15,16,17,18,19,20,21,22,23,24,25,26,27,28,29,30,31,32,33,34,35,36,37,38,39,40,41,42,43,44,45,46,47,48,49,50,51,52,53,54,55,56,57,58,59,60,61,62,63,64,65,66,67,68,69,70,71,72,73,74,75,76,77,78,79,80,81,82,83,84,85,86,87,88,89,90,91,92,93,94,95,96,97,98,99,100,101,102,103,104,105,106,107,108,109,110,111,112,113,114,115,116,117,118,119,120,121,122,123,124,125,126,127,128,129,130,131,132,133,134,135

T

Taco 3,5,21,24,34,65,110,123,126

Tomato 4,5,7,11,15,16,38,50,56,60,68,80,81,90,95,97,109,114,121,122,128,129,133

Tortellini 4,73

Turkey 3,5,10,18,51,55,77,84,85,94,118,130,131

V

Vegan 3,10

Vegetables 6,134

Vegetarian 3,4,6,23,53,134

Vinegar 53,128

Vodka 98

W

Worcestershire sauce 85,101

Wraps 3,42

Z

Zest 14,16,17,24,30,40,42,43,46,48,49,50,66,67,69,73,76,79,84,88,89,94,97,99,108,109,127,130

Conclusion

Thank you again for downloading this book!

I hope you enjoyed reading about my book!

If you enjoyed this book, please take the time to share your thoughts and post a review on Amazon. It'd be greatly appreciated!

Write me an honest review about the book – I truly value your opinion and thoughts and I will incorporate them into my next book, which is already underway.

Thank you!

If you have any questions, **feel free to contact at:** _author@shrimpcookbook.com_

Mary Taylor

shrimpcookbook.com

Printed in Great Britain
by Amazon